Elegy Written in a Royal Courtyard

A Facsimile Edition of Jagatprakāśamalla's *Gītapañcaka*

Elegy Written in a Royal Courtyard

A Facsimile Edition of Jagatprakāśamalla's *Gītapañcaka*

(Text, Translation, Commentary, Prosody, and Literary and Grammatical Notes)

Edited By

Professor Ramawatar Yadav, Ph.D.

Former Vice Chancellor

Purbanchal University, Nepal

ADROIT

Adroit Publishers

New Delhi

ISBN : 978-81-87393-61-0

Published by
ADROIT PUBLISHERS 4675/21, Ganpati Bhawan, Ansari Road, Daryaganj, New Delhi-110 002 Phone : 011-23266030
adroitpublishers@gmail.com

Printed at Thomson Press (India) Ltd.

Cover: Statues of King Jagatprakāśamalla(R) and Candraśeṣarasiṃha(L); courtesy of Prasant Shrestha

Typeset in Times New Roman by Arun, Akriti Graphic Solution, Delhi-110081 E-mail: arun263923@gmail.com, Ph: 9999414390

We look before and after,
And pine for what is not.
Our sincerest laughter
With some pain is fraught;
Our sweetest songs are those that tell of saddest thought.

Percy Bysshe Shelley (1792–1822) '*To a Sky–lark*' (1820)

In Memoriam

Ramswaroop Yadav
Radhakant Lal Das

Preface and Acknowledgements

Research for this work was carried out as an Alexander–von–Humboldt Senior Visiting Scholar at the Institut fuer Skandinavistik, Frisistik und Allgemeine Sprachwissenschaft (ISFAS), Christian–Albrechts–Universitaet Kiel, Germany during the summer months of July–September 2013. Grateful acknowledgements are due to the Alexander–von–Humboldt Stiftung, Bonn, Germany for offering me a three–month long Senior Visiting Scholar–level Postdoctoral Research Fellowship.

I am for ever in debt to Prof. Dr. John M. Peterson, Head of the Institut fuer Skandinavistik, Frisistik und Allgemeine Sprachwissenschaft, of the University of Kiel for offering me a two–way travel grant from Kathmandu to Kiel and for constantly consenting to discuss my research work and provide salutary suggestions over numerous cups of coffee.

Work on transliterations of the original Newari MS. into Devanāgarī and Roman scripts was carried out in different phases on different locations. Thus, a preliminary version of the Devanagārī transliteration of the Newari MS. of *Gītapañcaka* was completed on March 9, 2013 during my sojourn as Visiting Professor of English and Communications at the Novel Academy, Pokhara, while a preliminary version of the Roman transliteration of the text of *Gītapañcaka* was accomplished in my Lalitpur–residence, Kathmandu on March 18, 2013. The final versions of transliterations of the Newari MS. into Devanāgarī and Roman scripts were however prepared in Kiel, Germany during July–September 2013.

As regards the translation into English, the final version of translation of the Maithili text of Jagatprakāśamalla's *Gītapañcaka* into English was accomplished on 27 August 2013 in my apartment numbered D O2 at the Internationalesbegegnungszentrum (IBZ) of CAU arranged for me by Frau

Anke Baumann, the Sekretarin of the Institut fuer Skandinavistik, Frisistik und Allgemeine Sprachwissenschaft, Christian–Albrechts–Universitaet, Kiel, Germany. The translation of the Sanskrit *śloka*, however, was accomplished during mid June and early July 2015 at my Lalitpur–residence with the kind help and assistance of Prof. Dr. Shashinath Thakur, former Head of Sansktit Department of Tribhuvan University, Kathmandu, Nepal. Errors, if any, are mine.

I owe a special debt to the following individuals for their kind help and assistance in making available a number of valuable and rather difficult–to–acquire books and articles published in India, Nepal and abroad: Profesor John Peterson of the University of Kiel, Germany for gifting Zvabitel (1961) and Vaudeville (1986); Professor Ramdeo Jha of Laheriasarai, India for gifting Jha (ed. 2013); Dr. Ramanand Jha 'Ramaṇa' of Patna, India for gifting 'Śrīśa' (ed. Śāke 1896/1974 CE), Jha (1969), and Grierson (1884b); Professor Shrutidhari Singh of Ranti–Madhubani, India for gifting Thakur (1956/1988), Chaudhary (1976), and Singh (2013); Ayodhya Nath Chaudhary of Janakpur, Nepal for help in acquiring Shastri (ed. V.S. 2029/1972 CE); Naniram Khatri, Executive Director, Centre for Nepal and Asian Studies, Tribhuvan University, Nepal for gifting Nepāla (ed. V.S. 2040/1983 CE); Professor Kashinath Tamot of Kathmandu, Nepal for help in acquiring Paudel (V.S. 2065/2008 CE); Jñānamaṇi Nepāla of Kathmandu, Nepal for gifting Nepāla (ed. V.S. 2057/2000 CE); Professor Dinesh Raj Panta of the Nepal Academy, Kathmandu, Nepal for help in acquiring Bhattarai (ed. V.S. 2032/1975 CE); Professor Hetukar Jha of Patna, India for gifting Henry (1988); Professor Sudhir Thakur of Sacramento, USA for gifting Grierson (1886), and Dr. Jay Prakash Goit of the University of Tokyo, Japan for gifting Kitada (2014, 2015).

I am extremely thankful to Professor Emeritus Horst Brinkhaus of the Department of Indology of the University of Kiel for very kindly visiting me in my office room # 424 at the ISFAS, CAU, Kiel on more than one occasion and extensively discussing the MS. of *Gītapañcaka* with me as well as for allowing me to share a copy in his possession of the MS. # B 285/21 of *Gītapañcaka* for comparative purposes. I am indebted to Professor Shashinath Thakur, former Head of the Department of Sanskrit of Tribhuvan University for his kind help and assistance in rendering Sanskrit *śloka* into English. I would also wish to offer my grateful thanks to Professor Kashinath Tamot for help in locating as well as acquiring the MS. # B 285/21, MS. # B 285/22 and MS. # E 2924/24 of *Gītapañcaka*; he also helped in correctly deciphering the Newari text on a number of occasions and in determining the exact semantic connotations of a few of the rather less–known Newari and/or Sanskrit words used in the MS. of *Gītapañcaka*. Professor Dinesh Raj Panta, Member of the Nepal Academy, Kathmandu deserves special thanks for suggesting appropriate ways of correctly representing the written Sanskrit *śloka* used in the verse–text of *Gītapañcaka*.

A number of individuals have helped and assisted me in a variety of ways during the course of my research work on the present book. Prominent among them are: Dev Narayan Ray Yadav, Gopal Jha, Kashinath Tamot, Prakash Darnal, Devendra P. Chaudhary (Kathmandu); Bisheswor and Sita Acharya, Ram Jeewan and Laxmi Yadav, Krishna K. C., Jeevnath Pandey (Pokhara); Janardan Mandal, Ramesh Ranjan Jha, Shyam Sundar Shashi (Janakpur); Shrutidhari and Ratna Singh (Ranti–Madhubani); Govind Jha, Ramanand Jha 'Ramaṇa', Hetukar Jha (Patna); Irmgard and Eilhard Koppenhoefer, Peter Plewka, Erika and Otto Smolny, Angela Holst, Elisabeth and Klaus Reincke, Erika and Gebbard–von–Reibnitz, and the Sekretarin Frau Anke Baumann and the students of ISFAS, CAU, namely Christian Peters, Prajakta Pathak, and Jana Behrens (Kiel); Joern Kruhl (Munich); and Ulrike Koelver (Berlin). I offer them all profuse thanks.

Special thanks are due to my dear wife Nirupama and son Dr. (med.) Vijay, M.D. of the Vayodha Medical Hospital in Kathmandu and daughter–in–law Dr. (med.) Ṣarita who is pursuing her MD in Ophthalmology course at a Medical College affiliated to the Tribhuvan University of Nepal; and my daughter Usha, son–in–law Engr. Birendra – former General Manager of the Timber Corporation of the Government of Nepal, grandson Sushant who is in the final year of the MBBS course at a Medical College affiliated to the Kathmandu University, and granddaughter Yukta who is currently pursuing a course leading to the Bachelor's Degree in Corporate Law at a University in Bangalore, India, for their patience and understanding during my research tenure.

Ramawatar Yadav
Lalitpur–Residence
Xmas 2017

Table of Contents

1

Introduction

1. 1. Background

Ever since I came across a succinct remark made in right earnest by an Indian scholar of Maithili named Ramdeo Jha[1] (1971: 11) that to date no Nepali scholar had devoted their time and energy to the study and analysis of an amazingly vast wealth of hand–copied manuscripts of Maithili (an Indo–Aryan language) dramas and songs composed in Newari (a Tibeto–Burman language) script by the Newari–speaking royal men of letters of the Nepālamaṇḍala[2] in medieval Nepal and currently stored and preserved in the National Archives (known as the *Rāṣtriya Abhilekhālaya*) of the Government of Nepal in Kathmandu, I have had an ardent wish to undertake the rather arduous, punctilious, and onerous task of producing facsimile–cum–critical editions of a few of these manuscripts. As my research predilections were keenly focused on producing scientific linguistic descriptions of the sound pattern as well as the overall grammatical system of Modern Maithili (cf. Yadav 1984d; 1996, 2003), the task of linguistically analyzing and describing the literary texts of Middle Maithili hand–copied manuscripts composed by Newar kings and/or Maithil *paṇḍits* resident in Royal Courts in medieval Nepal was self–evidently deferred for the foreseeable future. My book entitled *A Facsimile Edition of a Maithili Play: Bhūpatīndramalla's Parśurāmopākhyāna–nāṭaka* (Yadav ed. 2011) was thus the first veritable essay in that direction. The present book, *Elegy Written in a Royal Courtyard: A Facsimile Edition of Jagatprakāśamalla's Gītapañcaka*, is a second such venture in the very same direction.

Before I move on to an analysis of literary traits and linguistic features of the verse–text of *Gītapañcaka* in detail, I deem it desirable to present a state–of–the–art historical overview of the dramas and collections and/or anthologies of verse compositions of the Malla kings in medieval Nepal published thus far across the globe. An eminent Indian scholar, Jayakanta Mishra (1960 'Introduction,' p. 1), reports that in all "as many as 300 old Mss. in Maithili" are found to have been stored in the National Archives in Kathmandu. A German scholar, Horst Brinkhaus (1987a), states that around 150 Newari and/or Mithilākṣara hand–copied manuscripts are stored in the National Archives in Kathmandu, while a senior Nepali archaeologist, Taranand Mishra (V.S. 2062/2005 CE; V.S. 2072/2015 CE), reports on the existence of 400 hand–copied manuscripts, including innumerable works on *Cikitsāśāstra* 'science of medicine' as well as a recently discovered gem of a hand–written manuscript of a treatise on *Āyurveda* titled *Vaïdyarahasya* by none other than the most eminent Maithili poet Vidyāpati, stored in the Āśā Archives, the Kaiser Library, private collections, and the National Archives of the Government of Nepal in Kathmandu. By a separate count, it is estimated that manuscripts of a total of 153 dramas (of which 26–30 are in Newari, 5–6 are in Bangla and Hindi/Braj Bhasha/Avadhi, and more than 115 are in Maithili) and a host of collections and/or anthologies of Maithili verse compositions of the poet–kings of the Malla dynasty written in Newari script in medieval Nepal are stored and preserved in the National Archives of the Government of Nepal in Kathmandu (Kamal P. Malla, *Personal communication*, *Email*, 2014). Indeed there are plenty more discoveries waiting to be unearthed; sadly only an infinitesimal number of these manuscripts have been published thus far.

It is common knowledge by now that August Conrady, a German scholar, was the first researcher ever to edit and publish the MS. of a Maithili (–cum–Bangla) play from medieval Nepal.[3] Towards the last decade of the 19th century, August Conrady (1891) published in Leipzig, Germany the Patan–king Siddhinarasiṃhamalla's (1620–1661) drama popularly held to be written in *Mischsprache* Maithili and Bangla under the rather confusing and somewhat ambiguous title of *Das Hariçcandranṛityam: Ein Altnepalesisches Tanzspiel* (after all, other than being an 'old' dance–play 'from' Nepal, this drama has virtually little to do with 'Old Nepali'!) with a 12–page *Einleitung* 'Introduction' in German, a transliteration of the main Newari text into Devanāgarī script, a transliteration of stage directions in Newari into Roman script along with a German translation thereof, and footnotes and commentary in German. However, in a highly scholarly and thoroughly researched article, Govind Jha (2005), with his characteristic systematic inquiry, steely accuracy, cool and invincible logic, and incisive and rather indisputable historical linguistic evidence, makes a vigorous claim to assert that the play *Hariścandranṛtyam* ought to be rightfully treated as a work of the Maithili language and not of Bangla. At any rate, the truth is that Dr. August Conrady submitted this published (it is customary in Germany and elsewhere in Europe to submit a "published" version of a dissertation to a University for a degree) research work as a *Habilitationsschrift* or "Professorial Dissertation" as Professor John Peterson dubs it, for the award of, what is commonly called in lighter vein, a "second" Ph. D. at 12 o' clock noon on Monday 23 November 1891 at the University of Leipzig in Germany, and indeed he won the award on that day. A curious observation springs to my mind presently: I deem it a little less than credible and quite astonishing to note that the–then most eminent British linguist as well as the saviour and the greatest exponent of the Maithili language – Sir George Abraham Grierson – was totally oblivious (or so it seems) of the existence of a vast wealth of hand–copied manuscripts of literary works of the Maithili language stored and preserved in the National Archives of the Government of Nepal in Kathmandu[4] as well as of the highly invaluable research work on Maithili language and literature then ongoing in Germany – in spite of the fact that around the same time Grierson was himself quite actively engaged in the act of getting his research work on Maithili folk–songs (collected from an itinerant wayfarer during a fieldtrip in the *tarāi* 'plains' of Nepal) published in a highly prestigious journal of linguistics in Germany titled *Zeitschrift der Deustchen Morgenländischen Gesellschaft* (cf. Grierson 1885) – which was published in the same city of Leipzig where Conrady's above–mentioned work was published some six years later.

In early 20th century, during the British Raj in India, a few Bengali (now Bangla) scholars of Calcutta (now Kolkata) and around followed suit and edited and published a number of medieval Maithili plays composed by Newar kings – sadly treating most of them as Bangla plays. Thus, Bandopadhyaya (ed. Baṅgābda 1324/1917 CE) edited and published Bhūpatīndramalla's (1696–1722) *Mahābhārata–nāṭaka*, 1702, and *Vidyāvilāpa–nāṭaka*, 1720, and Raṇajitmalla's (1722–1769) *Mādhavānala–Kāmakandalā–Nāṭaka* under the title of *Nepāler Bāṅgālā Nāṭaka* in Bangla script in Calcutta. Similarly, Bagchi (Baṅgābda 1347/1940 CE) edited and published Jagajjyotirmalla's (1614–1637) *Kuñjavihāra–nāṭaka* in a Bangla monthly journal, *Paricaya*, in Calcutta, and Datta (ed. 1980) edited and published a Bangla transliteration of Jagajjyotirmalla's

(1614–1637) Maithili play, *Muditakuvalayāśva–nāṭaka*, 1628, in a book titled *Prācīna Bāṅgālā–Maïthilī Nāṭaka* in Burdhman University of West Bengal.

In the meantime, a number of Maithili–speaking scholars of Bihar too are well–known to have taken up the onerous task of editing a number of Maithili plays written by the Newar kings of Nepālamaṇḍala – the most prominent among them being Ramdeo Jha. As a matter of fact, Ramdeo Jha has the singular distinction of editing and publishing a total of 5 Maithili plays of Jagajjyotirmalla (1614–1637): *Haragaürīvivāha–nāṭaka* (1970), *Kuñjavihāra–nāṭaka* (re–published, 1976), *Daśāvatāranṛtyam* (1988), *Ṣoḍaśagītam* (1988), and *Muditakuvalayāśva–nāṭaka* (re–published, 2013). Note that quite early on Jayakanta Mishra (ed. 1965) had re–published Bhūpatīndramalla's *Vidyāvilāpa–nāṭaka* under the title of *Vidyāvilāpa: Nepālīya Maïthilī Nāṭaka*; while Lekhanath Mishra (ed. 1972) had edited and published Jagatprakāśamalla's (1643–1673) play, *Prabhāvatīharaṇa–nāṭaka*.

Almost a century later than August Conrady, another German scholar, Horst Brinkhaus (1987a), published Jagatprakāśamalla's undated play, *Pradyumnavijaya–nāṭaka*, with a Roman transliteration and an English translation in Stuttgart, Germany.

Yadav (ed. 2011) published a facsimile–cum–critical edition of Bhūpatīndramalla's *Parśurāmopākhyāna–nāṭaka*, 1713, in Kathmandu; the book contained a distinctly readable facsimile of the Newari MS. (pp. 77–139), a Devanāgarī transliteration (pp. 141–194), a Roman transliteration (pp. 195–252), and a translation into English (pp. 253–320). More importantly, basing exclusively on the prose used in dialogues of the play, the book also presented a linguistic description culminating in a sketch of a grammar of Middle Maithili containing substantiated information on orthography, phonetics and phonology, morphology, and syntax and semantics (pp. 21–76).

More than three years ago, on 20 February 2014 to be exact, a young Japanese scholar named Makoto Kitada disclosed to me during a private lunch–meeting with him at my Lalitpur–residence that he too had put out a Japanese edition of king Jagajjyotirmalla's (1614–1637) Maithili play, *Madālasāharaṇa–nāṭaka*, with an introduction in Japanese and a transliteration of the original Newari MS. of the Maithili text into Roman script in a series of two articles published in a journal titled *Indomizokukenkyu* (roughly to be translated as *Indian Folk Culture Research*) of the Osaka

University Knowledge Archive: Osaka University, Japan (Kitada 2014, 2015). Fortunately, with great difficulty, I have been now able to avail the PDF versions of both of these articles with the kind help and assistance of Dr. Jay Prakash Goit of the Tokyo University.

Thus, of around 115 Maithili plays ascribed to have been composed by Newar kings of the Malla dynasty, altogether a toal of mere 13 plays are published to date.

Of around 26–30 extant Newari plays of the Malla period, a total of 6 plays are known to have been published to date. These are: Jayaprakāśamalla's *Ratneśvaraprādurbhāva* edited by Kasā (N.S. 1084/1964 CE), Bhūpatīndramalla's *Vikramacarita* edited by Jośī and Śākya (N.S. 1090/1970 CE), Jayaprakāśamalla's *Vīradhvajopākhyāna* (fragment) published in a Newari journal, *Situ*, in N.S. 1091/1971 CE, Raṇajitmalla's two plays *Madanacaritra* and *Kṛṣṇacaritra* – both of which were edited by Vajrācārya (N.S. 1103/1983 CE), and Jagatprakāśamalla's *Mūladevaśaśidevavyākhyāna*, edited with a transliteration into German and a 35–page long introduction in German by Brinkhaus (ed. 1987b). Raṇajitmalla's play *Kṛṣṇacaritra* was also re–published by Kāyastha (N.S. 1103/1983 CE).

To the best of my knowledge, a total of 4 plays of the Malla period written in the medium of Bangla are published to date. These are: Raṇajitmalla's *Rāmacarita* edited by Bandopadhyaya (ed. Baṅgābda 1324/1917 CE), *Gopīcandra–nāṭaka* edited by Mukherji (ed. 1970), Rāmabhadra's play titled *Lalitakuvalayāśva–Madālasopākhyāna–Śiva–Pārvatī–Mahimā–Nāṭaka* edited by Datta (ed. 1980), and *Kāśīvijaya–nāṭaka*, N.S. 717/1597 CE, of Rāmacandra composed during the reign of Gaṅgādevī, Traïlokyamalla, and Tribhuvanamalla (1561–1613) inadvertently and mistakenly edited as a Maithili play by Śreṣṭha (ed. N.S. 1124/2004 CE) – the play in question, in my opinion, is indeed a Bangla (occasionally interspersed with Maithili) play.

Be as it may, barring Jagatprakāśamalla's *Pārijātaharaṇa-nāṭaka* as reported in Brinkhaus (1987b: 12–13), to the best of my knowledge, no other play of the time written predominantly in the medium of Hindi/Braj Bhasha/Avadhi is reported to have been discovered and/or published as yet.

Similarly and curiously enough, as of now no play of the time written in the medium of Khas/Gorkhali/Parbate (Modern–day Nepali) has been reported to have been discovered.

This may be as good a place as any to make a brief account of a total of four published dramatic works of the early 14th century Nepal composed in the medium of languages such as Prakrit and Sanskrit. Thus, as indicated in Endnote # 3, based on a MS. also preserved in the National Archives of Nepal, a German scholar named Christian Lassen published with Notes in Latin a Two–Act Sanskrit farce–play titled *Dhūrtta–Samāgamaḥ* composed in c. 1320 CE by a Maithili scholar of great repute, namely Kaviśekharācārya Jyotirīśvara Ṭhākura (c. 1290–1350 CE), in 1838 in Bonn, Germany. A century and a half later, Bhattarai (ed. V.S. 2032/1975 CE) edited and published, along with a Nepali translation, a corrected version of the rather corrupt copy (apparently prepared by Amarendracandra and Devaju Abhaya – who were well–known to have been gifted with good handwriting) of a dated Prakrit play, *Rāmāṅka–nāṭikā*, of poet Dharmagupta of Lalitpur composed in N.S. 501/1381 CE during the reign of the first king of the newly–founded Kingdom of Lalitpur, namely Jayasiṃhamalla. We have also come to learn that the play *Rāmāṅka–nāṭikā* (that covers the story of Rāma's banishment to the forest up until the celebration of Rāma's ascension to the throne of the Kingdom of Ayodhyā as a king) was most likely staged to celebrate the solemn occasion of the establishment of the new Kingdom of Lalitpur as well as Jayasiṃhamalla's ascension to the throne as the first king of the Kingdom of Lalitpur. Eight years later, poet–playwright Jayata's Prakrit play, *Mahīrāvaṇavadha*, N.S. 457/V.S. 1394/1337 CE, was edited and published with a translation into Nepali by Nepāla (ed. V.S. 2040/1983 CE); the book also contained a gloss of Prakrit words into Sanskrit and Nepali (pp. 149–159) and a facsimile of the Prakrit MS. written in the Bhujiṃmol script of Newari (pp. 163–175). It is noteworthy that Jayata's play happens to be one of the first few dated plays to be discovered in Nepal. Nepāla (ed. V.S. 2057/2000 CE) edited and published yet another dated Prakrit play, *Bhaïravānanda*, of the Maithil poet Maṇika (also written as Māṇikyavarddhana and Māṇika in Sanskrit, and as Manaku in Vernacular) composed in N.S. 506/V.S. 1443/ 1386 CE along with a facsimile of a sample of 8 Folios of the Prakrit MS. written in the Bhujiṃmol script of Newari (pp. 203–204), a translation of the Newari MS. into Nepali (pp. 207–279), and a gloss of Prakrit words into Sanskrit and Nepali (pp. 280–296).

A cursory survey of the scantily published Middle Maithili verse compositions and inscriptions thereof carved on wood, metal, and stone tablets may be in order here. To begin with, Shailendra Mohan Jha (1969) was the first scholar from India to publish in Darbhanga a collection of 13 songs of king Siddhinarasiṃhamalla in a slim volume titled *Siddhi Narasiṃha Malla* (with a 4 + 16–page long introduction, and meaning and translation of songs into Modern Maithili prose) collated from such published and/or unpublished anthological sources as *Rāgataraṅgiṇī*, *Rāga–Bhajana–Saṃgraha*, and *Bhāṣā–Gīta–Saṃgraha*. Upon closer scrutiny, however, the book is found to consist of 12 (out of 13) songs from the hand–copied manuscript of the *Bhāṣā–Gīta–Saṃgraha* written in Tirhutā i.e. Mithilākṣara script. In an editorial to a Maithili journal titled *Maïthilī* (now out of print) and published from the city of Biratnagar in eastern Nepal, another Indian scholar, Praphulla Kumar Maüna (V.S. 2028/1971 CE), published a total of 3 rare Maithili songs (1 by king Pratāpamalla of Kantipur (now Kathmandu) and 2 by king Bhūpatīndramalla of Bhaktapur) preserved as inscriptions on stone tablets. In the same issue of the journal *Maïthilī*, Ramdeo Jha (V.S. 2028/1971 CE) published a highly scholarly article containing the Devanāgarī transliteration of a total of 18 rare songs (of Jagatprakāśamalla, Jitāmitramalla, and Pratāpamalla) preserved as stone–inscriptions in the cities of Bhaktapur and Kantipur in medieval Nepal. Sundar Jha Shastri (ed. V.S. 2029/1972 CE), however, turns out to be the first Nepali scholar ever to edit and publish a complete collection of an assortment of 109 numbered + 2 unnumbered *yuddha* and *daṇḍaka* songs (i.e. a total of 111 songs) of Jagatprakāśamalla titled *Nānārtha Deva Devī Gīta Saṃgraha* n.d. in a modest Maithili journal, *Phūla–Pāta*, (now out of print) that he edited and published in Kathmandu, while 'Śrīśa' (ed. Śāke 1896/1974 CE) was the first Indian scholar to edit and publish in Darbhanga a complete collection of 50 songs of Jagajjyotirmalla titled *Nṛpatijagajjyotirmalla–Kṛta Gīta–Pañcāśikā*, Śakābda 1550/1628 CE, in a slim volume containing an 8–page *prastāvanā* 'prologue' (pp. *ka–ja*) and an 8–page *ṭippaṇī* 'comments' (pp. 27–34). Three years later, 'Sumana' & Jha (eds. 1977) coedited and published in Patna an anthology of Old Maithili songs of Vidyāpati along with the songs of a large number of other rather less–known poets in a book titled *Maïthilī Prācīna Gītāvalī*, which contained, among others, a total of 10 songs (3 of which are from the play *Kṛṣṇacaritra–nāṭaka*) of king Siddhinarasiṃhamalla of Lalitpur. The same year, Jaimant Mishra (ed. 1977) edited and published in Patna an anthology of a total of 21 rare Maithili songs of a number of Newar kings, preserved in inscriptions on stone tablets in the cities of Kantipur and Bhaktapur, under the title of

Maïthilī Abhilekha Gītamālā. After a long gap of more than three decades, L. Mishra & Bh. Jha (eds. 2010) published a collection of 250 songs titled *Jagajjyotirmalla Padāvalī* containing *Gītapañcāśikā* (50 songs) – published earlier by Śrīśa in 1974 –, *Gītasaṃgraha* (148 songs), and selections from *Rāgabhajana* (52 songs). Sadly, L. Mishra and Bh. Jha (eds. 2010) make no mention whatsoever of Śrīśa (ed. 1974). The present book of mine is thus the fourth work to publish the complete collection of a verse composition of 40 Maithili panegyric elegiac songs (along with a corresponding number of Sanskrit *śloka*), *Gītapañcaka*, composed in c. N.S. 782/1662 CE, by king Jagatprakāśamalla.

None of the above–mentioned German and Indian (Shastri of Nepal included) editor–scholars of Maithili plays and/or verse compositions, however, deemed it desirable to publish the original Newari MS. as–the–manuscript–is in order for other scholars to see and investigate and interpret the Maithili language and its writing system of the time for themselves. Naturally, therefore, the authenticity of the Devanāgarī transliteration of the original Newari text continues to remain an object of grave doubt. As a matter of fact, two such published plays are known to have inadvertently contained a number of errors of incorrect reading of the text of the original Newari MS. viz. *Prabhāvatīharaṇa–nāṭaka* edited by L. Mishra (ed. 1972) and *Muditakuvalayāśva–nāṭaka* edited by Datta (ed. 1980). Here I might hasten to also add in passing that practically none of the editor–scholars of the greatest Maithili poet Vidyāpati have thus far been able to publish the *Padāvalī* along with its corresponding manuscript either – be it the *Nepāla Palmleaf MS.*, the *Rāmabhadrapura Palmleaf MS.*, or the *Taraünī Palmleaf MS.* I must nonetheless commend the highly scholarly and annotated edition of a total of 86 songs of the *Rāmabhadrapura Palmleaf MS.* by Sh. Thakur (ed. 1941) produced in the medium of Hindi, and the superb edition produced in the medium of English along with a translation into English of a total of 262 songs of the comparatively older *Nepāla Palmleaf MS.* by S. Jha (ed. 1954) – the doyen of Maithili linguistics. It pleases me to inform that U. Mishra and J. Mishra (eds. 1961) were in fact the first scholars to have published Vidyāpati's play, *Gorakṣavijaya–nāṭaka*, containing a facsimile of the 24–page original MS. composed in the Tirhutā i.e. Mithilākṣara script; sadly the published facsimile of the MS. is totally illegible due to poor quality of photo–printing. Self–evidently, my book entitled *A Facsimile Edition of a Maithili*

Play: Bhūpatīndramalla's Parśurāmopākhyāna–nāṭaka (Yadav ed. 2011) is the first–ever endeavor by a scholar – Nepalese or otherwise – to publish a facsimile edition of the Newari MS. of a Maithili play written by a Newar playwright of the Malla dynasty in medieval Nepal.

Now we move on to a discussion of the present book. The present book entitled *Elegy Written in a Royal Courtyard: A Facsimile Edition of Jagatprakāśamalla's Gītapañcaka* is a facsimile–cum–critical edition of the text of a MS. of *Gītapañcaka* (lit. 'consisting of five songs') written in a Newari script called *Nepālākhala* (Skt. *Nepālākṣara* and Modern–Newari *Nepā:akha:*, cf. Lienhard 1974/1992: pp. 2, 14) and containing a collection of Maithili lyrical songs and Sanskrit *śloka* penned by one of the most famous and illustrious Newar poet–kings of the Kingdom of Bhaktapur, namely Jagatprakāśamalla. Taking cue from and following the footsteps of such eminent Indologists as Grierson (1882a, b, 1884a, b, 1885, 1886, 1917, 1935), Shāstrī (1916), Bagchi (1938), Thakur (ed. 1941), Jha (ed. 1954), Bagchi & Śāstrī (eds. 1956), Mukherji (1963), Sen (1973, ed. 1977), Basu (1976), Kvaerne (ed. 1977/2010), Vaudeville (1986), Brinkhaus (1987a, b), Snell (1991/2006), and Nagasaki (ed. 2012), this work presents an English rendering of the text of *Gītapañcaka* and analyzes the literary traits and grammatical features of this collection of Maithili songs on modern linguistic principles. To begin with, as far as practicable, a thoroughly authentic and accurate transliteration of the Newari text into Devanāgarī and Roman scripts is made. Special care is taken to faithfully represent the original Newari text as–it–is; any scribal errors that may have inadvertently crept in due to carelessness and/or ignorance of the scribe are duly noted and correct forms immediately emended within square brackets and explanations thereof offered in appropriate places in the body of the text.

Chasing a hearsay trail augmented mainly by Taranand Mishra, I stumbled, as an act of sheer serendipity as it were, on a Newari MS. of *Gītapañcaka* in a private institution named the Āśā Archives in Kathmandu in mid–November of 2012 and I happened to order a CD of it on 7 December 2012. It needs to be known that the aforesaid Newari MS. of *Gītapañcaka* was kept for long in private possession of late Mr. Premabahādura Kasā in Kathmandu, and currently it is stored and preserved in a digitalized form in the Āśā Archives located at Raktakālī, Naradevī, in Kathmandu.

A cursory reading of the Newari MS. of *Gītapañcaka* almost instantaneously revealed that a total of eight *pañcaka* (i.e. 8 x 5 = 40) songs were indeed composed by the poet–king Jagatprakāśamalla. We also came to learn that these clusters of Maithili elegiac songs, accompanied with a corresponding number of Sanskrit *śloka*, were written to commemorate the sad and untimely demise of his friend, philosopher and guide Candraśeṣarasiṃha, to express his deep sorrow and poignancy of parting and separation from him, as well as to extol and highlight Candraśeṣarasiṃha's virtuous and glorious deeds. Unfortunately, the chronicles of Nepal are rather mute on the issue of who exactly Candraśeṣarasiṃha was and as to how and why he had been immensely successful in exerting an amazingly abiding and indelible influence on the character and personality of the Bhaktapur–king Jagatprakāśamalla.

To our utter dismay, on 13 January 2013, we discovered that the Newari MS. of *Gītapañcaka* made available to me courtesy of the Āśā Archives against payment of appropriate fee was rather fragmented and that Folios 1 Verso, 3, 11, 16, 18 Verso to 21 Recto, 23, 24, 25, 27, 31, 32, 34, 35, 36 as well as Folios 37 and 38 of the *patrāṅka* 'Table of contents' were sadly found to be missing. Further inquiry and search with the assistance of a few local scholars, most notably Professor Kashinath Tamot, led me to a discovery of the manuscript of yet another but complete and full text of *Gītapañcaka* containing a total of 40 Maithili songs and a corresponding similar number of Sanskrit *śloka* in the National Archives of the Government of Nepal in Kathmandu on 19 January 2013.

The present study is thus based on a digital copy of the full text of the MS. of *Gītapañcaka* (numbered B 285/22 in the Catalogue of the National Archives) officially made available to me courtesy of the National Archives of the Government of Nepal, Kathmandu against the payment of appropriate fees on 17 February 2013. On occasions, when deemed expedient, a comparison is also made with the text of the Āśā Archives as well as with other extant texts and variant copies of the manuscript of *Gītapañcaka* that are found to have been in existence either in the erstwhile Nepal–German Manuscripts Preservation Project (NGMPP) Office, Kathmandu or in the National Archives of the Government of Nepal, Kathmandu – in order to investigate, explicate, and establish the precise nature of textual variations and any scribal errors of omission, commission, and interpolation that may have inadvertently crept in due to carelessness and/or ignorance of the scribe as it so very often tends to happen in medieval Maithili texts stored and preserved in the Archives of Nepal. Such observations are duly made in the body of the text in appropriate places.

Knowledge about the existence and availability of this rare and therefore highly invaluable medieval Maithili literary work in the National Archives of the Government of Nepal as well as in a private Archive (albeit in a fragmented form) in Kathmandu came to light in not so remote past. Thus, barring a brief mention in Mishra[5] (1960, 'Introduction', p. 1), a stray and rather erroneous reference in Regmi[6] (1966/2007: 221), a casual reference in 'Śrīśa' (1983 CE: 129), a brief discussion in Mishra (ed. 1972: 26) and Jha (VS 2037/1980 CE: 98), a brief but pertinent observation in Brinkhaus (ed. 1987b: 12), and a brief but nonetheless authentic account in Jha (1971, 1990), precious little is known about *Gītapañcaka*. As a matter of fact, this collection of Maithili and Sanskrit lyrical songs is not thoroughly studied and linguistically analyzed as yet.

Published literature on Jagatprakāśamalla in the medium of English: (Mishra 1949, Regmi 1966/2007, Brinkhaus 1987a); Nepali: (Paudel V.S. 2065/2008 CE); Maithili: (Jha 1971, 1990, Shastri ed. 1972, Mishra 1977); and German: (Brinkhaus ed. 1987 b) is replete with speculative but conflicting anecdotes of an intense friendship, a rather deep bondage, and even ties of kinship between Jagatprakāśamalla and Candraśeṣarasiṃha: the episode of friendship attains all the more salience in view of the fact that Jagatprakāśamalla was a famous ruler of the Kingdom of Bhaktapur, while Candraśeṣarasiṃha, allegedly a brother[7] to his third queen Annapūrṇālakṣmī[8], happened to be a friend, guide, and mentor as it were as well as a Minister (may be even Chief Minister) in the Royal Court of the Kingdom of Bhaktapur. All available accounts suggest that in all likelihood king Jagatprakāśamalla was able to wed his third and youngest and dearest queen Annapūrṇālakṣmī with the sole aid of Candraśeṣarasiṃha[9].

Upon receiving the full and uncorrupted text of *Gītapañcaka* from the National Archives on 17 February 2013 and after having made a cursory perusal of it, I made an application to the Alexander–von–Humboldt Stiftung in Bonn, Germany on 3 March 2013 for an award to carry out a preliminary research on a facsimile–cum–critical edition of *Gītapañcaka* during the summer months of July–September 2013 at the Institut fuer Skandinavistik,

Frisistik und Allgemeine Sprachwissenschaft (ISFAS), Christian–Albrechts–Universitaet Kiel, Germany and, fortunately for me, I was offered the Senior Visiting Scholar–level Postdoctoral Research Fellowship on 7 April 2013. The present book is basically a result of the research carried out during July–September 2013 at the ISFAS of the University of Kiel in Germany.

1. 2. The Author: His Life and Works

Jagatprakāśamalla (1643–1673), son of Nareśamalla[10] – and not of Jagajjyotirmalla as was erroneously reported by Gyawali (V.S. 2019/1962 CE: 105) – and grandson of Jagajjyotirmalla, and one of the most illustrious kings of the Kingdom of Bhaktapur, was born on 26 Mārga, Saturday, *kārtika kṛṣṇa amāvasyā* in N.S. 759/V.S. 1695 (Paudel V.S. 2065/2008 CE: 21) corresponding to October 1639 CE, and died from the effects of a severe smallpox infection on 29 Mārga, Thursday, *mārgasīra kṛṣṇa caturthī* of N.S. 793/V.S. 1729 (Paudel V.S. 2065/2008 CE: 28) corresponding to 28 November 1673 CE (Jha 1990: 34) at the prime age of thirty–four.[11] Due to early demise of his father Nareśamalla on āś*vina vadī pañcamī* of N.S. 763/V.S. 1700 (Paudel V.S. 2065/2008 CE: 20) corresponding to 8 September 1643 CE, Jagatprakāśamalla is believed to have ascended to the throne of the Kingdom of Bhaktapur as a child–king at the age of four in 1643 CE, but his actual reign is believed to have lasted only for 18 years. In other words, his real regnal years are between 1655 CE to 1673 CE i.e. until his premature death at the prime age of 34 on Thursday, 28 November 1673 CE.

King Jagatprakāśamalla is sadly known to have led his tumultuous and rather short–lived life in terrible torment and strife due to incessant internecine dissension and personal aggrandizement and conflict between him and king Pratāpamalla (1641–1674) of Kantipur i.e. Kathmandu on the one hand and king Śrīnivāsamalla (1661–1684) of Lalitpur i.e. Patan on the other. In spite of it, he was able to produce an amazingly vast wealth of literary output of high merit in his short life. For more information on the trials and tribulations of Jagatprakāśamalla's strenuous life, the reader is referred to Ramdeo Jha's (1990) monograph on Jagatprakāśamalla published by the Sahitya Akademi in New Delhi, India.

Jagatprakāśamalla is known to have two wives: Candrāvatī and Padmāvatī[12]. As indicated above, it is also known by now that he received a third wife named Annapūrṇālakṣmī of Maithil descent by the sole aid of Candraśeṣarasiṃha. Unfortunately, the chronicles of Nepal do not offer us much information on the ancestral lineage either of Annapūrṇālakṣmī or of Candraśeṣarasiṃha or of Candraprakāśa (i.e. a pseudonym coined by adding *prakāśa* of king Jagatprakāśa to the initial *candra* of Candraśeṣarasiṃha), or of Jagatcandra (i.e. a pseudonym supposedly coined by adding the first part *candra* of Candraśeṣara to the first part *jagat* of king Jagatprakāśa). In *Gītapañcaka*, Jagatprakāśamalla makes an invariant and reverent reference to C̃ādaśeṣarasiṃha in the *bhaṇitā* 'author tag' of each Maithili song; he also makes an explicit reference to him by name without fail again and again in the Sanskrit *śloka* provided at the end of each *yāma* 'canto' avowedly stating in highly eulogical terms that these songs were indeed written to commemorate his life–like friend and brave 'brother' Candraśeṣarasiṃha and to extol and highlight his good and virtuous deeds. Copious references are indeed made to Jagatcandra and/or Jagaccandra in a great many of his dramas as well. Needless to say, the songs collected under the title of *Gītapañcaka* evoke the sentiments of tremendous intimacy with and awe and reverence for Candraśeṣarasiṃha – his *mamāgrayo, mamāgrajo* 'my elder brother' and *bhāi/bhāyi/bhāya* 'brother' – and of pangs of separation from and an irreparable loss of a person of the same lineage (*tohe mori ekahi kūla*, Fol. 14 R: 1). In *bhaṇitā* of a number of his dramatic works too, Jagatprakāśamalla is found to have described Candraśeṣarasiṃha as but one life or as one and the same: *jagataprakāśa bhana cāṃdaśekharasiṃha tohe hama ekahi parāna*, (*Malayagandhinī–nāṭaka*, Folio 59a); *jagataprakāśa nṛpa cāṃdaśekharasiṃha jānaha duhu jana eka*, (*Nalacaritra–nāṭaka*, Folio 53b).

In *Gītapañcaka,* Jagatprakāśamalla describes himself as a descendant of the solar dynasty (*bhānukulāvataṃsaḥ*, Folio 21 V: 4); he also uses such self–laudatory epithets as *nṛpati vara* 'Greater King' (Folio 6 R: 2), *bhūpati* 'Lord of Land' (Folio 8 R: 6), *mahīndra* 'Lord of Earth', and *nṛpacandra* 'Moon among Kings' (Folio 21 V: 4) for himself. Like in names of other Malla kings of the Nepālamaṇḍala, the epithet of *śriśrījaya* is consistently inserted prior to the name of Jagatprakāśamalla too.

Jagatprakāśamalla's dramatic works are to a large extent written in the medium of the Maithili language. Of the more than 10 dramas[13] ascribed to him, two very well–known and published Maithili dramas are:

Prabhāvatīharaṇa, 1656 (Mishra ed. 1972) and *Pradyumnavijaya*, c. 1666 (Brinkhaus 1987a). During 1987, Horst Brinkhaus also published a German edition of a Newari play, *Mūladevaśaśidevavyākhyāna*, n.d. in Stuttgart, Germany (Brinkhaus ed. 1987b). Other unpublished Maithili plays the manuscripts of which are currently stored and preserved in the National Archives of the Government of Nepal are: *Malayagandhinī*, circa 1663–65, NGMPP A 352/26; *Pārijātaharaṇa*, n.d., NGMPP 349/13: note that Brinkhaus (1987b: 12–13) claims *Pārijātaharaṇa* to be a play written in a dialect of Hindi (without specifying which one) "*... sowie das ganz in einem Hindi–Dialekt verfasste Stueck Pārijātaharaṇa geschrieben worden zu sein.*"; *Nalacaritra* (also called *Nalīyanāṭaka*), 1670, NGMPP B 275/7; *Uṣāharaṇa*, n.d. NGMPP B 398/9; *Madanacaritra*, c.1670, NGMPP B 275/14, written and staged on the solemn occasion of the *upanayana* i.e. the Sacred Thread ceremony of Jagatprakāśamalla's second son Ugramalla; *Mālatī–Mādhava*, n.d., NGMPP B 276/3, written and staged on the solemn occasion of the *upanayana* i.e. the Sacred Thread ceremony of Jagatprakāśamalla's first son Jitāmitramalla, while the play *Abhijñānaśākuntala*, NGMPP 346/26, was written and staged to celebrate the happy occasion of the birth of the eldest prince Jitāmitramalla. A few other plays which are either fragmented and/or incomplete, or are merely referred to by scholars but are generally untraced or elusive are: *Rāmāyaṇa*, *Vṛndācarita* (also called *Jālandharopākhyāna*), and *Kṛṣṇacarita* (also called *Kaṃśavadha*).

In addition to being a deft playwright, king Jagatprakāśamalla is also known to be a connoisseur of music and poetry of high order: *kavīndra* 'king of poets', *gandharvavidyāguru* 'preceptor of musical sciences', and *sāhityavidyāvid* 'expert on science of literature' were the sobriquets used for him. A large number of his Maithili songs are suitably preserved in carvings on metal, wood, and stone tablets in and around the cities of Kantipur, Lalitpur, and Bhaktapur (Jha 1971: 11–15; Mishra 1977) – sadly these precious inscriptions of Maithili songs might have been reduced to rubble in the massive earthquake of 25 April 2015 and in the successive equally massive aftershock of 12 May 2015. A great majority of his Maithili songs, along with the songs composed by other contemporary royal poets, are compiled in an assortment of verse anthologies produced later, while a considerably large number of his Maithili songs also form an integral part in the manuscripts of his plays preserved and stored in the National Archives of the Government of Nepal in Kathmandu. It is worth noting that even his well–known and complete Newari play, *Mūladevaśaśidevavyākhyāna*, happens to end in a Maithili devotional song beginning with *athira kaleval[r]a jānu he kamala pātaka jala tule* 'Be it known that (human) body/life is as unstable and infirm as a drop of water on lotus leaf' (Folio 50a–b) – a song that also happens to occur in *Gītapañcaka* (Folio 30 V: 6). He is credited to have authored a number of collections of Maithili verse compositions namely *Nānāraṃgagītaṃ* N.S. 780/1660 CE, *Gītāvalī* N.S. 781/1661 CE, *Padyasamuccaya*, n.d., *Nānārthadevadevīgītasaṃgraha* n.d. (Shastri ed. V.S. 2029/1972 CE), *Gītapañcaka* c. N.S. 782/1662 CE (the object of study in the present volume), and *Nānārāgagītaṃ* N.S. 790/1670 CE (also called *Puruṣokti Gītapañcakaṃ*, cf. Jha V.S. 2037/1980 CE: 82). A manuscript of a collection of 518 Newari verse compositions of Jagatprakāśamalla titled *Nepālabhāṣāgīta* is also reported to have been preserved and stored in the National Archives of the Government of Nepal in Kathmandu (Malla 1981: 54).

Jagatprakāśamalla's dramas and songs are an eloquent testimony to the fact that he was indeed a versatile author and a great musician. A polyglot as he was, Jagatprakāśamalla is known to have been highly proficient in the mastery of at least 6 languages (one may call him a *ṣaḍbhāṣāvijña*) such as Newari (his mother tongue), Sanskrit, Parbate/Khasa (Modern–day Nepali), Bangla, Hindi/Braj Bhasha/Avadhi, and of course Maithili.

For more information on Jagatprakāśamalla's literary achievements discussed at some length in three phases during the period prior to 1660, 1661–63, and 1664–73, the reader is referred to Brinkhaus (ed. 1987b).

1. 3. The Manuscript

To the best of my knowledge, a total of five extant texts of the MS. of the Maithili–Sanskrit verse–work *Gītapañcaka* are known to have been in existence in various Archives and private collections in Nepal; these are described below in some detail.

The National Archives of the Government of Nepal in Kathmandu houses a total of three manuscripts of *Gītapañcaka*. These are listed in the Catalogue under B 285/21, B 285/22, and B 283/23. The MS. B 285/21 contains 29 Folios and a *patrāṃka* 'Table of contents' of 2 Folios preceding the onset of the main text (printed in this book as an Appendix); the MS. B 285/22 contains 31 Folios sans *patrāṃka* 'table of contents'; while the MS. B 283/23, according to Professor Horst Brinkhaus of the Department of Indology, University of Kiel, Germany, contains Folios 97–113 and has only Maithili songs sans Sanskrit *śloka* (*Personal communication*, 2013). I have yet to ascertain and avail a copy of it. It is of no major consequence any way as I already possess a copy of the full text of the manuscript containing all Maithili songs (and Sanskrit *śloka*).

As was mentioned earlier, the Āśā Archives located at Raktakālī in Kathmandu preserves in its store a digitalized version of a rather fragmented and therefore incomplete text of the MS. of *Gītapañcaka* and it is listed in the Catalogue under DPN 1991. It is highly likely that this fragmented manuscript may also be available in the National Archives of the Government of Nepal, but I haven't deemed it necessary to ascertain and avail a copy of it as I already own a digital copy of the complete manuscript of it officially made available to me courtesy of the National Archives.

My explorations with the assistance of a few local scholars, most notably Professor Kashinath Tamot, have also led me to a discovery of the existence of the MS. of *Gītapañcaka* containing only the Sanskrit *śloka* sans Maithili songs. Currently it is preserved with the erstwhile NGMPP (Nepal–German Manuscripts Preservation Project) Office in Kathmandu and is listed in its Catalogue under E 2924/4. Fortunately, I have been able to avail a copy of it too. Based on this Sanskrit manuscript, we have also come to learn that the manuscript in question was copied out much later in N.S. 879/1759 CE i.e. around 86 years after the death of king Jagatprakāśamalla.

As indicated above, the present study of *Gītapañcaka* is based on the text of the MS. numbered B 285/22; in other words, of the five extant texts, the MS. of *Gītapañcaka* numbered B 285/22 has been used as A–text of this study. However, during my term as Alexander–von–Humboldt Senior Visiting Scholar at the Institut fuer Skandinavistik, Frisistik und Allgemeine Sprachwissenschaft, Christian–Albrechts–Universitaet Kiel, Germany during the summer of 2013, I happened to avail of an occasion to thoroughly examine and scrutinize the text of a photocopy of the MS. of *Gītapañcaka* numbered B 285/21 kept in private possession of Professor Horst Brinkhaus. The scrutiny led me to the conclusion that barring a few highly predictable and typically well–known orthographical variations relating, in particular, to *r~l, n~ṇ, n~ṃ, m~ṃ, s~ś~ṣ, i~ī, u~ū, t~ṭ, th~ṭh,, d~ḍ, dh~ḍh* etc., there existed practically no fundamental differences between the text of the MS. numbered B 285/21 and that of the MS. numbered B 285/22. Fortunately, by now upon return to Nepal, I have been able to avail a photocopy of the manuscript of *Gītapañcaka* numbered B 285/21 as well. In the present study, I have also been able to include the reprint of the *patrāṃka* 'Table of contents' contained in the manuscript numbered B 285/21 as an Appendix. The *patrāṃka* consists of 2 Folios listing *rāga* 'mode' and *tāla* 'beat', and it cites the first word and/ or the first couple of words of each *pañcaka* song. Thus, Folio 1 Recto has 2 columns and they consist of 6 lines each; instead, Folio 1 Verso and Folio 2 Recto have 3 columns and each column consists of 6 lines, whereas Folio 2 Verso has 2 columns: column 1 consists of 6 lines, while column 2 consists of the last 3 lines only. The *patrāṃka* is evidently written in a densely compact form in a somewhat differently altered handwriting using a rather sharp (bamboo) pen and having small–sized and rather thin letters suggesting that most probably the *patrāṃka* portion was interpolated into the manuscript as a Supplement as it were at a later date and in all likelihood by a different scribe altogether. Interestingly, the fragmented manuscript of the Āśā Archives also contains a one–page *patrāṃka* (the rest is sadly missing) at the end of the text.

The age and date of composition of the MS. of *Gītapañcaka* is unknown. A reference made to the date of death of the poet–king's dear friend Candraśeṣarasiṃha in the manuscript may nonetheless offer a clue. At the very outset, the first song of the first *yāma* 'canto' makes a cryptic reference to N.S. 782/1662 CE as the year of death of Candraśeṣarasiṃha in a chronogram in which numerals are expressed symbolically through rather puzzling code–ciphers ingeniously invented to "give proof of the poet's playfulness and love of enigmas" as it were (Lienhard 1992: 'Introduction,' p. 7):

> *jeṭha jivana sakhi, visalekhe bhela mori, mithuna piriti suka bāre,*
> *nepālaka saṃmate nara diṭhi vasu haya, se dina dura gela hāre //*
> *(Folio 2 R: 6 – 2 V: 1)*

Thus, Candraśeṣarasiṃha – the poet–king's very dear and life–like friend – apparently died on Friday in the month of *jeṭha* 'May–June' of *nara diṭhi* 'eyes' (i.e. 2), *vasu* 'saints/excellent ones' as in *aṣṭa vasu*[14] 'the eight saints or personifications of natural phenomena' (i.e. 8), and *haya* 'horse' as in ‘seven horses of God the Sun’ (i.e. 7); the numerals 287 yielded by the above chronogram are formulaically deciphered in a reverse order from left to right in order to construct the actual date – thus rendering 287 into N.S. 782 corresponding to 1662 CE. In other words, Candraśeṣarasiṃha died about eleven years earlier than the sad death of king Jagatprakāśamalla from the effects of a severe smallpox infection in 1673 CE. Based on the above evidence and the argument presented below, one would tend to surmise that the present collection of Maithili elegiac and panygeric lyrical songs, *Gītapañcaka*, was most probably composed in 1662 CE.

The name of the scribe of the manuscript is not mentioned either. We have come to learn from a different source (Professor Kashinath Tamot, *Personal communication*) though that the extant text of the present MS. of *Gītapañcaka* # B 285/22 was copied out in N.S. 836/1716 CE i.e. 43 years after the death of king Jagatprakāśamalla. A closer scrutiny of the script reveals that the entire manuscript was copied out in a uniform handwriting by a single scribe. In all fairness, it must be stated that the handwriting is distinctly neat, well–shaped, and highly legible. Judging by the orthographic peculiarities and/or anomalies evident in the manuscript, one may be emboldened to conclude that in all likelihood the scribe might have been a person of the Newar caste. More will be said about the orthographic peculiarities and/or anomalies contained in the manuscript in Section 1.7.1.

Gītapañcaka – a dirge, a threnody i.e. “a lamentation to the dead”, and quintessentially an elegy containing a total of 40 Maithili panegyric elegiac songs and a corresponding number of Sanskrit *śloka* – is divided into 8 *yāma* (literally meaning ‘cessation, end’); thus, for example, *prathama yāma*, under one reading, may simply mean ‘end of the (cluster of) first five songs’. In another interpretation, *yāma* is also believed to mean ‘watches’ or Skt. *prahara* (Maithili *pahara*) meaning ‘one–eighth of a day’ i.e. ‘three hours’. One may thus be tempted to surmise that in all likelihood king Jagatprakāśamalla, a versatile and spontaneous poet as he was, probably composed the *Gītapañcaka* within a time span of a total of 8 *yāma* ‘watches’ or *prahara* i.e. within 8 x 3 = 24 hours (most probably in the same year in which Candraśeṣarasiṃha died). In yet another interpretation, *yāma* may also represent the notion of Skt. *sargga* ‘canto’ (cf. the Skt. MS. of *Gītapañcaka* numbered E 2924/4, which happens to use *sargga* instead of *yāma*), suggesting thereby that the verse–work of *Gītapañcaka* containing a total of 8 *sargga* (or *yāma*) 'canto' may lay a legitimate claim to be rightfully classified as a Maithili *mahākāvya* 'epic' – for the simple reason that a *mahākāvya* 'epic' by definition has to have a total of 8 *sargga* (or *yāma)* 'canto'.

In the mean time, I have also come to learn of the existence of a rather new and independent genre of Middle Indo–Aryan versification (in particular in Middle Hindi/Braj Bhasha/Avadhi devotional poetry) popularly known as the *aṣṭayāma paramparā* (cf. Snell 1991/2006). It would behove to investigate in depth if the present Middle Maithili verse–work under study would fit into the scheme of this genre, and whether *Gītapañcaka* was at all influenced – howsoever feebly and remotely – by the Middle Hindi/Braj Bhasha/Avadhi *aṣṭayāma* tradition. Prima facie, Jagatprakāśamalla does seem to have tended to utilize the textural frame of the genre of *aṣṭayāma* in a number of songs (e.g. Folios 5 Verso; 9 Recto; 11 Verso; 15 Recto; 22 Recto; and 25 Verso) contained in *Gītapañcaka*: these songs do indeed appear to exhibit all the outward trappings and vestiges of the *aṣṭayāma* tradition. This investigation, nonetheless, is outside the purview of this work.

Gītapañcaka also contains a cluster of songs of an extremely popular and rather autochthonous genre of the folk oral–literature famously known as the *bārahamāsā* '(song of) the twelve months' in the 5th *yāma* 'canto' (Folios 17 R: 4 – 21 V: 3). The cluster of a total of twelve Maithili *bārahamāsā* songs, representing each month of the Vikramāditya Calendar currently in vogue in Mithilā and Nepal, is described in detail in Section 1.5.1. (See also Yadav 2014b). On the other hand, the Sanskrit *bārahamāsā* (written in the form of *śloka*) is very briefly discussed in Section 1.5.2.

In *Gītapañcaka,* at the end of each *yāma* 'canto', we invariably come across an expression like *bhāṣābhirlikhyate* – meaning thereby that these clusters of Maithili songs and Sanskrit *śloka* were indeed written in the mixed medium of two languages viz. Maithili and Sanskrit, respectively.

To sum up, the complete manuscript of *Gītapañcaka* is preserved in the National Archives of the Government of Nepal in Kathmandu. The MS. under study is listed in the Catalogue of the National Archives of the Government of Nepal under B 285/22; it contains a total of 31 Folios, and each Folio happens to contain a total of 6 exquisitely and neatly written lines.

Finally, the manuscript of *Gītapañcaka* (B 285/22) bears the royal insignia of *Śrī 3 Candra Samśera 1970* implying thereby that in all likelihood the present scribed version of the Newari *Nepālākhala* MS. of *Gītapañcaka* was enlisted in the Catalogue of the royal collection and/or library during the rule of the Rana Prime Minister Śrī 3 Candra Samśera in V.S. 1970, corresponding to 1913 CE.

1. 4. The Structure of the MS. of *Gītapañcaka*

At first sight, *Gītapañcaka* may read like a typical medieval Maithili lyrical drama penned by the Newari–speaking royal men of letters in the Nepālamaṇḍala. As a matter of fact, the opening of *Gītapañcaka* tends to bear all the trappings and vestiges of a typical lyrical play of the time.

The 'Preamble' to *Gītapañcaka* begins with a 'Song of Invocation' to Lord Śiva and his consort Pārvatī in a Sanskrit *śloka* beginning with *oṃ namo nāṭeśvarābhyāṃ* (Folio 1 V: 1). Immediately thereafter follows a song in Maithili – which describes Maheśvara, i.e. Lord Śiva, and his retinue of *gaṇas* 'attendants' including such votaries as Nandī, Gaṇeśa and Nārada. At the end of this song, we are explicitly told that king Jagatprakāśamalla sings this Maithili song out of sheer curiosity (*jagatprakāśa nṛpa kaütuke gābae* Folio 1 V: 5–6). The Maithili song is followed by a Sanskrit *śloka* in the form of a *nāndī stuti* 'Song of Blessing' – which acts as a 'Prologue' to *Gītapañcaka*. The Sanskrit *śloka* presents a highly dramatic and powerful portrayal of *tāṇḍava nṛtya* 'a frantic dance with violent gesticulations' of Lord Śiva and of his retinue of *gaṇas* 'attendants' including such votaries as Nandī, Serpent–King, Kārtikeya, Kārtikeya's mount–the–Peacock and so on, and it contains a plethora of vibrantly vivid and graphic imagery in it. The agile movement and shaking in quick rhythmic succession of the *kakubha* 'a lump of fatty flesh forming a hump on the Bull's neck', and the *gaṇḍoḍḍi* 'a long leathery fan–like cartilage dangling in front of the face and temple of the throat of the ecstatic Bull' while dancing and playing *maruja* 'a *mānari* or a *mṛdaṅga*–like drum', and the Bull's *citkāra* 'loud shrieks' of joy and happiness billowing out a "blessing of protection" for all and everyone are all portrayed with gusto and a vivid poetic imagination. In a similar vein, a breathtakingly superb description of the Serpent–King quivering and struggling to squeeze and wriggle the entire volume of his seemingly bellicose body into his own two flared up nostrils out of sheer fear, nay *angst*, of being devoured by Kārtikeya's mount–the–

Peacock is both picturesque and piteously and hilariously graphic. Without meaning to accuse the poet–king Jagatprakāśamalla of plagiarism, the afore–mentioned Sanskrit *śloka* is stated to have been lifted verbatim unabashedly from Bhavabhūti's classic Sanskrit work *Mālatī–Mādhava* (Jha 1990: 52); similarly, the first *śloka* of the 5th *yāma* 'canto' (Folio 15 V: 1–3) is also known to have been lifted verbatim from Kālidāsa's famous dramatic work *Abhijñāna Śākuntalam* (Professor Shashinath Thakur, *Personal communication*, 2015).

Gītapañcaka pursues a rather consistently systematic structural pattern. Thus, each *yāma* begins with the word *atha* 'thus begins' in a statement made in Sanskrit and it ends in a statement made in Sanskrit beginning with the word *iti* 'finis'. Indeed, we also notice that each *yāma* begins with a Maithili song followed by a Sanskrit *śloka*, and again with a Maithili song followed by a Sanskrit ś*loka*, and so on until the end of the *yāma*. Then it states:

candraśeṣarasiṃhasya, guṇaṃ jñātvā prakāśyate,
gītaślokādibhāṣābhirlikhyate gītapaṃcakaṃ ||
(Folio 5 V: 1–2)

"Knowing the attributes of Candraśeṣarasiṃha and in a bid to extol and highlight them, I have composed the *Gītapañcaka* containing songs in Maithili and *śloka* in Sanskrit."

The end of a *yāma* is characterized by a statement such as the following:

iti śrīgītapañcake, candraśeṣaraviyoge,
śrīśrījayajagatprakāśakṛte, prathamayāmavarṇṇanā samāptā ||
(Folio 5 V: 3–4)

"Thus ends the description of the first *yāma* 'canto' of *Gītapañcaka* composed in sad and loving memory of Candraśeṣara by śrīśrījaya Jagatprakāśamalla."

Here it would probably be apt to note in passing that although king Jagatprakāśamalla avowedly states that the present collection of verse–songs, *Gītapañcaka*, was indeed composed to mourn the sad and untimely death as well as to extol the glorious deeds of his close friend, Candraśeṣarasiṃha, a number of songs contained herein do tend to express rather intensely emotional and highly intimate feelings – suggesting thereby that in all probability a few of these songs might, just might, have been composed to also mourn the sad and untimely death of his third and youngest and dearest queen, Annapūrṇṇālakṣmī – who apparently also died earlier than Jagatprakāśamalla but not yet known exactly when, where, and under what circumstances.

This act of the poet–king's to dedicate the present verse–work in memoriam to an awe–inspiring and highly revered friend appears to be quite in tune with the literary and poetical convention of the time, as is ably exemplified by Jha (1995: 23) in the following lines:

> *maïthilī gīta–paramparāme dekhala jāita achi je kavi apana gītaka bhaṇitāme apana nāmaka saṃga apana guṇagrāhī rasajña āśrayadātā vā mitraka ullekha karaïta chathi.*

> "In the tradition of Maithili song–writing, it is noticed that in the *bhaṇitā* 'author tag' of his song, the poet, along with his own name, happens to make a reference either to the name of his admirer–patron (under whose patronage he serves and flourishes) who is knowledgeable about *rasas* 'sentiments', or to his friend."

The verse–work then states: Now the second *yāma* 'canto' containing a description of good and virtuous deeds of Candraśeṣara begins:

> *atha dvitīyaj[y]āmakṛtyavarṇṇanā (Folio 5 V: 4)*

> "Thus begins the second *yāma* 'canto' describing the (glorious) deeds (of Candraśeṣarasiṃha)."

This structural pattern is followed consistently throughout till the end of the text of *Gītapañcaka* except in the 5th *yāma* 'canto' which tends to suddenly violate as it were the overall structural pattern of this collection of lyrical songs. Thus, in addition to a total of the usual five songs, the 5th *yāma* 'canto' also contains a cluster of 12 *bārahamāsā* '(song of) the twelve months' songs embedded in it. The actual number of songs contained in *Gītapañcaka* may thus add up to 52 (40 + 12). If one also chooses to include a Maithili song provided in the 'Preamble' prior to the onset of the main text, *Gītapañcaka* may be said to contain a total of 53 Maithili songs. Nonetheless, quintessentially, *Gītapañcaka* ought to be viewed as a collection of verse compositions containing 40 Maithili lyrical songs as was the wont of the poet.

Note should also be made of a strangely curious fact that the reader is all of a sudden confronted with the poet–king's virtuosity as well as his versatile ability to compose 1 song in the medium of the Bangla language and 2 songs in the medium of Middle Hindi/Braj Bhasha/Avadhi i.e. the language of Midlands in India in the 5th *yāma* (Folio 15 V: 3 – 16 R: 2) and the 7th *yāma* (Folio 26 R: 2 – 26 V: 6), respectively. Apparently, the custom to insert songs written in Bangla and Braj Bhasha was practiced even earlier: king Jagatprakāśamalla's illustrious grandfather, king Jagajjyotirmalla, too had tended to unhesitatingly embed a total of 7 songs in Bangla and 1 song in Braj Bhasha in his famous collection of verse–songs, *Gītapañcāśikā*, Śakābda 1550/1628 CE ('Śrīśa' ed. Śāke 1896/1974 CE; Mishra & Jha eds. 2010).

In consonance with its original scheme of structural parallelism, *Gītapañcaka* also contains a total of 5 Sanskrit *śloka* in each of the 8 *yāma* (8 x 5 = 40) except in the 5th *yāma* wherein, along with the 12 *bārahamāsā* Maithili songs, it also contains an additional number of a total of 12 corresponding Sanskrit *bārahamāsā śloka* – thus totalling the number of Sanskrit *śloka* to 52 (40 + 12). If one also chooses to count a Sanskrit *śloka* contained in the 'Prologue' prior to the onset of the main text, *Gītapañcaka* may be said to contain a total of 53 Sanskrit *śloka*. In all, then, *Gītapañcaka* may be said to contain a total of 53 Maithili songs and a total of 53 Sanskrit *śloka* (53 + 53 = 106). In essence, though, *Gītapañcaka* ought to be viewed as a verse–work containing a total of 40 Maithili panegyric elegiac songs and a total of corresponding 40 Sanskrit *śloka* as was the wont of the poet. That this was the real intent of the poet is evident at the end of the text of the 8th *yāma* of the manuscript wherein it categorically states as follows:

> *// iti śrīgītapañcake, candraśeṣaraviyoge, śrīśrījayajagatprakāśakṛte aṣṭamayāmavarṇṇanā samāptā // (Folio 31 V: 2–3)*

> "Thus ends the description of the 8th *yāma* 'canto' of *Gītapañcaka* composed by śrīśrījaya Jagatprakāśamalla in sad and loving memory of Candraśeṣara."

Thus also ends the *Gītapañcaka* – an elegy written in a royal courtyard in the Kingdom of Bhaktapur – by the poet–king Jagatprakāśamalla in loving memory of his dear friend Candraśeṣarasiṃha.

1.5. Textual Analysis: Literary

This section discusses, in main, the Maithili *bārahamāsā* song and the Sanskrit *bārahamāsā* written as *śloka* and succeeding each of the Maithili *bārahamāsā* song, and states that *Gītapañcaka* may indeed be viewed as an early sample of a "long" Maithili poem in general and as a panegyric elegy in particular.

1. 5. 1. Maithili *Bārahamāsā*

Bārahamāsā (composed of two constituent elements *bāraha* 'twelve' and *māsā* 'month') '(song of) the twelve months' is an extremely well–known and extraordinarily popular and prototypical genre of oral folk–literture – folk or literary, secular or devotional, but highly romantic and intensely emotional – in practically all of Modern Indo–Aryan languages, including Maithili. Indeed, the childhood memories of the amorous sound and sweet cadence of bucolic young male folks of my village rocking themselves in the swing tied tightly with a rope onto two stark bamboo poles in mango groves while singing the Maithili *bārahamāsā* beginning with *caïta he sakhi*... linger vividly in my mind till today.

Extant old *bārahamāsā* texts in Indo–Aryan languages such as Old Rajasthani (Varma ed. V.S. 1982/1925 CE; Nahta ed. 1953), Old Gujarati (Dalal ed. 1956), Old Marathi, Old Braj Bhasha, Old Avadhi (Mullā Dāūd's *Candāyan*, composed in 1375), Classical Bangla (Zbavitel 1961), and Bhojpuri (Grierson 1884) are both well–attested and sufficiently reliably studied and analyzed (Zbavitel 1961; Vaudeville 1986). As a matter of fact, the *bārahamāsā* song, with its three hallmark traits, has tended to serve as a "template" for poets of all Modern Indo–Aryan languages of north India, including the national language, Nepali, of Nepal (and I might add, for Tibeto–Burman Newari speaking poet–kings of medieval Nepal: cf. Lienhard 1992, Song # 67, p. 159) for centuries, as was ably observed by Orsini (2010). In her own words:

> Today barahmasas are perceived only as a kind of folk song, but a significant literary tradition attests to the attractiveness of this template for poets in all the literary languages of north India for centuries...The female voice, her pining for and loyalty to, her absent lover and the calendrical cycle are the core elements of a matrix that poets from a wide variety of cultural backgrounds took up and modulated according to their specific taste and inclination. (Orsini 2010: 143)

The earliest analysis of folk–songs, including *bārahamāsā* songs, of an Indo–Aryan language that I happened to have come across thus far is by

Grierson (1884b, 1886). In a seminal article titled "Some Bihārī Folk–Songs," Grierson (1884b) analyzes Bhojpuri folk–songs such as *Sohar* (Song # 9–11), *Vivāha–Gīta* (Song # 12), *Jhūmar* or *Pūrwī* (Song # 13–15), and *Jat'sār* (Song # 16–18); in addition, he also analyzes a total of 7 Bhojpuri *bārahamāsā* (actually 6 "*Bārah Māsas*" and 1 "*Catur māsa*") songs in sufficient detail and provides some piercing and highly illuminating observations on the form of these songs:

> The first seven of these songs belong to a class well known throughout India from the earliest times...My own knowledge of modern vernacular folk–songs is confined to Eastern Hindūstān and the Bengal Presidency, and with regard to this tract I can assert that several songs of the class are popular in every district between Banāras and the Brahmāputra. These songs are at the present day called '*Bārah Māsas*' or '(songs of) the twelve months.' Their form is always the same. Some woman laments the absence of her beloved or of her son. Each verse is devoted in order to a month of the Hindū year; in it she describes the peculiar woe which she experiences at that season. Thus she goes through the round of the twelve months, and at the last month her patience is generally rewarded by the return of her husband, or of her son, as the case may be. (p. 200)

It is claimed, and in my mind rightly so, that the earliest Maithili *bārahamāsā* – pronounced by Maithili speakers as [bərə'masa][15] – songs were composed during the first quarter of the 15th century by the greatest Maithili poet Vidyāpati (circa 1352–1448). As a precursor as it were to a practice carried out some three centuries later by such eminent poet–kings of medieval Nepal as Jagajjyotirmalla (1614–1637) and Jagatprakāśamalla (1643–1673), these songs are found to have been embedded in a collection of mellifluous lyrical songs of Vidyāpati famously known as the *Padāvalī*. Thus, in a footnote # 51, Zbavitel (1961: 607) alludes to a Maithili *bārahamāsā* song occurring in a publication of Vidyāpati's *Padāvalī* edited by Basumati (1935, pp. 194–195) and published in Calcutta. Similarly, a Maithili *bārahamāsā* song depicting all the twelve months of the year is found to have been inserted in a masterly collection of a total of 710 mellifluous songs of Vidyāpati edited by Govind Jha (1981: 229–230, Song # 569). Upon inquiry, Govind Jha (*Personal communication*: *Emails*, dated the 19 and 20 November 2014) has very kindly and graciously informed me that he had lifted the above–mentioned *bārahamāsā* song from Nagendranath Gupta's edition of Vidyāpati's songs titled *Bidyāpati Ṭhākurer Padāvalī* (Song # 729) and that Nagendranath Gupta had indeed acknowledged to have acquired the song in question from a source in Mithilā – implying therby that in course of his research Govind Jha had never ever come across this song in any earlier source – hand–copied manuscript or otherwise – prior to that of Nagendranath Gupta's. Nagendranath Gupta's classic edition included two types of songs: songs contained in the *Taraünī Palmleaf MS.* as well as the songs collected at large in Mithilā; the second category of songs were arranged under the rubric *Mithilār Pada* and the *bārahamāsā* song in question was placed under this rubric (it is common knowledge by now that Nagendranath Gupta had indeed received the collections of both varieties of songs courtesy of the Mahārājādhirāja of Darbhanga). All this leads us to the inescapable conclusion that the *bārahamāsā* song contained in Govind Jha's (1981) erudite edition does not form part of a hand–copied manuscript. Towards the fag end of the time for submission of the final draft of this book for publication to the press, I chanced to lay my hand on a copy of Govind Jha's (ed. 2012) seminal work titled *Vidyāpati–Gīta–Samagra* – a compendium of 866 songs, with annotations and index, compiled from a total of 15 known and/or acknowledged sources that happen to contain songs composed by or ascribed to the greatest Maithili poet Vidyāpati. Not much therefore will be said about the aforesaid book except that it too contains a total of 1 *bārahamāsā* song listed under Nagendranath Gupta's collection (Song # 735: pp. 533–34). Similarly, to the best of my knowledge, no hand–copied manuscript of *bārahamāsā* songs composed by the greatest Maithili poet, Vidyāpati, or copied out by scribes of a later date, has been discovered as yet. Strangely enough, such masterly compilers and editors of Vidyāpati's songs as George Abraham Grierson (1882), Shivanandana Thakur (ed. 1941), and Subhadra Jha (ed. 1954) – to name only the famous few – tend not to contain even a single *bārahamāsā* song in their collections and/or anthologies. It is quite likely that there may be more *bārahamāsā* songs in existence published in anthologies that are beyond my reach at the moment, but, thus far, I have been able to locate the published versions of a total of only four *bārahamāsā* songs categorically bearing the name of the poet Vidyāpati in their *bhaṇitā* 'author tag' as composer; these are: a song contained in Basumati (1935: 194–195) as cited in Zbavitel (1961: 607, Footnote # 51); Govind Jha (1981: 229–230, Song # 569); Kāmeśvarī

Devī (1999: 175, Song # 405); Amar Nath Jha (2008: 329, Song # 1021) – a variant version of which is also reprinted in Vishweshwar Mishra (2014: 94–95, Song # 191). Interestingly, Amar Nath Jha's most voluminous collection, containing a total of 1521 songs of Vidyāpati, also includes a *bārahamāsā* song without explicitly bearing the name of Vidyapati as composer in its *bhaṇitā* 'author tag' (Amar Nath Jha 2008, 232–234, Song # 735). One only wishes that these published *bārahamāsā* songs of Vidyāpati may not turn out to be spurious interpolations by later rather less–known poets.

Maithili *bārahamāsā* songs constitute an opulently rich and impressive heritage of oral literary tradition par excellence. Nonetheless, contemporary and colloquial versions of a number of *bārahamāsā* songs, occasionally bearing the names of composers, are printed in a number of anthologies of Maithili *loka* 'folk' and *saṃskāra* 'rite of passage' songs but tend to shun bearing any reliable references to the source and mode of collection and/or time of composition. Mention may be made of two such extremely famous and highly remarkable anthologies viz. Rāmiqbālasiṃha 'Rākeśa' (V.S. 1999/1942 CE) and Kāmeśvarī Devī (1999), and of a book mistakenly titled as *Maïthilī* [sic] *Saṃskṛti* by Ram Dayal Rakesh (1999). Thus, under the rubric *bārahamāsā*, 'Rākeśa' (V. S. 1999/1942 CE: 404–467) lists a total of 20 songs and subcategorizes them as *bārahamāsā* proper (14), *bārahamāsā chandaparaka*[16] (1), a scaled–down version of a *bārahamāsā* known as *caümāsā* 'song of the four months (of the rainy season)' (1), and *caümāsā chandaparaka* (3). Interestingly, 1 song (i.e. Song Number 11) compiled herein makes no mention of any months whatsoever. Names of poets such as Kũvara, Sūra, Babana, Sukavidāsa, Gopāladāsa, Nebālāla, Kulapati, Jayadevasvāmī, and Mādhava are mentioned in the *bhaṇitā* of songs. A total of 14 songs bear the names of composers in their *bhaṇitā*, while 6 songs are by composers who have apparently wished to remain anonymous. Kāmeśvarī Devī (1999: 171–181) lists a total of 16 songs, and subcategorizes them as *caümāsā* (5), *chandaparaka caümāsā* (2), another scaled–down version of a *bārahamāsā* known as *chaümāsā* 'song of six months' i.e. from Jyeṣṭha to Kārtika corresponding to May–June through October–November (1), *bārahamāsā* proper (7), and *chandaparaka bārahamāsā* (1). Names of poets such as Rāmakṛṣṇa, Baṭenātha, Kṛṣṇa, Śambhudāsa, Jayadevasvāmī, Vidyāpati, Mādhava, Ramānanda, Nebālāla, and Kulapati are mentioned in the *bhaṇitā* of songs. A total of 11 songs bear the names of poets in their *bhaṇitā*, while 5 are anonymous. Similarly, Ram Dayal Rakesh (1999) lists a total of 17 *bārahamāsā* songs of which only one categorically bears the name of Sūradāsa as composer in its *bhaṇitā* 'author tag' (p. 62) while the rest are anonymous: he also lists scaled–down versions such as *tinamāsā* (1), *caümāsā* (3), *pañcamāsā* (1), *chaümāsā* (1), and even a *satamāsā* (1) without labeling it to be so. The so–called verse fillers and what Grierson (1884) mirthfully calls "unmeaning burdens" such as *re*, *rī*, *he*, *ho*, *ne*, *me*, *ge, nā re*, *e*, *yo, yaü* are commonly used in these *bārahamāsā* songs. Grierson's mirthful observations in this regard are worth quoting here:

> The uneducated, and especially women, have a great reverence for the unintelligible, and love for "that blessed word Mesopotamia" is just as great in the East as it is in the West. (1884: 198)
>
> Like folk–songs in other languages, these songs abound in unmeaning burdens, like the English "Sing heigh, sing ho, the linden tree,"... (1884: 199)
>
> Examples are the unmeaning phrases ललना in Song No. 9. and हू रे जी in Song No. 16. These, as a rule, I have left untranslated. To translate them would seem only ridiculous, and to translate them would be impossible without destroying the Oriental colour of the picture which I attempt to present to view. (1884: 199)

As indicated above, the Maithili *bārahamāsā* song under study does not form a separate and independent identity of its own; instead it is found to be embedded, as a veritable mark of virtuosity, versatility and craftsmanship of the poet as it were, in the manuscript of the Maithili 'epic' poem *Gītapañcaka* composed by Jagatprakāśamalla in a Newari script. This is after all not the first occasion when Jagatprakāśamalla has done so: in another collection consisting of an assortment of devotional verse compositions titled *Nānārtha Deva Devī Gīta Saṃgraha* n.d. (Sundar Jha Shastri V.S. 2029/1972 CE), the poet–king has tended to insert a *bārahamāsā* song laced with *Megha Mallāra Rāga* and *Kharjjati Lāṃjati Tāla* (Song # 63, pp. 18–19). This custom to embed a song of a totally different and independent genre in a long epic poem may not be as unusual as it appears prima facie; after all the Newar poet–kings did habitually compose Newari *bārahamāsā* songs in skilful imitation of the pattern of North Indo–Aryan languages (Lienhard 1974/1992, Song # 67, p.

159). Mention must also be made of a similar custom practised much earlier even by Jagatprakāśamalla's illustrious grandfather, Jagajjyotirmalla, who has highly ingeniously inserted a number of indigenous Maithili "folk tunes" such as *laganī* 'song sung while grinding grains under two heavy stone slabs' (Song # 46), *kobara* 'wedding song' (Song # 47), and *jhūmari* 'song sung on swings' (Song # 49) in his collection of verse–songs laced with classical *rāga* 'mode' and *tāla* 'beat', *Gītapañcāśikā*, Śakābda 1550/1628 CE, ('Śrīśa' ed. Śāke 1896/1974 CE, pp. 22–24). We have also come to learn from Zbavitel (1961) that this practice to embed songs was "of considerable antiquity" (p. 587) in classical Bangla literature, that it was after all "no chance addition or insertion" (p. 588) in course of development of the Bangla narrative *Baromasi*, and that even Bangla *Baromasi* of *viraha* 'separation' was found to be "best suited to be interpolated into longer epics" (p. 590).

In course of my investigation, thus far, I happen to have come across a total of two *bārahamāsā* songs penned by poet–king Jagatprakāśamalla: as indicated above, one *bārahamāsā* song is inserted in his collection of an assortment of devotional verse compositions titled *Nānārtha Deva Devī Gīta Saṃgraha* (Sundar Jha Shastri ed. V.S. 2029/1972 CE, Song # 63, pp. 18–19), while the other is embedded in the collection of lyrical songs under study titled *Gītapañcaka* (Folios 17 R: 4 – 21 V: 3). Both of the above–mentioned verse–works are no doubt undated. Based on the arguments presented above in Section **1.3** and suggesting that *Gītapañcaka* was more than likely composed in the same year in which Jagatprakāśamalla's life–like friend Candraśeṣarasiṃha died (i.e. 1662 CE), I have tended to arrive at the conclusion that the hand–copied Newari manuscript of the present cluster of *bārahamāsā* songs, found to be embedded in the manuscript of the collection of lyrical songs, *Gītapañcaka*, composed by the Bhaktapur–king Jagatprakāśamalla in c.1662 CE, may claim to be the oldest extant hand–copied text of the Maithili *bārahamāsā* songs, to date.

Most *bārahamāsā* are what is called *viraha–bārahamāsā*; in other words, they tend to express an ardent longing for reunion among the separated lovers. These folk–songs are both secular and sectarian/devotional. The secular *bārahamāsā* songs dwell on the popular theme of "the pain of separation (*viraha*) endured by a young wife pining for the return of her beloved all the twelve months of the year" (Vaudeville 1986: x). The acute pain of separation described therein is pitched against the background of a highly moving description of nature's (i.e. season's) face aggravating the pain of separation during each month of the year – the rainy season of four months being most un–bearing. On the other hand, the so–called religious/devotional *bārahamāsā* songs depict the separation of Rādhā (or a Gopī) from Kṛṣṇa and describe her acute pining for reunion with Kṛṣṇa. Occasionally a few songs also tend to describe Maïnā's acute anguish over choosing a highly unusual and rather cumbersome bridegroom in the form of Śivaśaṃkara for her daughter Gaüri. A *bārahamāsā* is also said to depict a mystical conflict of 'within' with 'beyond': an Article of the Month – September 2009 and posted in an online *Exotic India Newsletter* states as follows:

> Nature affords to Barahmasa poetry its canvas, all pictures and colours, love, its spirit and essence, and endless continuity of its pangs month–after–month, its narrative technique and epical stretch and binds into one thread the two confronting worlds, the worlds of man and nature. (No page number given)

Nonetheless, the present cluster of *bārahamāsā* songs representing all the twelve months of a year and embedded in the manuscript of an 'epic' poem, *Gītapañcaka*, makes a clear departure from the literary convention in that it is avowedly written to commemorate the sudden and untimely demise of king Jagatprakāśamalla's life–like and dear friend Candraśeṣarasiṃha and to express deep sorrow and grief over the loss of and separation from the loved one as well as to extol his fine attributes and virtuous deeds.

Composers of Maithili *bārahamāsā* are at variance with regard to the issue of the structure of their songs; in other words, there is no apparent unity of structure with regard to precisely which month of the Vikramāditya Calendar currently in vogue in Nepal and Mithilā a typical *bārahamāsā* song ought to begin with. Thus, 5 out of 7 *bārahamāsā*–proper songs compiled in Kāmeśvarī Devī's (ed. 1999) anthology begin with a description of the month of *Caïta* and end with a description of the month of *Phāguna*. Of the remaining two songs, one song begins with a description of the month of *Baïsākha* and ends with a description of the month of *Caïta*, while the other song begins with a description of the month of *Asāḍha* and ends with a description of the month of *Jeṭha*. The only *chandaparaka bārahamāsā* song contained in this anthology begins with a description of the month of *Sāona* and ends with a description of the month of *Asāḍha*. Similarly, as indicated above, the anthology edited by 'Rākeśa' (ed. V.S. 1999/1942 CE) contains a total of 14 *bārahamāsā*–proper songs which describe all the twelve months of the year. Apparently, these songs observe no uniform unity of structure either. Thus, of the 14 *bārahamāsā*–proper songs, 7 begin with a description of the month of *Asāḍha* and end with the description of the month of *Jeṭha*; 6 songs describe the months of *Caïta* to *Phāguna*; and 1 song describes the months of *Jeṭha* to *Baïsākha*. One additional song, labeled as *bārahamāsā chandaparaka*, begins with the description of *Sāona* and ends with a description of the month of *Asāḍha*, The remaining *caümāsā* and *caümāsā chandaparaka* songs too display a similar discrepancy with regard to the unity of structure. As indicated earlier, Ram Dayal Rakesh's (V.S. 2056/1999 CE) work cites a total of 17 *bārahamāsā* songs depicting all the twelve months of the year; these songs too observe no uniform unity of structure either. Similarly, the *tinamāsā*, *caümāsā*, *pañcamāsā*, *chaümāsā*, and *satamāsā* songs too display a stark discrepancy with regard to the structural unity.

It is worth noting though that the present *bārahamāsā* song of Jagatprakāśamalla specified with *Nāṭa Mallāra Rāga* and *Kharjati Lāṃjati Tāla* and the two *bārahamāsā chandaparaka* songs contained in the anthologies referred to above observe a peculiarly striking analogy of unity of structure. In other words, all the three *bārahamāsā* songs that are laced with information on the musical *rāga* 'mode' and *tāla* 'beat' begin with a description of the month of *Sāona* (Skt. *Śrāvaṇa*) and end with a description of the month of *Asāḍha* (Skt. *Āṣāḍha*).

Another structural peculiarity that tends to characterize the present *bārahamāsā* of king Jagatprakāśamalla as unique is that each stanza of the song of twelve months contains a total of four *caraṇa* (roughly speaking, lines) and that the third *caraṇa* begins with a reduplication of the last *pada* (roughly speaking, word) or parts of the last *pada* of the second *caraṇa* – thereby lending flexibility and cadence to the sonorous voice of the singer. Needless to say, this feature is stridently lacking in other *bārahamāsā* songs – be they the songs collected in Grierson (1884) or the ones compiled in other anthologies referred to above.

In a study of the first Urdu *bārahamāsā* song titled *Bikaṭ Kahānī* and composed by Afzal Jhinjhanvi in the early 17th century, Rakhshanda Jalil (2012) comes as it were to "the rescue of the rich and important but largely ignored literary form" of *bārahamāsā* and asserts that it is in essence almost entirely rural and that it survives in the form of a *loka gīta*. Jalil (2012: 3) also lists a total of three hallmark traits of a *bārahamāsā* in this study; in her own words, these are: *gharelu lehja* 'domestic style', *dramai tarz* 'dramatic tone', and *khud-kalami* 'use of the first person'. Decrying the rather slanted and lopsided thrust of contemporary literary criticism and research, Jalil (2012: 5) concludes:

> Had the literary historian not created this artificial distinction between high and low literature, a great deal of folk–related literature whose roots go back to an orally–transmitted cultural legacy would not have been marginalized. However, it is still not too late. Even now, if we abandon the parameters of 'high' culture and 'high' literature and begin to study the small and the simple and the natural we can avert some of the dangers of separatism.

Needless to say, Jalil's succinct remarks will provide a proper perspective on the scientific study of the Maithili *bārahamāsā* song in particular and the Maithili folk–literature in general, especially in view of the fact that the age–old tendency to mistakenly dichotomize *loka sāhitya* 'oral/folk literature' as "folksy" and written literature, composed mainly by Brahmins, as *śiṣṭa sāhitya* 'cultured literature' woefully continues to persist till today (cf. Malangiya 2004: 54, Mishra 2008: 4, Jha 2010: 82, and 'Ramaṇa' ed. 2014 'Editorial', page number not indicated).

Finally, the main question that raises itself is: Is the genre of *bārahamāsā* poetry an autochthonous form, or is it derived from some other source? It may not be easy to come up with a definitive statement with regard to the genesis of the genre of *bārahamāsā*. It is commonly held that the earliest form of the *bārahamāsā* song may be traced back to the *ṛtuvarṇana* 'the portrayal of a season', in particular the *ṣaḍṛtuvarṇana* 'the portrayal of six seasons' depicted in the *Ṛg Veda* and the Vedic *Saṃhitās*, and later in the great epics of Classical Sanskrit – the *Rāmāyaṇa* and the *Mahābhārata* –, and still later in Kālidāsa's *Ṛtusaṃhāra*, a work that describes the six seasons of the Indian lunar calendar in sufficient detail (cf. *WWW.exoticindiaart.com*). Nevertheless, basing himself on a strict scrutiny of around two hundred Bangla *Baromasi* in different parts of Bengal and of a host of texts of the folk–poetry and literature of Rajasthan, Punjab, Gujarat, Orissa, Tamilnad and a number of tribal areas, including those of Chhattisgarh, of India, Zbavitel (1961: 615) has arrived at a succinct and credible conclusion:

> At present, it seems most probable that the Baromasi existed in the folk–poetry of India in a very remote past, that it was preserved by oral tradition and that it spread all over India, developing in each of its numerous national and tribal literatures in a different way.

In the light of the above firm assertion of Zbavitel's, it would be both apt and proper to view the *bārahamāsā* song (and for that matter the Maithili *bārahamāsā* song) as an autochthonous genre of the oral folk–liteature.

1. 5. 2. Sanskrit *Bārahamāsā Śloka*

It is hard to determine with certitude if *bārahamāsā* songs *per se* and modelled either on the pattern of the maxim of the "template" so ably described by Orsini (2010) or on the pattern of Afzal Jhinjhanvi bearing the three hallmark traits referred to in Jalil (2012) were ever composed in the medium of the Sanskrit language – Vedic or Classical. Most probably they were not. Upon gleaning the available accounts, it is discerned that much of the available information tends to hinge on the possible connection subsisting between the *bārahamāsā* and the *ṛtuvarṇana*, in particular, the *ṣaḍṛtuvarṇanā* – so dexterously delineated in the Vedic and Classical Sanskritic literary texts. All we have been able to ascertain thus far is that with the decline of Prakrit, Pali and Apabhraṃśa around the turn of the 1st millennium, *bārahamāsā* as an autochthonous genre of the oral folk–poetry began to be composed independently in a variety of ways in a number of newly emerging regional Vernacular languages of India. Therefore, without further ado, I propose to add a very brief note below on the Sanskrit *bārahamāsā śloka* found to have been embedded in the verse–text of *Gītapañcaka*.

The 5th *yāma* 'canto' (Folios 17 R: 4 to 21 V: 3) of *Gītapañcaka* contains a total of 12 *bārahamāsā śloka* – covering all the twelve months of a year – beginning with a description of the month of *Śrāvaṇa* (July–August) and ending with a description of the month of *Āṣāḍha* (June–July). The pattern of structural arrangement happens to be as follows: first occurs the Maithili song of a stanza of four *caraṇa* (roughly speaking, lines) and then occurs a Sanskrit *śloka* (of two lines). This custom is uniformly observed throughout without exception.

Content–wise, the Sanskrit *śloka* is not quite an exact replica of the preceding Maithili song – although both the Maithili song and the Sanskrit *śloka* reinforce as well as complement each other, and together they tend to express king Jagatprakāśamalla's deep sense of loss and his poignantly genuine pain and bereavement of separation from his most intimate and dear friend Candraśeṣarasiṃha. What distinguishes the Sanskrit *śloka* most is the copious use of similes and metaphors, occasionally bordering on hyperbolic extremity and even verbosity – cf. especially the Sanskrit *śloka* contained in Folios 19 V, 20 R, 20 V, and 21 R.

Thus, to sum up our brief discussion on the literary traits of the present verse–text under study, it can be safely surmised that the collection of lyrical songs, *Gītapañcaka*, is a panegyric elegy of superb quality evoking deeper feelings of extreme loss and sadness in great measure. One may also venture to describe *Gītapañcaka* as a veritable sample of an early 'long" poem, nay a *mahākāvya* 'epic', of reasonably good poetic quality composed in Middle Maithili during the mid 17th century.

1. 6. The Prosody

This section will list the *rāga* 'mode' and *tāla* 'beat' indicated in *Gītapañcaka* and make a brief commentary and a rather sweeping remark on the age–old conventional mode of prosodic analysis carried out in the literature.

As indicated above, the lyrical songs contained in the *Gītapañcaka* are laced with *rāga* 'mode' and *tāla* 'beat'. Following is a list of a total of 23 *rāga* indicated in *Gītapañcaka*:

1. Dhanāchi/Dhanāśrī
2. Aherāṇī
3. Vibhāsā
4. Bhaïrava
5. Velāvala/Verāvara
6. Kaüśika
7. Kedāra Mālava
8. Mālava
9. Gopivallabha

10. Gaürī
11. Korāva
12. Gujjarī
13. Sorathī
14. Varāḍi
15. Bhathyārī
16. Nāṭa Mallāra
17. Pathamañjari
18. Kāmoda
19. Nāṭa
20. Āsāvari
21. Sorathi Pahaḍiyā
22. Vasanta
23. Sāraṃgī Pañcama

Following is a list of a total of 8 *tāla* indicated in *Gītapañcaka*:

1. Cokha
2. Kharjjati (A Newri calque for the Gauḍian *drutayati*)
3. Paratāl[r]ā
4. Raghuśeṣara
5. Lāṃjati (A Newari calque for the Gauḍian *mantharayati*)
6. Eka (tāla)
7. Kharjjati Lāṃjati (A combination of two *tāla*)
8. Jati (Is it a truncated form of Kharjjati or of Lāṃjati?)

To the best of my knowledge, no scientific description dealing with the versification and metrical analysis of aspects of Maithili prosody of a *mahākāvya*, a *khaṇḍakāvya*, or of a poem – long or short – is available to date. A number of primers masquerading as works on Maithli *chandaśāstra* in the Indian market turn out to be indeed a mere description of the Sanskrit prosody written in the medium of the Maithili language. This may not be as surprising as it appears. After all, almost all Maithili metres derive from those of Sanskrit, Prakrit and Apabhraṃśa, and are described wholly on the pattern of the Sanskrit terminology.

The age–old practice of conventional prosodic analysis based on restricting itself to mechanically compute the number of *laghu* 'short' and *guru* 'long' syllables in each line of a stanza may turn out to be less efficacious and even vacuous, as was observed much earlier in a monumental work by Mukherji (1976). Regretting the absence of a scientific and/or systematic analysis of the metres, Mukherji described the state of affair as follows:

> Only superficial features like the number of syllables in a verse and the particular sequence of longs and shorts in it were considered, and metres with widely different rhythmic qualities were lumped together in the same group. (p. 1)

In the same breath, Mukherji concluded that:

> Except sometimes in the name, there is no indication of the rhythmic character of a particular metre or of the considerations that may have led to the acceptance of the metrical scheme as **the objective correlate of an emotional mood** (Boldness added). (p. 2)

More than a century earlier than Mukherji, Grierson (1884: 198–199) too had made some highly pertinent remarks on the prosody of the Bhojpuri *bārahamāsā* folk–songs; these are worth quoting here:

> Another point to be noted in these songs is that they by no means follow the strict and complicated metric laws of Tulsī Dās and B[*sic*]idyāpati. Nor, considering their singers and preservers, can they be expected to do so. Probably, when they were written, each line may have contained its orthodox supply of long and short *mātras*, but now they are, and for generations they have been, remembered by the melody to which they are sung, and by that alone. Any number of syllables, long or short, can be crowded into a line, so long as the need of a musical *ictus* is satisfied. Hence no study of the *Prākrit Pingal* nor of the *Chhandodīpak* will avail for reading these songs, though, as Mr. Beams so happily says, "they trip off the tongue with a lilt and grace which are irresistable".

As a matter of fact, a fresh analysis based on assessing as to how precisely the *rāga* 'mode' and *tāla* 'beat' manouevre to incrementally contribute to enhancing the poetical quality of a poem/song in general and the lyricality and/or musicality in particular needs to be carried out; it is indeed the dire need of the day. Unfortunately, however, a study modelled on Sen (1973), Snell (1991/2006), Nagasaki (ed. 2012) and Kitada (2012) delineating the versification and the metrical structures of Middle Maithili verse–compositions as well as describing and/or classifying the structure of songs according to use, text, scale/melody or rhythm and providing the musical notations of Middle Maithili lyrical songs on the pattern of Henry (1988: 291–310; 1998) is beyond the scope of the present work. Indeed, all this would form the subject matter of a separate study altogether.

1.7. Textual Analysis: Grammatical Notes

Basing exclusively on the spelling system of the *Nepālākhala* Newari script used in the verse–text of *Gītapañcaka*, this section will dwell briefly on the Middle Maithili sound system that may obtain, and will also attempt to present a sketch of a morphological analysis of nouns, pronouns, numerals, adjectives, gender, verbs (including auxiliary verbs, compound verbs, and converbs), adverbs, emphatic clitics, and vocatives and/or verse–fillers of Middle Maithili. A few sentence types will also be described in brief.

1.7.1. Script and Sound System

To an initiate not fully conversant with, and not quite adept in, reading the Newari script – in particular with how to flawlessly decipher it and as to how to correctly interpret a host of intricate ways in which the graphemes and various and curious combinations of *mātrā* of the Newari script represent the sound system of Middle Maithili – it is recommended that the reader go through my earlier work (Yadav ed. 2011, pp. 22–42). Nonetheless, a few pertinent observations delineating the prominent features of the Newari orthography discerned in the verse–text of *Gītapañcaka* are made below.

a) A closer scrutiny of the script reveals that the entire manuscript was copied out in a uniform handwriting by a single Newar scribe. In all fairness, it must be stated that the handwriting is distinctly neat, well–shaped, and highly legible.

b) Like in other medieval manuscripts of the Nepālamaṇḍala stored in the National Archives in Kathmandu, in the manuscript of *Gītapañcaka* too, all words are interconnected and characterized by absence of space between words until a pause mark occurs – thereby causing tremendous difficulty of word–division; this also ensues forth considerable room for ambiguity on a number of occasions. Examples of <*na*> and <*hi*> may be cited. In particular, the character <*na*> tends to pose more difficulty as it may stand as: (i) a negative marker, (ii) a locative case marker, and (iii) an intrinsic part of a word itself.

c) Consonant characters are less problematic and pose no difficulty in general; nonetheless, there is room for confusion between the following pairs of consonant characters, e.g. <*ya*> and <*pa*>; <*ca*> and <*ra*>; <*cha*> and <*kṣa*>; and also between <*ḍa*> and the vowel character <*u*>. Characters such as <*jha*>, <*cha*>, <*bha*>, and <*pha*> are equally problematic for accurate decipherment, while <*va*> and <*ba*> are almost always inseparable. A Newar scribe also typically tends to alternate between such grapheme pairs as <*tha*> for <*ṭa*>, <*dha*> for <*ḍha*>, <*ra*> for <*la*>, <*la* > for <*ra*>, <*ṭa*> for <*ta*>, and so on. Similarly, a few consonant combinations that pose considerable difficulty in correct decipherment are: <*ttha*>, <*ṣṭa*>, <*tpra*>, <*khya*>, and <*pta*>. Most of such ambiguities are however suitably disambiguated in the context by an expert reader of the text.

d) Vowels too are rather straightforward: both short and long graphemes are available in the text. Unlike in other hand–copied Newari manuscripts of Middle Maithili that I happen to have investigated thus far, distinct and unambiguous use of *mātrā* indicating long <*ī*> and long <ū> are attested in the text throughout. Thus, for example, the words <*sūkha*>, <*bhūkha*> (Folio 9 V: 3), <*dūkha*> (Folio 18 R: 6) and <*pūṣa*> (Folio 19 R: 2) typically bear the distinct use of the *mātrā* indicating long <*ū*>, while <*tasu*>, <*mukha*> (Folio 9 V: 3) and <sukha> (18 V: 1) display a clear and unambiguous use of the *mātrā* indicating short <*u*>. Similarly, the following words <*peyasi mori sajani sakhi*> (Folio 7 V: 5) all indicate a clear use of the *mātrā* indicating short <*i*>, while words such as <*bhīna*>, <*vihīna*> (Folio 9 R: 4–5), <*tohī* > (Folio 8 R: 3) and <*hīta*> (Folio 12 R: 1) display a distinct use of the *mātrā* indicating long < ī >. The long vowel grapheme ई (also written ईा) is attested but only twice in the text, while the long vowel grapheme ऊ is observed to have occurred but once in the text, and that too for the sole purpose of rhyme.

e) Punctuation Marks: In addition to the copious and rather indiscriminate use of the punctuation mark for a (single) comma, including double commas (indicated by a rather reversed sign of a usual comma) and a semi full stop and a full stop (indicated by a single vertical bar and double vertical bars, respectively), a total of three other rather unusual punctuation marks that are used in the text deserve special mention here. Thus,

(i) A punctuation mark consisting either of three dots written in the fashion of a colon, or of three hyphens written from above and upside down is used to indicate that a little space is left empty or unfilled after a consonant character (C) or after a consonant cluster (CC) or after a consonant vowel cluster (CV) at the end of a line. This attests to the meticulousness with which the scribe of the present manuscript observes the principle of uniformity and symmetry and neatness on a written page. Examples occur on: Folios 1 V: 5, 4 R: 3, 6 R: 6, 10 V: 3, 14 R: 6, 23 V: 4, 31 R: 5, and so on.

(ii) A mini v–like mark is used to indicate that a character (or a cluster of characters) that is unawares left out unwritten by a scribe is inserted or written as a second thought above the line. Examples are: <*e*> Folio 4 R: 1, <*du*> Folio 8 R: 5, <*sa*>, <*na*>, <*ja*> Folio 8 V: 4, <*u*> Folio 18 V: 4, and <*pa*> Folio 18 V: 6, and so on.

(iii) A set of two mini bars placed on the inadvertently written item(s) above the *śirorekhā* is used to indicate that the written item(s) ought to be treated as superfluous and thus be indeed deleted. Thus, the diacritic of two mini bars placed on the *visarga* in the word <*pathikaḥ*> (Folio 17 R: 3) indicates that the *visarga* ought to be deleted and that this word should be written and read instead as <*pathika*>. The correct reading is shown as such in the transcription – both Devanāgarī and Roman.

(iv) A lengthened *repha*–like curvy diacritic over a consonant character above the *śirorekhā* is used to indicate the *mātrā* representing the long vowel <*ā*> succeeding a consonant. Examples occur on: Folio 13 R: 4, 16 R: 3, 17 V: 5, 20 R: 3, and 22 R: 4. On one occasion, a tilde–like curve on the line (the *śirorekhā*) representing the *mātrā* <*e*> (which is usually marked by a postposed <*e*> attached with a conaonant) coupled with a lengthened *repha*–like curvy diacritic above a consonant character together represents the *mātrā* <*o*>. The example occurs on Folio 15 V: 4.

f) *Anusvāra*, a term used for postvocalic nasals homorganic with the following consonant, is defined by Varma (1929/1961: 148) as "a dependent word, which can manifest itself only on the basis of another sound". Similarly, Allen (1953: 40) argues that *anusvāra* may be literally translated as 'after sound' or 'subordinate sound'.

In the verse–text of *Gītapañcaka*, the diacritic *anusvāra*, indicated by a small circle above the character and shown as <ṃ> in the Roman transliteration, is profusely used to serve a number of disparate functions. Thus:

(i) *anusvāra* is used to denote a palatal nasal <*ñ*> preceding a homorganic palatal consonant, e.g. <*anuraṃjana*> for <*anurañjana*> Folio 2 V: 3, <*khaṃjana*> for <*khañjana*> Fol. 2 V: 3, and <*gītapaṃcakaṃ*> for <*gītapañcakaṃ*> (throughout) .

(ii) *anusvāra* is used to denote a velar nasal <*ṅ*> preceding a homorganic velar consonant, e.g. <*aṃge*> for <*aṅge*> Folio 1 V: 2; <*raṃga*> for <*raṅga*>; <*saṃga*> for <*saṅga*> Folio 28 R: 4–5, <*saṃkha*> for <*śaṅkha*> Folio 29 V: 4–5, and so on.

(iii) *anusvāra* is also used to denote a dental nasal <n> preceding a homorganic dental consonant, e.g. <*aṃta*> for <*anta*>, <*kāṃtayā*> for <*kāntayā*> Folio 14 R: 1–2, etc.

(iv) Finally, *anusvāra* is used to denote nasalization represented by the final nasal <*m*> in a word of Sanskritic origin, e.g. <*Gītapañcakaṃ*> for <*Gītapañcakam*> (throughout).

g) *Candravindu*, on the other hand, is used to denote vowel nasalization represented by a phonologically distinctive nasal vowel; in the Roman transliteration, it is indicated by a tilde above the vowel in question. Examples are: <*cā̃daśeṣara*> (Folio 14 V: 4), <*hā̃si hā̃si* > (3 R: 4), <*vihū̃si vihū̃si*> (Folio 9 R: 2), <*jhā̃khi*> (Folio 19 R: 3), <*ā̃dhakāra*> (Folio 29 V: 4), <*tẽ*> (Folio 17 V: 4), and so on.

h) *Visarga*, indicated by two small circles succeeding a consonant character in the fashion of an English colon, is represented by <*ḥ*> in the Roman transliteration, e.g. <*yaḥ*>, <*manīndraḥ*> and <*skhalitaḥ*> (Folio 4 R: 5– 6).

i) Like in other manuscripts of the time, the MS. of *Gītapañcaka* too does not indicate the punctuation mark for interrogation; instead, the overt presence of an interrogative pronominal form helps in interpreting the structure as an interrogative clause.

1.7.2. The Noun

1.7.2.1. Case

A total of six case forms attaching to nouns are attested in the text of *Gītapañcaka*. These are: Nominative, Instrumental, Ablative, Allative, Genitive, and Locative.

Nominative: -*ø*

Examples:

1. jagataprakāśa–*ø* (NOM) nṛpa kaüituke gābae Folio 1 V: 6
   'King Jagatprakāśa sings out of sheer curiosity'
2. hari lelī īsari–*ø* (NOM) hamara adhāri Folio 4 V: 2–3
   'The goddess abducted the axis of my (life)'
3. kamalini–*ø* (NOM) mudali kumuda prakāsa Folio 15 R: 3–4
   'The lily flower squeezed itself in as the moon light spread out'
4. torite torite bijuri–*ø* (NOM) camakala Folio 17 R: 5
   'The lightning kept shining in quick succession'
5. kha–*ø* (NOM) ati niramala hoeta ehi beri Folio 18 R: 2
   'The sky is very clear at this time (of the year)'
6. nisi dina sājani–*ø* (NOM) raha mohi sātha Folio 28 V: 6
   'Day and night (my) friend used to be with me'

Instrumental: *-e; -te*

Examples:

1. tua pun–*e* (INSTR) hame raha sātha Folio 13 V: 4–5
   '(O goddess!) It was due to the grace of your (supreme feet) that I received the company (of my friend)'

2. janani kṛpā–*te* (INSTR) priya hame punu pābe Folio 20 R: 5
   'If by the grace of Mother Goddess I get to be re–united with my friend again'

Ablative

In this verse–text, the semantics of the ablative case is not expressed through the suffixation of case markers to noun forms; instead it is accomplished by the use of the postposition *saño*, as shown below.

Examples:

1. ayalahu priya ghare–*saño* (ABL) duhu mohi ghare Folio 22 R: 3–4
   '(Then) both of us came over to my house from the house of my friend'
2. ehana priyatama hama–*saño* (ABL) dūra Folio 25 V: 4–5
   'Such a dear friend is now away from me'

Allative

The semantics of the allative case denoting the English 'with' is also not conveyed through the suffixation of case markers to noun forms in this text; instead it is conveyed through the use of independent word–like postpositions such as *laga* 'with, near' and *saṃga* 'with'.

Examples:

1. vilāsa karaba sakhi–*laga* (ALL) raha ābe Folio 20 R: 4–5
   'I would (definitely) rejoice in the company of my friend'
2. sakhi–*saṃga* (ALL) khelayite ādha nisi gela Folio 25 V: 3
   'While playing with my friend half of the night was gone'

Genitive: *-ø, -ka, -hi, -ka[e]r* (*-ka* being the most common affix).

Examples:

1. bhavana kanaka–*ø* (GENIT) Folio 30 V: 6–31 R: 1
   'Gold palace (lit. House of gold)'
2. sunalahu pika–*ø* (GENIT) bola Folio 29 R: 6
   'I heard the (sweet) voice of a cuckoo'
3. dura gela piya sakhi–*ø* (GENIT) bola Folio 29R: 6–29V: 1
   'The (sweet) voice of my dear friend is gone far away'

4. kanaka–ø (GENIT) śaṃkha sama Folio 29 V: 4–5
   'As shapely as a conch–cell of gold'
5. caïta–ø (GENIT) candana–ø (GENIT) parama śītala keśari–ø (GENIT) suvāsa Folio 20 R: 3–4
   '(The month of) *Caïta*'s extreme coolness of the sandalwood paste and the sweet fragrance of *Kesari* flowers'
6. kakhane dekhaba hame priya sahi–ø (GENIT) kāya Folio 15 R: 6
   'When after all shall I (be able to) catch a glimpse of the figure of my dear friend?'
7. c̃ādaśeṣara pema–*ka* (GENIT) ã̄[ā]kara Folio 14 V: 4
   ''C̃ādaśeṣara is a repository of love'
8. khana mani dura gela hṛdaya–*ka* (GENIT) hāra Folio 4 R: 4–5
   'All of a sudden my best friend and the necklace of my heart went far away'
9. pūsa punima–*ka* (GENIT) śaśi–*ka* (GENIT) sama mukha Folio 19 R: 2
   'In the month of *Pūsa*, (your) face beamed like that of the full moon'
10. c̃ādaśeṣara mohi ūra–*ka* (GENIT) hāra Folio 28 V: 1–2
    'C̃ādaśeṣara is the necklace of my heart'
11. duhu jana–*ka* (GENIT) duhu kāya Folio 31 R: 4–5
    'Both of our bodies (lit. the two bodies of the two of us)'
12. prema–*hi* (GENIT) rasa tasu jāna Folio 14 V: 3–4
    'He who knows about the sentiment of love'
13. dura–*ka[e]ra* (GENIT) śaśi kichu śītala dela Folio 22 R: 5
    'The far-off moon offered us a little coolness'

Locative: Case affixes: *-ø, -e, -hu, -na, -si*

Postpositions: *-para, -tala, -tara, -pae/paya*

Examples:

1. harakhe vasaṃta–ø (LOC) vilāsa Folio 20 R: 4
   '(My friend and I experienced) such happiness (as one would expect to have) in a spring season'
2. gal–*e* (LOC) muṇḍa māla Folio 1 V: 3
   'A string of human skulls in his neck'

3. hamahi praṇavi piya uth[ṭh]ali parāt–*e* (LOC) Folio 3 V: 6
   'As soon as my best friend came to me, I woke up in the morning and offered obeisance to him'
4. je binu nija ghar–*e* (LOC) bhelahu ucāṭa Folio 7 R: 2–3
   'Without him/whom I felt utterly lonesome in my house'
5. mohi kara sakhi śir–*e* (LOC) āsana dela Folio 25 V: 3–4
   'I offered my hand as a head-rest to my friend'
6. dina–*hu* (LOC) jhā̃khala toha hṛdaya–*hu* (LOC) jehi sakhi
   Folio 13 V: 3
   'The friend whom I glanced upon daily inside my heart'
7. kara juga kiśalaya hṛdaya–*na* (LOC) dhari mori Folio 2 V: 4
   'Having held his two lotus–like hands on my heart'
8. sakhika pāṇi lae ura–*si* (LOC) dhari kahu Folio 14 R: 5–6
   'Holding the hands of my friend and placing them on my heart'
9. cāru karaṇa *para* (LOC) Folio 29 V: 6
   'In (your) shapely ears'
10. muruchi vasudhā *para* (LOC) re Folio 24 R: 5
    'I (may even) swoon (lit. having swooned) on the ground'
11. karaṇa *para* (LOC) kuṇḍala d[ḍ]ola Folio 1 V: 3–4
    'Ear–rings dangle in ears'
12. rākhaha janani duhu caraṇa kamala *tara* (LOC) Folio 30 V: 1
    'Allow the two of us O Mother to be under your two lotus–feet'
13. hamara yahi mati sakhihi *pae* (LOC) gati Folio 5 R: 5
    'In my view my deliverance rests on (my) friend'
14. sumati hamara gati cā[ā̃]daśeṣarasiṃha tohe *pae* (LOC) hṛdayaka hāra
    Folio 13 R: 4
    'O benevolent Cā̃daśeṣarasiṃha! My deliverance rests on you; I lay the necklace of my heart on you'

1.7.2.2. Number

No grammatical number exists in the Middle Maithili verse–text of *Gītapañcaka*; apparently the category of number was already lost a few hundred years earlier in Eastern Indo–Aryan languages, including Bangla and

Maithili (cf. Grierson 1881, Chatterji 1926, and Jha 1954, 1958). Nonetheless, a number of independent full words of Sanskritic origin such as *gana/gaṇa, ādi, jana, juga/yuga, jora, dala*, etc. combine with nominal constructions in order to convey what might be loosely interpreted as expressing the semantics of plurality and/or aggregativeness in Middle Maithili.

Examples:

1. raha saṅga bhūta *gana* Folio 1 V: 3
   'Spirits accompany (him)'
2. nārada *ādi–hi* gita gābe Folio 1 V: 5
   'Nārada and all others sing a song'
3. budha *jana* Folio 20 V: 6
   'Those who are wise'
4. duhu *jana* Folio 3 R: 4
   'We/Both of us'
5. nayana *juga* Folio 3 R: 3
   'The two eyes'
6. kara *yuga* kiśalaya Folio 29 V: 5–6
   'The two lotus–like hands'
7. tāri *dala* Folio 20 V: 6
   'The stars/ the starry universe'
8. jahena cakevā *jora* Folio 29 R: 5–6
   'Just as the Cakevā couple'

1.7.3. Pronoun

Personal Pronouns: First, Second, and Third personal pronoun forms are attested in this verse–text. According to case inflection, the following matrix may be formulated for personal pronouns used in the *Gītapañcaka* songs.

First Person: Stem forms: *mo*, *hama*

	mo	*hama*
Nominative:	---	hama–ø, ham–e
Dative:	mo–hi	hama–rā, hama–ke, ham–e
Genitive:	mo–ra, mo–ri (FEM)	hama–ra
	mo–hi	hama–rā

Examples: mo

1. nida na ābae *mo–hi* (DAT) Folio 29 V: 1
   'I could no longer sleep (lit. Sleep does not come to me)'
2. *mo–hi* (DAT) dhani teji kata kayala payāne Folio 29 R: 4
   'My friend forsook me and went away I know not where'
3. ābe bhela *mo–hi* (DAT) baḍa parama kudīna Folio 23 R: 6
   'Now all of a sudden very bad days are here for me'
4. ke kara *mo–hi* (DAT) paripāti Folio 18 R: 2
   'Who will take care of me (now)?'
5. *mo–hi* (DAT) teji nāka payāne Folio 22 V: 3–4
   'Forsaking me (he) left for the heavenly abode'
6. e vidhi kata *mo–hi* (DAT) kayala tarāne Folio 4 R: 3
   'In this manner he did many such favors to me'
7. kī śaśi mukha cā̃daśeṣara raha *mo–hi* (GENIT) sukha Folio 6 V: 4–5
   'Will moon–faced Cā̃daśeṣara continue to remain (the source of) my happiness?'
8. kī *mo–hi* (GENIT) thala nayana dekhala hame sādara Folio 5 V: 5
   'Then all of a sudden at my place I devoutly caught a glimpse of you'
9. abhimata *mo–hi* (GENIT) tahni pāsa Folio 30 R: 6–30 V: 1
   'But in my thoughts I am constantly with him'
10. cā̃daśeṣara *mo–hi* (GENIT) ūraka hāra Folio 28 V: 1–2
    'Cā̃daśeṣara is the necklace of my heart'
11. *mo–hi* (GENIT) sukha pari hari lela Folio 7 V: 1
    'My happiness was taken away'
12. āna na *mo–ra* (GENIT, MAS) gati Folio 2 V: 5–6
    'None else can offer me (lit. my) deliverance'
13. jehi chala jiva sama sājani *mo–ra* (GENIT, MAS) Folio 27 R: 2–3
    'My friend who was equal to my life'
14. jeṭha jivana sakhi visalekhe bhela *mo–ri* (GENIT, FEM) Folio 2 R: 6
    'My life–long friend parted from me (i.e. left for the heavenly abode) in the month of *Jeṭha*'
15. hari lela jehi piya *mo–ri* (GENIT, FEM) rata Folio 6 V: 3–4
    '(What had I done after all that) God took away my dear friend from me?'

16. pati binu rati *mo–ri* (GENIT, FEM) bhela upamāna
    Folio 28 R: 6–28 V:1
    'I am likened to (lit. my condition is quite like) a wife without a husband'
17. sajani jivaka sama *mo–ri* (GENIT, FEM) jehi Folio 22 V: 3
    'My friend who was equal to my life'
18. prakāsa bhana *mo–ri* (GENIT, FEM) dura geli hāra Folio 23 V: 1
    Prakāśa says: my necklace is gone far away'
19. *mo–ri* (GENIT, FEM) baḍa tasu mukha dekhayake bhūkha
    Folio 9 V: 3
    'I have a great desire to see his (beautiful) face (once again).

Examples: hama

1. vidhu bina nisi *hama–ø* (NOM) bhela Folio 10 R: 1
   'I have become (like) a night without moon'
2. toha binu *hama–ø* (NOM) bhela hamara vihina Folio 3 V: 1
   'Without you I am bereft of my self'
3. māsa mādhava sahi na pāraba suniya *hama–ø* (NOM) pika sora
   Folio 20 V: 1–2
   'In the (hot) month of *Vaïśākha* I can no longer bear to hear the plaintive love wails of a cuckoo'
4. se sakhi binu *ham–e* (NOM) jioba ki kāja Folio 23 V: 5
   'What use is for me now to (continue to) live without such a friend?'
5. sukha pāoba *ham–e* (NOM) jehi laga pāya Folio 21 V: 2–3
   'I will receive happiness in his company'
6. tua pune *ham–e* (NOM) raha sātha Folio 13 V: 4–5
   '(O Goddess!) It was by your grace that I was able to receive the company of my friend'
7. *ham–e* (NOM) nahi bisaraba sakhi guṇa sūkha Folio 9 V: 2–3
   'I will never forget the merit and the pleasure of the company of my friend'
8. kahu khane sahacari *ham–e* (DAT) nahi tejaya Folio 30 R: 5
   'May my friend never ever forsake me!'

9. he sakhi *ham–e* (DAT) janu bisaraha tohi Folio 28 V: 5
   'O friend! Don't you ever forget me'
10. hari na harala *ham–e* (DAT) Folio 12 V: 4
    'God did not abduct me'
11. abase priya binu sabahi saṃśaya bhelahu *hama–rā* (DAT) dī[hī]na Folio 27 V: 2–3
    'For sure everything looks meaningless (to me) without my friend; I have become the poorer'
12. jaño hoa *hama–rā* (DAT) sadanaka kāja Folio 9 R: 3–4
    'If I ever felt the need of (his) company'
13. *hama–rā* (DAT) tohahi adhāri Folio 3 V: 4
    'To me you alone are the axis (of my existence)'
14. kāya vacana mana *hama–ke* (DAT) daya gela
    Folio 30 R: 6
    'He went away leaving his body, speech and mind to me'
15. c̃ādaśeṣara *hama–ke* (DAT) deha punu Folio 27 V: 5
    (O lord!) Give back C̃ādaśeṣara to me again'
16. hoyata *hama–ra* (GENIT) kāja Folio 30 R: 5
    'My work will be done'
17. ke kara *hama–ra* (GENIT) vicāra Folio 29 V: 3
    Who will take care of me/my life (now)?'
18. ke kara *hama–ra* (GENIT) tarāne Folio 29 R: 5
    'Who will offer me deliverance?/Who will be the instrument of my deliverance?'
19. abasahi dura bhela *hama–ra* (GENIT) parāne
    Folio 29 R: 4–5
    'For sure my life is gone'
20. punu sakhi kaya dela *hama–ra* (GENIT) sam[n]āne
    Folio 4 R: 2–3
    'Then my friend bathed me/arranged for my bath (a younger peson as I was)'
21. *hama–ra* (GENIT) yahi mati sakhihi pae gati Folio 5 R: 5
    In my view my deliverance rests on (my) friend'

22. hari hari *hama–rā* (GENIT) dith[ṭh]i ati pāpi Folio 9 V: 3
    O lord! I have very sinful eyesight (lit. my eyesight is very sinful)'

In the first person pronouns, the followimg case relations are also observed to have been expressed through the use of a combination of a (genitive) case affix and a postposition and/or a case affix in that order, eg.

Dative:	---	hama–ra laga
Instrumental:	---	hama–ra kāraṇ–e
Locative:	---	hama–rā/ra pās–e

Examples:

23. *hama–ra laga* (DAT) kumati jehi māre Folio 8 R: 5
    'As I was smitten with ill thoughts'
24. *hama–ra kāraṇ–e* (INSTR) priye jiva daya gela Folio 7 V: 1
    It was due to me that my friend left me to live on'
25. Jakhane sajani raha *hama–rā pās-e* Folio 7 V: 1
    'When my friend is near me'

Second Person: Stem forms: *tu*, *to*, *toha*

Nominative:	---	to–hi	toha–ø
Dative:	---	to–hi, to–he, to–ra	toha–ø
Genitive:	tu–a (tu–va)	---	toha–ra

Examples:

1. he sakhi hame janu bisaraha *to–hi* (NOM) Folio 28 V: 5
   'O friend! Don't you ever forget me'
2. dura kara nora jata *to–hi* (NOM) Folio 10 V: 1–2
   '(You used to) wipe away all my tears (of sorrow)'
3. priye mori *to–hi* (NOM) priye mori *to–hi* (NOM) teji janu na ḍābaha mohi Folio 8 R: 1
   'My dear, you alone are dearest to me; (you) do not forsake me and leave me (all of a sudden)'
4. harihi hari lela *to–hi* (DAT) Folio 11 R: 1–2
   'It was God who took you away'
5. aïsana priyatama *to–hi* (DAT) Folio 29 V: 3
   'Such was the state you were in, dear friend!'

6. tir[l]a bhari *to–he* (DAT) binu rahaya na pāraba Folio 29 R: 5
   'I cannot live without you even for the fraction of a moment'
7. *to–he* (DAT) tyaji dūra gela sūkha Folio 23 R: 2
   'After you left me my happiness went away for good'
8. *to–he* (DAT) binu mori bhela dhana jana hāni Folio 23 V: 6
   'Without you, I lost all my wealth and all my men'
9. maheśvara he *to–he* (DAT) nāṭaka sohābae Folio 1 V: 5–6
   'O Maheśvara! The dance becomes/behoves you so'
10. *to–he* (DAT) binu hame nahi pāraba sā̃bhāri Folio 17 V: 5
    'Without you I cannot gain control of myself'
11. avakāśa karabahu hama sakhi *to–ra* (DAT) Folio 19 V: 6–20 R: 1
    'How will I ever abandon you, O friend?'
12. *tu–a* (GENIT) pada paya mati Folio 2 V: 6
    'May my mind be ever devoted to your feet!'
13. sumane nisi dina karaba japa *tu–a* (GENIT) nāma Folio 5 R: 2
    '(Happily) I will repeatedly rehearse/recite your name day and night'
14. caraṇa *tu–a* (GENIT) vārijaṃ Folio 7 V: 5
    'Your feet are lotuses'
15. toritahi *tu–a* (GENIT) tanu pāoba mohi Folio 28 V: 5–6
    'Soon I will be reborn as you (lit. receive your body)'
16. *tu–a* (GENIT) pune pūrathu mori mati kāma Folio 17 R: 6–17 V: 1
    'By your grace may my wishes be fulfiled!'
17. kī mohi dhana *tu–va* (GENIT) tula nahi thika jata jana Folio 5 V: 6
    'Of all my wealth/possession and of all my men no one is equal to you'
18. cā̃daśeṣarasiṃha hita mori *toha–ø* (NOM) bhāya Folio 30 R: 2
    'O my benefactor Cā̃daśeṣarasiṃha! You are my brother'
19. *toha–ø* (NOM) mohi bhāya Folio 25 V: 5–6
    'You are my brother'
20. dinahu jhā̃khala *toha–ø* (DAT) hṛdayahu jehi sakhi Folio 13 V: 3
    'I glanced upon you, dear friend, daily inside my heart'
21. *toha–ø* (DAT) binu hama bhela hamara vihina Folio 3 V: 1
    'Without you I am bereft of my self'

22. jagatprakāsa āsa kaela *toha–ra* (GENIT) cā̃daśeṣarasiṃha bhāya
    Folio 31 R: 3–4
    'O brother Cā̃daśeṣarasiṃha! Jagatprakāśa (had) pinned high hopes on you'
23. kanaka śaṃkha sama *toha–ra* (GENIT) rucira gala Folio 29 V: 4–5
    'Your lovely neck was as shapely as a conch–cell of gold'
24. *toha–ra* (GENIT) bhaüha dhanu darasana binu Folio 22 V: 5
    'In absence of a glimpse of your arrow–like eyebrows'
25. *toha–ra* (GENIT) uru kadali sama jāne Folio 7 V: 5–6
    'Your thighs are known to be as shapely as the banana tree–trunk'
26. prakāśa kayalahu *toha–ra* (GENIT) dheyāna Folio 4 V: 4–5
    'Prakāśa (has) remembered you'

Note though that in one instance at least the so–called dative form *to–he* also conveys the semantics of the genitive case, e.g.

27. cā̃daśeṣarasiṃha *to–he* mori ekahi kūla Folio 13 V: 6–14 R: 1
    O Cā̃daśeṣarasiṃha! Our (lit. yours and mine) ancestry is the same"

Note must also be made of the fact that the Middle Maithili second person honorific form <*ihāña*> 'you' attested in Bhūpatīndramalla's play *Parśurāmopākhyāna–nāṭaka* (1713) as well as the Modern Maithili second person honorific form <*ahā̃*> 'you' and the high honorific form <*apane*> 'you' are not attested in the text of *Gītapañcaka*, c. 1662.

Third Person/Demonstrative Pronouns

Proximal: *e* 'this', *eha/yaha* 'this', *e–he* 'only this', *ī* 'he'

Distal: *o* 'that', *o–he* 'only that'

Examples:

1. *e* vidhi kata mohi kayala tarāne Folio 4 R: 3
   'In this manner he did many such favors to me'
2. *e* vidhi jānuha je hoa budha jana Folio 20 V: 6
   'All who are wise know it to be so'
3. jeṭha jīva mori tejala *e–he* tanu Folio 20 V: 5
   'In the month of *Jeṭha* my life–like friend left his body (lit. this body of his)'

4. prakāśa nṛpa *e–he* gābe Folio 17 R: 2
   'King Jagatprakāśa sings this (song)'
5. kathi lāyi *eha* tanu kalevara sājani binu saṃśaya gela Folio 23 R: 1
   'I began to nourish doubts as to what for would I need my body any more in absence of my friend'
6. kahalahu ore jagataprakāśa nṛpati *yaha* dukha Folio 6 V: 4
   'King Jagataprakāśa said this woeful tale'
7. se binu hame *e–hi* sobhe Folio 10 R: 3
   'I am likened to that (bee) without him'
8. kha ati niramala hoeta *e–hi* beri Folio 18 R: 2
   'The sky is very clear at this time (of the year)'
9. jaño *o–he* sājani rahao samāja Folio 12 R: 5–6
   'If I could re–live in the company of the very–same friend'
10. *o–he* rajanī ābe kata cali gela Folio 15 R: 4–5
    'Where is the very–same night gone now?'
11. *ī* saṃga kae devi abhimata pūra Folio 11 V: 6
    'O Goddess! Fulfill my wish and get me re–united with him'

Relative Pronouns	**Correlative Pronouns**
je, je–ha, je–he, je–hi, ja–kara	*se, se–hi, so, tẽ*
jahni (Hon), *jahni–ka* (Hon)	*tahni* (Hon), *tahni–ka/kā̃* (Hon)

Examples:

1. e vidhi jānuha *je* hoa budha jana Folio 20 V: 6
   'All who are wise know it to be so'
2. kulaka vadhu karae *je* so bhāve Folio 8 V: 2
   Lit. 'Even if the daughter–in–law of the (royal) progeny does as she pleases'
3. *je* vidhi jata nadi tiruhu jhā̃pala Folio 17 V: 3–4
   'Just as a full–flowing river engulfs even its banks (in the rainy season)'
4. jhūlahi *je* priye niya kare hid[ḍ]olā Folio 14 R: 4
   'My friend who rocks on a swing unaided'
5. *je–ha* sakhi nāśaya mohi pada dhūra Folio 11 V: 6
   'The friend who removed the dust off my feet'

6. hari lela *je–hi* piya mori rata Folio 6 V: 3–4
   '(What had I done after all that) God took away my dear friend from me?'
7. hamara laga kumati *je–hi* māre Folio 8 R: 5
   '(As) I was smitten with ill thoughts'
8. *je–hī* pavane parasi sukha bhela Folio 14 V: 1
   'The touch of the very–same breeze that gave us happiness'
9. sukha pāoba hame *je–hi* laga pāya 21 V: 2–3
   'In whose company I will receive happiness'
10. *je–hi* chala jiva sama sājani mora Folio 27 R: 2–3
    'My friend who was equal to my life'
11. *ja–kara* pūne hamahi jhiki leha Folio 14 V: 2
    'By virtue of those (good deeds) I will be able to snatch him back'
12. *jahni* bujhi śiraka āsana mori Folio 22 V: 4–5
    'He whom I always thought of as a place of my head–rest'
13. hari hari *jahni–ka* hari sama vege raha Folio 12 V: 6
    'What a pity! The friend who was blessed to walk fast with an elephantine gait'
14. *se* dina dura gela hāre Folio 2 V: 1
    'On that day my necklace went far away'
15. *se* piya khana dura gelā Folio 3 R: 3
    'All of a sudden the dear friend went away'
16. *se* binu darasane rahalāhu kā̃pi Folio 9 V: 4
    'No wonder that without him I was deprived of catching even a glimpse of him'
17. *se* binu na jioba re Folio 24 V: 6 – 25 R: 1
    'Without him I will no longer live'
18. *se* beri priya sakhi ayalahu pāsa Folio 15 R: 4
    'It was at that time that my friend visited (lit. came to) me'
19. *se* binu mahi tar[l]a purar[l]ihu nora 27 R: 3
    'Without him I filled the earth with my tears (of sorrow)'
20. kulaka vadhu karae je *so* bhāve Folio 8 V: 2
    Lit. 'Even if the daughter-in-law of the (royal) progeny does as she pleases'

21. *se–hi* piya khana ābe gelihu dūra Folio 11 V: 5
Now the same friend has suddenly gone far away'

22. jata jana mori lekhe *tahni* piya mūla Folio 11 V: 5
'Of all my men he was for me the pivot'

23. sukṛta bhaya *tahni* pābe Folio 14 V: 3
'By performing good deeds I will be re–united with him'

24. kathi lāyi *tahni* binu mānika hīra Folio 18 V: 6
'Of what use are the gems and diamonds without him any way?'

25. sahi na pārabe *tahni* guṇa bujhi Folio 22 V: 4
'Realizing his merit I can no longer bear it'

26. *tahni* binu kathi lāyi hamarā jiva Folio 28 V: 5
'Without him of what use is my life anyway?/What for should I (continue to) live any longer?'

27. pāoba *tahni–ka* saṃga bāṭa Folio 7 R: 3
'I will find a way to be in his company'

28. bhelahu *tahni–kā̃* bhūla Folio 20 V: 6
'(But) they are at fault'

29. *tẽ* vidhi bādh[ḍh]ala sineha Folio 17 V: 4
'In a similar manner our love overpowered (us)'

Interrogative Pronouns

The following interrogative pronoun forms are attested in the text of *Gītapañcaka*: *ke* 'who', *kañona* 'who', *ki* 'what', *kata* 'where'.

Examples:

1. *ke* kara mohi paripāti Folio 18 R: 2
'Who will take care of me (now)?'

2. *ke* kara hamara tarāne Folio 29 R: 5
'Who will offer me deliverance?'

3. ṛju dekhi *ke* nahi bhūle Folio 2 V: 3–4
'Who would not be oblivious of themselves after the cast of even a cursory glance at an honest and upright person like him?'

4. sakhi teji *ke* kara hamara saṃtāra Folio 12 R: 4–5
'Who else but my friend can offer me deliverance?'

5. sehi nayana juga *kañona* hari lela Folio 27 R: 4–5
   'Who abducted those two (lovely) eyes (of yours)?'
6. bola bolaba hame *kañona–ka* pāse Folio 20 V: 2–3
   'Who to would I speak (about my feelings)?'
7. raṃga viraṃga saba ehana *ki* kāja Folio 21 R: 4–5
   'What use is such fun after all?'
8. ohe rajanī ābe *kata* cali gela Folio 15 R: 4–5
   'Where is the very–same night gone now?'
9. ehana priya sakhi *kata–hu* geli ābe Folio 14 V: 1–2
   'Where did such a dear friend suddenly go away?'

Reflexive Pronouns

The reflexive pronouns are: *apana*, *apanu*, *niya* 'self'.

Examples:

1. sajani *lapana* [*apana*] hame śaśi sama jāna Folio 23 R: 4–5
   I knew that my friend was like a moon'
2. jāni karaya ohe *apanu–ka* kāja Folio 9 R: 4
   '(He used to offer me company) considering it as his own duty'
3. bhanayi prakāśa nṛpa *apanu–ka* vedana Folio 30 R: 1
   'King Jagatprakāśa says (about) the sorrow of his self'
4. jata jana nahi rākha *niya* visavāse Folio 20 V: 3
   'Where no one seems to have self–confidence/self–trust'

1.7.4. The Numerals

The following numerals are used in the text of *Gītapañcaka*.

The **Cardinal** numerals 1 <*eka, eka–hi*> 'one', 2 <*duhu*> 'two', 4 <*cāri*> 'four', 8 <*āṭha*> 'eight', 10 <*dasa, daha*> 'ten', and <*ādha*> 'a-half' are attested in the text.

Examples:

1. tribhuvana mori lekhe tahni *eka* mūla Folio 25 V: 5
   'In Three Worlds he alone was the pivot for me'
2. tohe mori *eka–hi* kūla Folio 14 R: 1
   'You and I are of one and the same ancestry'

3. kara priya *eka* mane hama paya devā Folio 9 R: 3
   'Single–mindedly the dear friend did favors to me'

4. mohi sakhi *eka* gati Folio 16 V: 5–6
   'My friend (alone) is single-minded'

5. cāru *duhu* khaṃjana jāne Folio 2 V: 3
   '(His) two pretty (eyes) were well–known to be as (agile as those of) a wagtail'

6. *duhu–ka* ekahi parāna Folio 14 V: 4
   'We both have but one life'

7. *duhu* jana jānala tanu nahi bhīna Folio 9 R: 4
   'Both of us knew that (our) bodies were but inseparable'

8. ekahi bhela *duhu* deha Folio 17 V: 3
   'The two bodies became but one'

9. *cāri* pahara dina sājani bola Folio 11 V: 4
   'Up until the fourth 'watch' (i.e. the end) of the day my friend kept talking'

10. *āṭha* pahara sakhi raha mori saṃga Folio 28 R: 4–5
    'My friend stayed with me twenty–four hours (day and night)'

11. phāguṇa *daśa* guṇa vedana bāḍhala Folio 19 V: 5
    'In the month of *Phāguna* my sorrow increased ten–fold'

12. *daha* diśa ore malina dekhala abe jagata Folio 6 V: 3
    'In (all) ten directions the world looked gloomy to me now'

13. sakhi saṃga khelayite *ādha* nisi gela Folio 25 V: 3
    'While playing with my friend half of the night was gone'

The **Ordinal** numerals <*prathama*> 'first', <*dosari, dvitiya, dutiya*> 'second', and <*titiya*> 'third' – usually the Sanskritic and/or semi–Sanskritic forms – are also used in the text.

Examples:

1. sakhi saṃga khelayite *prathama* pahara gela Folio 22 R: 2–3
   'The first 'watch' (i.e. the early part) of the day was gone while playing with the friend'

2. tohe vara sahacari jivaka *dosari* thika[i] Folio 3 R: 2
   'You are my best friend – a second embodiment of my life'

3. *dvitiya* pahara beri āyala Folio 5 V: 5
   'The second 'watch' of the day arrived'
4. *dutiya* pahara duhu jana jāni Folio 22 R: 3
   'Both of us came to realize (lit. having realized) that it was now the second 'watch' of the day i.e. the midday'
5. *titiya* pahara bhela jānala sāya Folio 9 R: 1-2
   'The friend came to realize that it was now the third 'watch' of the day i.e. the evening hour'

1.7.5. The Adjective

The following adjectival forms – largely of Sanskritic origin, but not necessarily so – are attested in the text of this verse–work. A few examples are given below for illustration.

1. tohe *vara* sahacari, jivaka dosari thika[i] Folio 3 R: 2
   'You are my best friend – a second embodiment of my life'
2. duhuka piriti dekhi, śaśadhara kumudini, kayalaha mati *ati* lāje
   Folio 3 R: 5–6
   'Seeing our love and affection, the moon and the white water–lily felt deeply abashed in their minds'
3. mohi laga sājani nahi bhela *thīra* Folio 4 V: 2
   'My friend could not remain steady with me (for long)'
4. *sujana suhṛdaya*, *suguna saṃjuta*, *sukaṭi ati abhirāma* Folio 5 R: 1–2
   'Benevolent, good–hearted, endowed with good virtues, possessed with a suitably thin waist, and very handsome'
5. kapola *niramala*, civuka *sundara*, vadana punimaka canda
   Folio 5 R: 3–4
   'Pure and clean cheeks, beauteously–shaped chin, your face is (like) a full moon'
6. *priya* sakhi ore Folio 5 V: 4–5
   'O dear friend!'
7. śaśi binu ore, rajani sahaje *ati malina* Folio 6 R: 6
   'Without the moon, the night is naturally awfully dull'
8. je binu nija ghare bhelahu *ucāṭa* Folio 7 R: 2–3
   'Without whom I felt utterly lonesome in my own house'

9. jagataprakāśa bhana, sabahi *athira* thika Folio 13 R: 3
   'Jagatprakāśa says: all is unsteady'
10. sabaka *caṃcala* mati re Folio 16 V: 5
    'Every one is fickle–minded'
11. sājani vadana bhela, *parama suhema* Folio 23 V: 4
    'My friend's complexion was very golden'
12. bujhite bhela tanu *khīna* Folio 27 V: 3–4
    'Reminiscing (about those happy times) made me unhappy'
13. sahaje *dukhita* hama, sakhi bodhi gamāvala 29 V: 3
    'Realizing that I had lost my friend I was naturally sad'

A number of pronominal, adverbial, and numeral – both cardinal and ordinal – forns used as adjectives are also attested in the text; so are the genitive–case– marked forms used as adjectival forms. These forms are discussed in appropriate places in **1.7**.

1.7.6. The Gender

In Old Maithili and Middle Maithili, grammatical gender was rampant. Modern Maithili, however, does not show grammatical gender distinctions; traces of limited grammatical gender inflections in the past and future verb forms, auxiliary forms, genitive case–marked forms, and nominal and adjectival forms in some high styles nonetheless exist. As early as 1950, Dinabandhu Jha had succinctly remarked that gender is sex–specific and not grammatical in Maithili. In his own words: "*mithilābhāṣāme śabda laŭkike puṃsatvādi liṅga achi śāstrīya nahi*" (Jha 1950, 'Introduction', p. 8). Eight years later, Subhadra Jha (1958) summarized the loss of grammatical gender distinctions in Modern Maithili in explicitly clear terms as follows:

> For the present purpose Maithili nouns indicative of animate objects are masculine, if they refer to the names of male things, whilst those that indicate the female sex are feminine. (p. 281)
>
> So it may be concluded that the grammatical gender has disappeared to a great extent from Maithili. (p. 282)

Remnants of Old Maithili grammatical gender distinctions are attested in the Middle Maithili verse–text of *Gītapañcaka* as well. A few examples are given below for illustration.

Genitive case-marked forms: *mo-r-i*

1. c᷈ādaśeṣarasiṃha hita *mo–r–i* (I–GENIT–FEM) toha bhāya
   Folio 30 R: 1–2
   'O my benefactor, C᷈ādaśeṣarasiṃha! You are my brother'
2. āṭha pahara sakhi raha *mo–r–i* (I–GENIT–FEM) saṃga Folio 28 R: 4–5
   'My friend stayed in my company twenty–four hours i.e. day and night'
3. sagari janama *mo–r–i* (I–GENIT–FEM) vedana bhela Folio 18 V: 1–2
   'My entire life became sorrowful'

Verb forms

1. *r[l]e-l-a-hu* (take–PST–MAS–1) kula vadhu bhāva, je kari priya sakhi pāba Folio 16 V: 1
   'Finally I sensed the feelings of my friend (lit. of the respectable lady); (now) I will do whatever it takes to get my dear friend back'
2. gagaṇa *pura–l–a–ø* (fill–PST–MAS–3) meghahi ehi khana
   Folio 24 V: 1–2
   'Suddenly the sky was covered with clouds'
3. se binu mahi tar[l]a *pura–r[l]–i–hu* (fill–PST–FEM–3) nora
   Folio 27 R: 3
   'Without him I filled the earth with my tears (of sorrow)'
4. *pura–l–i–ø* (cover–PST–FEM–3) mahihi tusāra Folio 24 V: 6
   'The earth covered itself with ice/frost'
5. *phur[l]a–l–i–ø* (blossom–PST–FEM–3) madhurī jāti Folio 18 R: 2
   'Many kinds of fragrant flowers blossomed in full'
6. ehana priya sakhi katahu *ge–l–i–ø* (go–PST–FEM–3) ābe
   Folio 14 V: 2–3
   'Where did such a dear friend suddenly go away?'

Auxiliary forms

1. śiva śiva *bhe–l–a–hu* (AUX–PST–MAS–1) malāne Folio 22 V: 4
   'O lord! I became so sad/forlorn'
2. ābe *bhe–l–a –ø* (AUX–PST–MAS–3) mori baḍa parama kudīna
   Folio 23 R: 6
   'All of a sudden very bad days were here for me'

3. jehi *cha–l–a–ø* (AUX–PST–MAS–3) jiba sama sājani mora
   Folio 27 R: 2–3
   'My friend who was equal to my life'
4. tribhuvana nahi *thik–i* (AUX–PRES–FEM–3) hama sani pāpini
   Folio 13 V: 5
   'No one is more sinful than me in Three Worlds'
5. kha ati niramala *ho=e–ta* (AUX=Link–FUT–MAS–3) ehi beri
   Folio 18 R: 2
   'The sky is (lit. will be) very clear at this time (of the year)'
6. vedana ghara *thika–ø* (AUX–PRES–MAS–3) hamarā kāe
   Folio 9 V: 4–5
   'My body is home to pain'

Adjective forms

1. tribhuvana nahi thiki hama *san–i* (like–FEM) pāpini Folio 13 V: 5
   'No one is more sinful than me in Three Worlds'
2. *sumat–i* (well–disposed–FEM) sājani guṇaka *āgar–i* (repository–FEM)
   Folio 11 R: 4
   '(My) good–natured friend – a repository of virtues'
3. *sagar–i* (all–FEM) janama mori vedana bhela Folio 18 V: 1–2
   'My entire life became sorrowful'

Nominals

1. *sumati sājan–i* (friend–FEM) guṇaka *āgari* Folio 11 R: 4
   '(My) good–natured friend, a repository of virtues'
2. *purali mahi–hi* (earth–EMPH–FEM) tusāra Folio 24 V: 6
   'The earth covered itself with frost/ice'
3. *phular[l]i madhur–ī jāti* (flowers of fragrant types–FEM) Folio 18 R: 2
   'Many kinds of fragrant flowers blossomed in full'
4. *gagaṇa* (sky–MAS) *purala* meghahi ehi khana Folio 24 V: 1–2
   'Suddenly the sky was covered with clouds'
5. *kamal–ini* (lily–FEM) *mudali* kumuda prakāśa Folio 15 R: 3–4
   'The lily flower squeezed itself in as the moon light spread itself out'

1.7.7. The Main Verb

1.7.7. 1. Tense

Present Tense: *-ø, -e/<ae, aya>, -a, i/<yi>, -hi, -ño*

Examples:

-ø

1. jagataprakāsa *kaha–ø* (say–PRES–3) nite ehi cita Folio 9 V: 5
   'Jagatprakāśa says: I should bear it in my mind everyday'
2. kathi lāi ābe besa kuṇḍala *dora[ḍola]–ø* (dangle–PRES–3) Folio 20 R: 1
   'Now why would it be at all nice to let my ear–rings (continue to) dangle?'
3. śiśira samaya sājani jaño *raha–ø* (be–PRES–3) Folio 25R: 1
   'If during the winter season one is with one's friend'
4. jagataprakāsa nṛpa vedana *bhāna–ø* (say–PRES–3) Folio 27 R: 5
   'King Jagatprakāśa says in sorrow'
5. jata jana nahi *rākha–ø* (keep–PRES–3) niya visavāse Folio 20 V: 3
   'Where no one seems to have self–confidence/self–trust'

-e <ae, aya>

6. se binu hame ehi *sobh–e* (behove–PRES–1) Folio 10 R: 3
   'Without him it behoves me to be like that (bee)'
7. je binu mori ati ehi tanu *tāb–e* (burn–PRES–3) Folio 18 R: 3
   'Without him my body burns grievously'
8. sahi nahi *ho=a–ya* (be=Link–PRES–1) prema vihīna Folio 23 R: 5–6
   'I can no longer bear (to live) a love–less (life)'
9. nida na *ā=b–ae* (come=Link–PRES–3) mohi Folio 29 V: 1
   '(Lit: Sleep does not come to me) I could no longer sleep'
10. ravihi *tāp=a–ya* (burn=Link–PRES–3) sarira *kā̃p=a-ya* (shiver=Link–PRES–3) Folio 24 R: 5–6
    'The sun heat is scorching and my body is shivering in sheer heat'
11. māsa agahana *khel=a–ya* (play=Link–PRES–1) upavana Folio 18 V: 4
    'In the month of *Agahana* I used to play (lit. play) out into the garden'

12. jagataprakāsa *bhan=a–ya* (say=Link–PRES–3) vedana Folio 27 V: 4–5
'Jagatprakāśa says (this) in sorrow'

13. *pahir=a-e* (wear=Link–PRES–3) bāgha chālā Folio 1 V: 4
'He wears a tiger–hide'

-i/<yi>

14. *bhana=y–i* (say=Link–PRES–3) prakāśa nṛpa Folio 13 V: 6
'King Jagatprakāśa says'

-hi

15. *jhula–hi* (frolick–PRES–3) je priye niya kare hid[ḍ]olā Folio 14 R: 4
'(Unaided) my friend frolicks on a swing with his own hands'

-ño

16. khina tanu *sumara–ño* (remember–PRES–1) sakhika sunāma
Folio 17 R: 6
'It is with a sad heart that I repeatedly remember/recite the name of my friend'

Past Tense: *-la*, *-li* (FEM), *la-hu*, *li-hu* (FEM), *-la, -la-ha*

First Person (Unmarked)

17. toha tyaji hama *bhe–l–a–ø* (become–PST–MAS–1) tela binu dīpa
Folio 19 V: 3
'After you left I became a lamp without oil'

18. aneka sukha hame *bhũja–l–a–ø* (experience–PST–MAS–1)
sakhi saṃge Folio 27 V: 3
'I experienced many happy times together with my friend'

19. hṛdaya *rākha–l–a–ø* (keep–PST–MAS–1) hame kiśalaya jāni
Folio 4 V: 3
'Knowing them to be lotuses, I put those tender hands on my heart'

Third Person (Unmarked)

20. jagataprakāśa *ka=e–l–a–ø* (do=Link–PST–MAS–3) tua āsa
Folio 11 R: 3
'Jagatprakāśa held high hopes on you'

21. se binu *upaja–l–a–ø* (grow–PST–MAS–3) atihi karūna Folio 12R: 4
'Without him, compassion grew aplenty'

22. prathama pahara *ge–l–a–ø* (go–PST–MAS–3) Folio 22 R: 3
    'The first 'watch' i.e. the early part of the day was gone'

    -li (also *lī*)

23. hamahi praṇavi piya *uth[ṭh]a–l–i–ø* (arise–PST–FEM–3) parāte Folio 3 V: 6
    'I woke up early in the morning and offered obeisance to my friend'

24. *suta–l–i–ø* (sleep–PST–FEM–3) jāmini duhu kare tana binu jhā̃pi Folio 29 V: 1
    'At night (the friend had) slept (well) turning on both sides without even covering the body'

25. priya anurāge *lāga–l–i–ø* (attach–PST–FEM–3) mori jīva Folio 28 V: 4
    'My whole life was devoted to the love of my dear friend'

26. *hari le–l–ī–ø* (abduct take–PST–FEM–3) iśari hamara adhāri Folio 4 V: 2–3
    'The Goddess abducted the axis of my (life)'

27. sakhi he katahu na *ge–l–ī–ø* (go–PST–FEM–3) mati mori Folio 12 V: 4
    'O friend! Nowhere did my mind wander off'

    -la-hu

First Person (Marked)

28. *a=ya–la–hu* (come=Link–PST–1) priya ghare saño Folio 22 R: 3
    '(Then both of us) came (over to my house) from the house of my friend'

29. hamarā *bhe–la–hu* (become–PST–1) paramahi sūkha Folio 21 V: 2
    'I became extremely happy'

30. priya bujhi *teja–la–hu* (spend–PST–1) rāti Folio 13 V: 3
    'Reminiscing about (the sweet memory of) my friend, I managed to spend the night (somehow or other)'

Third Person (Marked)

31. *uga–la–hu* (rise–PST–3) śiśu hari *bhe–la–hu* (become–PST–3) vihāna Folio 4 R: 1
    'The baby–sun rose, the morning dawned'

32. parakāśa *ka=ya–la–hu* (do=Link–PST–3) tohara dheyāna Folio 4 V: 4–5
'Jagatprakāśa (has) remembered you'

-li-hu

Third Person (Marked for Feminine gender and person)

33. sakala diśa ābe sita *baha–l–i–hu* (blow–PST–FEM–3) Folio 24 V: 5
'Suddenly the cold wind blew in all directions'

34. se binu mahi tara *pura–r[l]–i–hu* (fill–PST–FEM–3) nora Folio 27 R: 3
'Without him I filled the earth with my tears (of sorrow)'

35. hamari puruba *ge–l–i–hu* (go–PST–FEM–3) dura sakhi Folio 11 R: 2–3
'My friend died (lit. went away) ahead of me'

-lā

Note: This form may apparently be viewed as a precursor to and an antecedent form of the Modern Maithili elaborated honorific form <-*lā-ha*>).

Exanples:

36. śiva śiva sehe mori pari *hari le–lā* (abduct take–PST–MAS–3 Hon+3) Folio 7 R: 2
'Alas, the very–same (Lord) abducted my (friend)'

37. jehi daive dukha *de–lā* (give–PST–MAS–3 Hon+1) Folio 7 R: 2
'The Lord gave me sorrow'

38. abe mukha dekhiya na *bhe–lā* (become–PST–MAS–1+2 Hon) Folio 3 R: 2–3
'I could no longer (bear to) look at you/your face'

39. se piya khana dura *ge–lā* (go–PST–MAS–3 Hon) Folio 3 R: 3
'All of a sudden the dear friend went far away'

Note: I happen to personally know a native speaker of Maithili in my home town of Janakpur named Guruśaraṇa Rohitā of about 72 years of age who invariably uses the honorific transitive and intransitive past tense forms *–lā* (without *–ha)* throughout in his idiolect even today.

-la-ha

40. duhuka piriti dekhi śaśadhara kumudini *ka=ya–la–ha* (do=Link–PST–3) mati ati lāje Folio 3 R: 5–6
'Seeing the love and affection of the two of us, the moon and the white lily felt deeply abashed in their minds'

Future Tense

First Person: *-ba*

41. hame nahi *bisara–ba* (forget–FUT–1) sakhi guṇa sūkha Folio 9 V: 2–3
 'I will never forget the merit and pleasure of the company of my friend'

42. *pā=o–ba* (get=Link–FUT–1) tahni saṃga bāsa Folio 11 R: 3–4
 'I will receive his company'

43. ehana priyatara hame na *teja–ba* (abandon–FUT–1) Folio 19 V: 1–2
 'I will never ever forsake such a dearer friend'

44. se binu na *ji=o–ba* (live=Link–FUT–1) re Folio 24 V: 6–25 R: 1
 'Without him I will no longer live'

Third Person: *-ta*

45. *ho=ya–ta* (be=Link–FUT–3) kata kata sūkha Folio 25 R: 1–2
 'Much happiness will ensue forth'

46. *ho=ya–ta* (be=Link–FUT–3) hamara kāja Folio 30 R: 5
 'My work will be done'

47. kha ati niramala *ho=e–ta* (be=Link–FUT–3) ehi beri Folio18 R: 2
 'The sky is (lit. will be) very clear at this time (of the year)'

Note: A couple of grammatical structures containing the present tense marker also tend to denote the semantics of the future tense, e.g.

48. ke *kara–ø* (do–PRES–3) mohi paripāti Folio 18 R: 2
 'Who will take care of me (now)?'

For more information on the profusely complex Modern Maithili verbal agreement system, the reader is referred to Stump & Yadav (1988) and Yadav (1996, 2003).

1.7.7.2. The Auxiliary verb

The practice to use auxiliary verbs as carriers of present tense affixes – so characteristic of Modern Maithili (cf. Yadav 1996) as well as of Middle Maithili of the early 18th century (cf. Yadav ed. 2011) – does not seem to have obtained by the time (i.e. 1662 CE) the present verse–work of *Gītapañcaka* was composed. Thus, the auxiliary verbs are used as full verbs and these have indeed separate and distinct forms for present, past, and future tenses, e.g.

	acha Present tense
Auxiliary	*cha-* Past Tense
	ho- Future Tense, and
	thika
	thik-i (FEM)

Note though that while the Present tense auxiliary form *acha* is a composite present tense form and it takes no obvert suffixes as tense markers, the Past and the Future auxiliary verb forms, *cha–* and *ho–,* do. Indeed, the tense markers are attached onto auxiliary forms *cha–* (e.g. *cha–la*) and *ho–* (e.g. *ho–a, ho=a–e*, written <*hoaya*>, and *ho=e–ta*). Mention ought to be made of the fact that the present tense form *acha* occurs but 2 times, the past tense form *cha–* and its derived forms occur only 2 times, while the future tense form *ho–* and its derived forms occur 5 times in the text. The following examples are illustrative.

acha–ø

1. sa[ṃ]mukha *acha–ø* (AUX–PRES–3) ṛtu pati Folio 24 R: 5
   '(After all) the master of seasons – spring – is right here'
2. ratana khacita *acha–ø* (AUX–PRES–3) kuṇḍala d[ḍ]ola Folio 27 R: 4
   '(Your) gem–studded ear–rings dangle (beautifully)'

cha–la

1. jehi *cha–la* (AUX–PST–3) jiva sama Folio 27 R: 2–3
   'He who was equal to my life'
2. jakhane sājani mani *cha–la* (AUX–PST–3) mori saṃge Folio 3 V: 6
   'As soon as my best friend came to (lit. was still with) me'

ho–a

1. sakhika guṇa bujhi dhaïraja nahi *ho–a* (AUX–FUT–1) Folio 19 V: 6
   'Realizing the merits of my friend, I cannot hold patience'
2. e vidhi jānuha je *ho–a* (AUX–FUT–3) budha jana Folio 20 V: 6
   'All who are/ may be wise know it to be so'
3. purar[l]i upavana dekhi nahi *ho–a* (AUX–FUT–1) Folio 24 R: 4
   'I cannot bear to see the garden in full bloom'

ho=a–e (written <*hoaya*>)

1. sahi nahi *ho=a–ya* (AUX=Link–FUT–1) prema vihina Folio 23 R: 5–6
   'I can no longer bear to live in a love–less (life)'

ho=e–ta (also written <*hoyata*>)

1. kha ati niramala *ho=e–ta* (AUX=LINK–FUT–3) ehi bera Folio 18 R: 2
   'The sky is (lit. will be) very clear at this time (of the year)'

Note: The analysis of *ho–* as a future auxiliary form may tend to run into difficulty. Even if the auxiliary paradigm suggests *ho–* (and its derived forms) to be categorized as a future auxiliary form, the English rendering of utterances containing *ho–* form lends them a modal reading. In other words, *ho–* may also be viewed as a modal auxiliary verb form in the above context. Note also the use of a negative marker in utterances consisting of *ho–* as a modal auxiliary in compound verb constructions (cf. **1.7.7.3**. below).

The auxiliary forms *thika* (and *thiki*, FEM) – stereotyped markers of the Brahmin caste idiolect and often a butt of ridicule of late – occur as rather frozen forms for a total of 5 and 3 times, respectively, in this verse–text.

thika

1. bhaüha kuṭila priya manamatha dhana *thika–ø* (AUX–PRES–3)
   Folio 2 V: 3
   'His eyebrows had a beautiful arrow–like curve; they were a gift of Kāmadeva (Hindu Eros)'
2. tohe vara sahacari jivaka dosari *thika–ø* (AUX –PRES–3) Folio 3 R: 2
   'You are my best friend – a second embodiment of my life'
3. kī mohi dhana tuva tula nahi *thika–ø* (AUX–PRES–3) jata jana
   Folio 5 V: 6
   'Of all my wealth and of all my men no one is equal to you'
4. vedana ghara *thika–ø* (AUX–PRES–3) hamarā kāe Folio 9 V: 4–5
   'My body is home to pain'
5. jagataprakāśa bhana sabahi athira *thika–ø* (AUX–PRES–3)
   Folio 13 R: 3
   'Jagatprakāśa says: all is unsteady'

thik–i (FEM)

6. tohahi sājani parasamaṇi *thik–i* (AUX–PRES– FEM–2)) Folio 5 R: 4–5
   'You, my friend, are a touchstone'
7. tohahi *thik–i* (AUX–PRES–FEM–2) tejaba nahi hamahī Folio 8 V: 1
   'You alone are (my) real friend; I will never forsake you'
8. tribhuvana nahi *thik–i* (AUX–PRES–FEM–3) hama sani pāpini
   Folio 13 V: 5
   'No one is more sinful than me in Three Worlds'

1.7.7.3. The Compound Verb

One of the strident typological features of Modern Indo–Aryan languages, including Maithili, is the overwhelming use of compound verbs in their verbal sytems (cf. Masica 1976). It should not come as surprise, therefore, to witness the occurrence of a few compound verb constructions in Middle Maithili texts as well. Below is given a list of a few of the compound verb constructions attested in the verse–text of *Gītapañcaka.*

Examples:

1. kī gatāgata *har=i le–la* (abduct=Link take–PST–3) jehi piya mori rata
   Folio 6 V: 3–4
   'What had I done after all that (God) took away my dear friend from me?
2. sukha sakhi *par=i har=i le-la* (abduct=Link take–PST–3) Folio 10 R: 2
   '(My) happiness was snatched away by my friend'
3. hari tula *uḍ=i ge–la* (fly=Link go–PST–3) sāya Folio 12 V: 6–13 R: 1
   'My friend disappeared from view into thin air'
4. harihi visalekha *ka=e de–la* (do=Link give–PST–3) priya saṃga
   Folio 13 R: 2–3
   'It was God who separated me from the company of my friend'
5. ohe rajanī ābe kata *cal=i ge–la* (walk/go=Link go–PST–3)
   Folio 15 R: 4–5
   'Where did the very–same night go now?'
6. cā̃daśeṣarasiṃha *la=e ge–la* (take=Link go–PST–3) sūkha
   Folio 15 R: 6–15 V: 1
   'Candeaśeṣarasiṃha took away (all) the happiness'

7. paripāti priya sakhi *ka=e ge–la* (do=Link go–PST–3) ābe Folio 18 R: 3
   'True, my dear friend had taken good care of me earlier'

Note also that the morphophonemic stem alternations are the same as in Modern Maithili. In addition, as indicated above, Modern Maithili compound verb constructions obtaining a modal reading always occur with a negative marker; a similar practice is observed in Middle Maithili compound verb expressions as well, e.g.

8. *sah=i na pāra–ba* (bear=Link NEG Modal–FUT–1) priya bujhi tejalahu rāti Folio 13 V: 2–3
   'Reminiscing about the (sweet memory of) my friend, I could not spend the night (with ease)'
9. tohe binu hame *nahi pāra–ba sãbhār=i* (NEG Modal–FUT–1 hold=Link) Folio 17 V: 5
   'Without you I cannot gain control of myself'
10. ḍāḍhala anale tanu *sah=i nahi jā–ya* (bear=Link NEG Modal–PRES–1) Folio 15 R: 5
   'I can no longer bear the fiery heat (of separation) that is burning my body'

For an elaborate analysis of compound verb constructions in Modern Maithili, the reader is referred to Yadav (1996: 191–208).

1.7.7.4. The Converb

The converbal affixes are: a) *–i*, b) *–e*, and c) *–kahu*. The precise form of a converbal affix is determined by whether the verb stem happens to be bound (i.e. consonant–ending) or open (i.e. vowel–ending), e. g.

a) *–i* (attached to consonant–ending verb stems), e.g.

1. priya *bujh–i* (realize–CONV) tejalahu rāti Folio 13 V: 3
   'Reminiscing about (the good deeds of) my friend I barely managed to spend the night (somehow or other)'
2. toha *tyaj–i* (forsake–CONV) hama bhela tela binu dipa Folio 19 V: 3
   'After you left, I became (like) a lamp without oil'
3. jehi pavane *paras–i* (touch–CONV) sukha bhela Folio 14 V: 1
   'The touch of (lit. having touched) the very–same breeze that gave us happiness'

4. karaba *mir[l]–i* (meet–CONV) duhu bhāve Folio 14 V: 2–3
   'Being together (lit. having met) we will offer prayers with devotion'
5. sakhi pada *dekh–i* (see–CONV) Folio 29 V: 6
   'Gazing at the feet of (my) friend'
6. duhu jana *hā̃s-i* (smile-CONV) *hā̃s-i* (smile-CONV) bolalahu eka jiva *jān–i* (know–CONV) Folio 3 R: 4
   'Smiling sparingly the two of us laughed and spoke to each other treating each other as but one life'
7. je *kar–i* (do–CONV) priya sakhi pāba Folio 16 V: 1
   'I will do whatever (it needs to be done) to get my dear friend back'
8. *harakh–i* (please–CONV) sājani samipa *bas–i* (sit–CONV) duhu Folio 14 R: 5
   'Feeling happy and sitting close to each other'

b) *–e/<ya>* (attached to vowel–ending and to *r*–ending verb stems upon deletion of the word–final *–r*), e.g.

9. sakhika pāṇi *la–e* (take–CONV) Folio 14 R: 5–6
   'Holding (lit. having held) the hands of the friend'
10. pemaka basa *bha–ya* (become–CONV) Folio 10 V: 5–6
    'Out of sheer love and affection'
11. hamahi sā̃ga *ka–ya* (do–CONV) karu sā̃tāre Folio 8 R: 2
    'Keeping (lit. having kept) me in (your) company, offer me deliverance'
12. cā̃daśeṣara *pā–ya* (receive–CONV) hamarā bhelahu paramahi sūkha Folio 21 V: 2
    'After having received the company of Cā̃daśeṣara, I became extremely happy'

c) *–kahu* is a historical antecedent full form of the Modern Maithili truncated converbal form *–ka* upon the deletion of *–hu*. Note also the stem alternation upon addition of *–kahu* in the verb stems in the utterances cited below.

Examples:

13. ura-si *dhar=i kahu* (keep=Link–CONV) Folio 14 R: 6
    'Placing (them) on my heart'
14. kariya *mil=i kahu* (meet=Link–CONV) raṃga Folio 21 R: 4
    'Together (lit. having met) we will have fun and amusement'

For more information on an exhaustive diachronic analysis of the origin and development of converbs in Maithili through ages, the reader is referred to Yadav (2004).

1.7.8. Adverbs, Emphatic Clitics, Vocatives, and Verse–Fillers

1. 7. 8. 1. Adverbs

Adverb of Time: A few of the adverbs of time attested in the verse–text of *Gītapañcaka* are given below.

abe/ābe 'now, all of a sudden'

khana (*khan-e, khana-hi, khana-hu*) 'at that moment/all of a sudden'

ekhana 'now'

kakhan-e 'when'

kakhan-e-hu na/nahi 'at no time/never'

kañon-e khan-e 'at which time/when'

na kahu khana 'never ever'

kahu khane na 'never ever'

jakhan-e 'as soon as/now'

takhan-e 'then'

se beri 'at that point of time/then'

janam-e janam-e 'in all (subsequent) births'

Examples:

1. *abe* mukha dekhiya na bhelā Folio 3 R: 2
   'Now I could no longer behold/look at your face'
2. *ābe* bhela mohi baḍa parama kudīna Folio 23 R: 6
   'All of a sudden very bad days are (lit. were) here for me'
3. ehana hita priya *ābe* kata gela 28 R: 5–6
   'Where did such a dear benefactor disappear all of a sudden?'
4. ohe rajanī *ābe* kata cali gela Folio 15 R: 4–5
   'Where did the very–same night go now?'
5. vedana bāḍhala sājani teji *ābe* Folio 27 V: 2
   'Now upon losing my friend my sorrow grew aplenty'

6. nayana hari ati medani parala *abe* Folio 13 R: 1
   'With eyes very pretty and lotus-like (the friend) was now lying (unconscious/dead) on the ground'
7. *abe* nahi dhaïraja hamara pā[a]rāna Folio 28 R: 6
   'My life has no endurance/forbearance any longer'
8. *khana* mani dura gela hṛdayaka hāra Folio 4 R: 4–5
   'All of a sudden my best friend and the necklace of my heart went away'
9. se piya *khana* dura gelā Folio 3 R: 3
   'All of a sudden the dear friend went far away'
10. *khana–hu* sājani hamahi na tejaya Folio 27 V: 4
    'My friend may never leave me even for a moment'
11. gelahu dura *khana–hi* mani mohi Folio 8 R: 4
    'All of a sudden my gem was gone far away'
12. *jakhan–e* sājani mani chala mori saṃge Folio 3 V: 6
    'As soon as my best friend came to me'
13. *jakhan–e* sajani raha hamarā pāse Folio 7 V: 1
    'When my friend is near me'
14. *kakhan–e* bhelahu dina *kañone khan–e* rāṭ[t]i Folio 7V: 1–2
    '(Irrespective of) when the day dawned and when the night arrived'
15. *kakhan=e–hu na* tejaya sakhi mori sevā Folio 9 R: 2–3
    'My friend never ceased to serve me'
16. *kakhan=e–hu nahi* teja ṣevā niyema Folio 23 V: 4–5
    'He never quit performing his daily rite of passage'
17. *takhan–e* saño priya sakhi nida basa bhela Folio 25 V: 3
    'Just then my friend began to fall asleep'
18. hṛdaya *na kahu khana* manda Folio 29 V: 5
    '(Your) heart/mind was never cheerless'
19. e[hi] *khan–e* sakhi mori cira hari lela Folio 4 R: 1–2
    'Right then my friend took off my garment'
20. *kahu khan–e* sahacari hame na tejaya Folio 30 R: 5
    'May my friend never ever forsake me'

21. *se beri* priya sakhi ayalahu pāsa Folio 15 R: 4
'It was at that time that my friend visited (lit. came to) me'

22. *janam–e janam–e* cā̃daśaṣara bhāya Folio 22 V: 1
'May I have Cā̃daśeṣara as my brother in rebirth after rebirth'

Adverb of Comparison

sana (*san–i* FEM) 'like'

sama 'like'

baḍa/bara 'very/extremely'

jata/jat–i (FEM) 'all'

tula 'as/like'

adhika 'very much/a lot'

ati 'very much/a lot'

Examples;

23. sājani jivaka *sama* mori jehi Folio 22 V: 3
'My friend who was equal to my life'

24. tāri dala hamarā *tula* mukha bhela Folio 20 V: 6 –21 R: 1
'The starry universe looked as sad as my face'

25. dekhala jagata hame *ati* ā̃dhakāra *sana* Folio 3 V: 2
'The world looked very dark–like (gloomy) to me'

26. tribhuvana nahi thiki hama *san–i* pāpini Folio 13 V: 5
'No one is as sinful as me in Three Worlds'

27. sājani cikul[r]a bhela *baḍa* ā̃dhakāra *tula* Folio 29 V: 1–2
'(At night) the friend's locks of hair looked very dark–like'

28. cā̃daśeṣara *bara* sundara Folio 23 R: 2
'Cā̃daśeṣara is extremely handsome'

29. ehana dukha *adhika* bhela sahi nahi pāra he Folio 8 R: 5–6
'The agony increased more and more, I couldn't bear it any longer'

30. locana dekhala *jata* priya sakhi jāni Folio 23 V: 6
'The more I looked at my eyes mistaking them as those of my dear friend's'

31. tejala *jat–i* mori sūkha Folio 18 R: 6–18 V: 1
 'I forsook all my happiness'

Adverb of Place

kata, kata–hu 'where/at which place'

dura 'far'

laga 'near'

samipa 'near'

pāsa 'near'

heṭha-hi 'at this spot'

Examples:

32. mohi dhani teji *kata* kayala payāne Folio 29 R: 4
 'Forsaking me where did my friend go away?'
33. ehana priya sakhi *kata–hu* geli ābe Folio 14 V: 1–2
 'Where (after all) did such a dear friend suddenly go away?'
34. jagata janani pada *heṭha–hi* rākhaha Folio 31 R: 4–5
 'May the Mother–World put her feet here (and no where else) i.e. (on both of our bodies)!
35. suniya *dura* priya bor[l]a Folio 20 V: 2
 '(My friend) will (probably) hear the wail of my anguish from a far off place'
36. *laga* leha hame dhani hamahi nihāri Folio 9 R: 5–6
 'Look (lit. having looked) at me and keep me close to you, O friend!'
37. harakhi sājani *samipa* basi duhu Folio 14 R: 5
 'Feeling happy and sitting close to each other'
38. abhimata mohi tahni *pāsa* Folio 30 R: 6
 'In my thoughts I am constantly with (lit. near) him'

Adverb of Manner

ehana 'such'

sahaj-e 'easily/naturally'

e vidhi "this way/in this manner'

jahene 'such'

torit-e torit-e 'soon/in a hurried manner/in quick succession"

dhire dhire 'slowly/gently'

je vidhi 'as/just as'

ke vidhi 'in which manner/how'

tẽ vidhi 'in that manner'

Examples:

39. *je vidhi* jata nadi tiruhu jhā̃pala Folio 17 V: 3–4
'Just as a (full–flowing) river engulfs (lit. engulfed) even its banks (in the rainy season)'

40. *tẽ vidhi* bādh[ḍh]ala sineha Folio 17 V: 4
'In a similar manner, our love overpowered (us)'

41. *e vidhi* kata mohi kayala tarāne Folio 4 R: 3
'In this manner he did many such favors to me'

42. *ke vidhi* tejaba sājani binu ṛtu Folio 24 V: 4
'How shall I spend the (autumn) season without my friend?

43. san[m]ipa śītala jalaka dhārā, pavana *dhire dhire* pāse
Folio 14 R: 6–14 V: 1
'Nearby was a sprout of cold water and a breeze of wind passed gently by us'

44. *torit–e torit–e* bijuri camakala Folio 17 R: 5
'The lightning kept shining in quick succession'

45. *sahaj–e* dukhita hama sakhi bodhi gamāvala Folio 29 V: 3
'Realizing that I had lost my friend, I was naturally sad'

46. *ehana* sukha duhu kaela anubhava Folio 20 R: 4
'Both my friend and I experienced such happiness (as one would expect to have in the spring season)'

Adverb of Condition

jaño 'if', *taño* then'

Examples:

47. kāja karaba *jaño* priya raha thīra Folio 18 V: 5
'One can (lit. will) experience love only if the dear friend is steady'

48. rati pati rati saṃge, *jaño* raha eka thala, *taño* raha duhukā̃ sohe
Folio 13 V: 1–2
'If the Lord of Love (Kāmadeva) gets to live with his consort Rati at one place, then that so suits them both'

Adverb of Reason

kathi lāi/kathi lāyi 'why/for what reason'

Examples:

49. *kathi lāi* abe besa kuṇḍala dora[ḍola] Folio 20 R: 1
'Now why would it be at all nice to let (my) ear–rings (continue to) dangle?'

50. tahni binu *kathi lāyi* hamarā jība Folio 28 V: 5
'Without him, of what use is my life any way?'

In addition, adverbs such as *binu* 'without'; *lekhe* 'for'; *abase* 'for sure/ definitely'; *hina/vihina* 'without' are also attested in the text of *Gitapancaka.*

Examples:

51. *abase* priya *binu* sabahi saṃśaya Folio 27 V: 2–3
'For sure all things looked doubtful/meaningless (to me) without my friend'

52. tribhuvana mori *lekhe* tahni eka mūla Folio 25 V: 5
'In Three Worlds he alone was the pivot for me'

53. *vihina* parama dūkha, kakhane dekhaba mūkha 16 R: 5–6
'Without (you), (I experience) great sorrow; when shall I (get to) see (your) face?'

1. 7. 8. 2. Emphatic Clitics

The emphatic clitics attested in the text of *Gītapañcaka* are: *–hi* 'only', *–hu* 'too, even', *–e* 'alone', and *–u* 'also' – the emphatic clitic *–hi* being the most common and the emphatic clitic *–u* being the least common occurring but only once in the text.

Examples:

1. *nandi–hi* muruja bajābe Folio 1 V: 4–5
'Nandī plays the *mṛdaṅga*–drum'

2. *sakhi–hi* pae gati Folio 5 R: 5
   '(My) deliverance rests only on (my) friend'
3. *hama–hi* rodana ka[e]ra dura kara mora sakhi Folio 3 R: 4–5
   'My friend, wipe away my tears of sorrow'
4. jagataprakāsa bhana *toha–hi* hīta Folio 11 V: 6–12 R: 1
   'Jagatprakāśa says: You alone are (my) benefactor'
5. jagataprakāśa nṛpa rasa *e–hi* dūkha Folio 15 R: 6
   'King Jagataprakāśa suffers from this sentiment of sorrow'
6. *je–hi* chala jiva sama sājani mora Folio 27 R: 2–3
   'My friend who was equal to my life'
7. guṇamata ore *guputa–hi* bhela mani hamara Folio 6 V: 1
   'My wise and jewel–like friend disappeared all of a sudden'
8. jagata janani pada *heṭha–hi* rākhaha Folio 31 R: 4–5
   'May the Mother World put her feet here (and no where else) (i.e. on both of our bodies)'
9. *kakhan=e–hu* na tejaya sakhi mori sevā Folio 9 R: 2–3
   'My friend never ever ceased to serve me'
10. ehana priya sakhi *kata–hu* geli ābe Folio 14 V: 1–2
    'Where did such a dear friend suddenly go away?'
11. *du–hu* jana jānala tanu nahi bhīna Folio 9 R: 4
    'Both of us knew that (our) bodies were but inseparable'
12. prakāśa nṛpa *e–he* gābe 17 R: 1
    'King Jagatprakāśa sings this (song)'
13. *to–he* mori ūraka mani maya hāra Folio 19 R: 4
    'You are (indeed) the gem-studded necklace of my heart'
14. jaño *o–he* sājani rahao samāja Folio 12 R: 5–6
    'If I could re–live in the company of the very–same friend'
15. parasi *pavan–e* mudita *du-hu* jana Folio 18 V: 4–5
    'The two of us were very happy to feel the brush of a breeze of wind'
16. *abas–e* śarira vināsa Folio 19 V: 5–6
    'This will for sure ruin my body'
17. ehana sukha *du–hu* kaela anubhava *harakh–e* vasaṃta vilāsa
    Folio 20 R: 4

'My friend and I experienced such happiness (as one would expect to have) in a spring season'

18. *pun–u* sakhi kaya dela hamara sam[n]āne Folio 4 R: 2–3
'Thereafter my friend bathed me (a younger person as I was)'

19. ehana priya sakhi *kata–hu* geli ābe Folio 14 V: 1–2
'Where did such a dear friend suddenly go away?'

For more information on a detailed morphosyntactic analysis of clitics in Modern Maithili, the reader is referred to Yadav (1991, 1996)

1.7.8.3. Vocatives and Verse–Fillers

It would be worthwhile to recall once again the mirthful remark of Grierson's (1884b) referred to earlier with regard to the fondness for that "blessed word Mesopotamia" and of the untranslatability of the "unmeaning burdens/phrases" and/or verse–fillers in order to preserve "the oriental color" of these folk songs. In the verse–text of *Gītapañcaka*, the vocative *he* and the verse–fillers *he*, *re*, and *ore* are attested. The following sentences are illustrative.

Examples:

he

1. maheśvara *he* tohe nāṭaka sohābae Folio 1 V: 5–6
'O Maheśvara! The dance suits you so'

2. athira kalevara jānuka[jānu] *he* kamala pātaka jala tūle Folio 30 V: 6
'Be it known that (our) body is as unsteady as a drop of water on a lotus leaf'

3. ehana dukha adhika bhela sahi nahi pāra *he* Folio 8 R: 5–6
'The agony increased more and more and I couldn't bear it any longer'

re

4. sakhi binu tanu ḍāḍhala *re* Folio 24 R: 5
'Without my friend, my body burned'

5. hama[e] janu bisaraha *re* cā̃dakiraṇe deha *re* Folio 24 V: 1
'Do not ever forget me; give me the soothing moon beams, i.e. Candraśeṣara'

ore

6. priya sakhi *ore* dvitiya pahara beri āyala Folio 5 V: 4–5
   'O dear friend! The second 'watch' i.e. the midday (has) arrived'
7. toha binu *ore* pati visalekhe hama rati Folio 6 R: 1
   'Without you I am likened to a beloved suffering from the pain of separation from the husband'
8. guṇamata *ore* guputahi bhela mani hamara Folio 6 V: 1
   'My wise and jewel–like friend disappeared all of a sudden'
9. je binu *ore* jivaka kalesa ati bādh[ḍh]ala Folio 6 V: 2
   'Without whom my life's misery grew in great measure'

1.7.9. Sentence Types

As the work under study is composed in verse laced with *rāga* and *tāla* in which inversion of word order for purposes of rhyme and poetic effect turns out to be a constant feature, full regular sentences bearing the standard Subject Object Verb (**SOV**) word order are rather hard to come by in it. Nonetheless, an attempt is made below to discern and list samples of a few distinct sentence types that may be retrieved from the verse–text of *Gītapañcaka*.

Declarative Clauses

1.

raha–ø	saṅga	bhūta	gana	Folio 1 V: 3
live–PRES (3)	with	spirit	PL	

'Spirits accompany (him)'

2.

pahira–e	bāgha	chāla	Folio 1 V: 4
wear–PRES (3)	tiger	skin	

'Tiger–hide is his attire (Lit. He wears tiger skin)'

3.

ham–e	nahi	bisara–ba	sakhi	guna	sūkha
I–NOM	NEG	forget–FUT (1)	friend	virtue	pleasure

Folio 6 V: 2–3

'I will never ever forget the pleasure of the friend's virtue'

4.

tohe	binu	ham–e	nahi	pāra–ba	saṃbhāri
You	without	I–NOM	NEG	can–FUT (1)	control

Folio 17 V: 5

'Without you I can no longer control myself'

5. jagataprakāśa–ø bhana–ø toha–hi adhāra
Jagatprakāśa–NOM say–PRES (3) you–EMPH axis
Folio 28 V: 1
'Jagatprakāśa says: You alone are the axis (of my existence)'

Interrogative Clauses

1. ṛju dekh–i *ke* nahi bhul–e Folio 2 V: 3–4
person of honor see–CONV who NEG forget–PRES (3)
'Who would not be oblivious of themselves after a cast of even a cursory glance at my honorable friend?'

2. sakhi tej–i *ke* kara–ø hama–ra saṃtāra
friend leave–CONV who do–PRES (3) I–GENIT deliverance
Folio 12 R: 3–4
'Who else but my friend can offer me deliverance?'

3. ehana priya sakhi *kata–hu* ge–l–i ābe
such dear friend where–EMPH go–PST–FEM (3) now
Folio 14 V: 1–2
'Where did such a dear friend suddenly go away?'

4. bola bola–ba ham–e *kañona–ka* pāse
speech speak–FUT (1) I–NOM who–GENIT near
Folio 20 V: 2–3
'Who to (Lit. in whose company) would I speak (now)?'

5. se sakhi binu ham–e ji=o–ba *ki* kāja
CORREL friend without I–NOM live=LINK–FUT (1) what purpose
Folio 23 V: 5
'What use is there to (continure to) live without the very–same friend?'

6. tahni binu *kathi lāyi* hama–rā jī–ba Folio 28 V: 5
REL (H) without what for I–ACC/DAT live–FUT (1)
'Why should I continue to live without him any way?'

7. *ke* kara–ø hama–ra vicāra Folio 29 V: 3
who do–PRES (3) I–GENIT care
'Who will take care of me (now)?'

Imperative Clauses

1. hama–hi rodana–ka[ke]ra dura *kara–ø* mo–ra sakhi
   I–DAT cry–GENIT remove do–IMP (2NH) I–GENIT friend
   āṃcala kiśalaya pāni Folio 3 R: 4–5
   hem of a dress tender hand
   'Wipe away my tears of sorrow with the tender hem-like hands of yours'

2. hama–hi saṅga ka–ya *kar–u* saṃtāre
   I–ACC/DAT with do–CONV do–IMP (2H) deliverance
   Folio 8 R: 2
   'By keeping me in your company offer me deliverance'

3. cāṃdaśeṣarasiṃha *kar–u* avadhāna Folio 12 V: 1
   Candraśeṣarasiṃha do–IMP (2H) attention
   'Candraśeṣarasiṃha! Take a heed'

4. khana–hu na *teja–ø* mohi Folio 10 V: 1
   moment–EMPH NEG forsake–IMP (2NH) I–DAT
   'Do not forsake me even for a moment'

5. dura *kara–ø* nora jata tohi Folio 10 V: 1–2
   remove do–IMP (2NH) tears all you–NOM
   'Wipe away all my tears (of sorrow)'

6. jani bisara–ha *ceta–ha* piya paripāti
   NEG forget–IMP (2MH) be alert–IMP (2MH) friend custom
   Folio 11 R: 2
   'Do not forget your friend and be warned about it'

7. ham–e janu *bisara–ha* Folio 16 R: 6
   I–ACC/DAT NEG forget–IMP (2MH)
   'Do not ever forget me.

8. ham–e janu *bisara–ha* re cāṃdakiraṇa
   I–ACC/DAT NEG forget–IMP (2MH) VOC Cā̃dakiraṇa
   de–ha re Folio 24 V: 1
   give–IMP (2MH) VOC
   'Do not ever forget me; give me back Candraśeṣarasiṃha'

2

Gītapañcaka: Facsimile of the MS. B 285/22

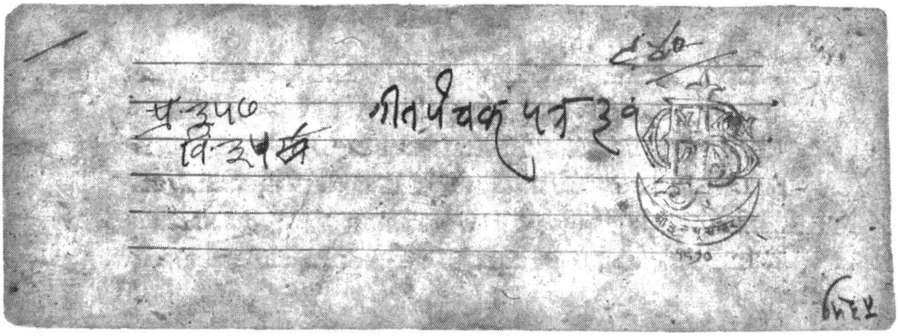

Folio 1V

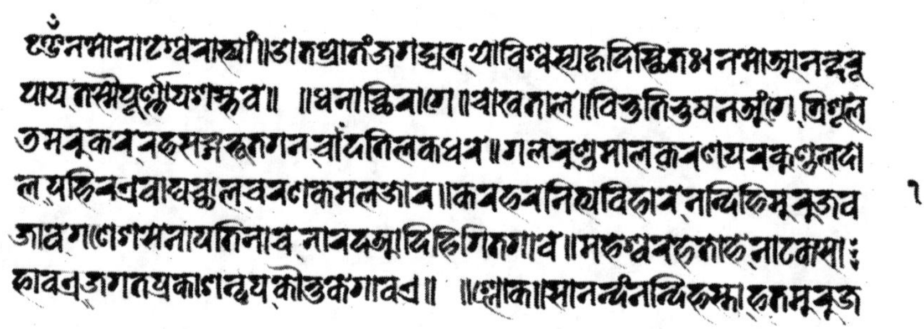

Folio 2R

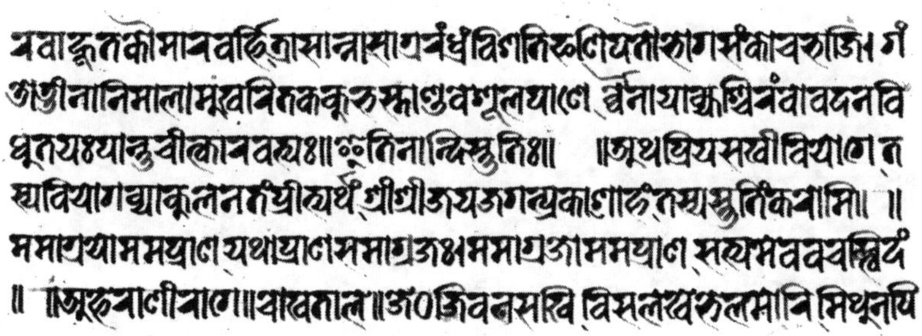

Folio 2V

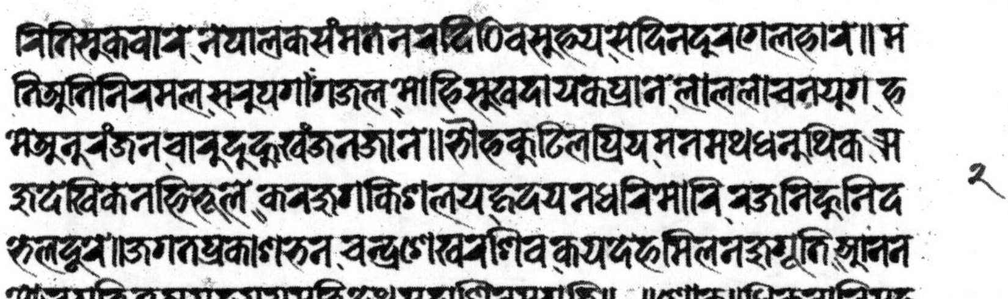

Folio 3R

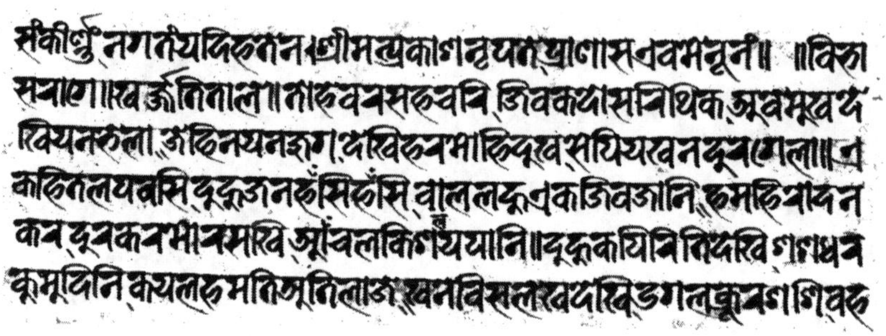

Folio 3V

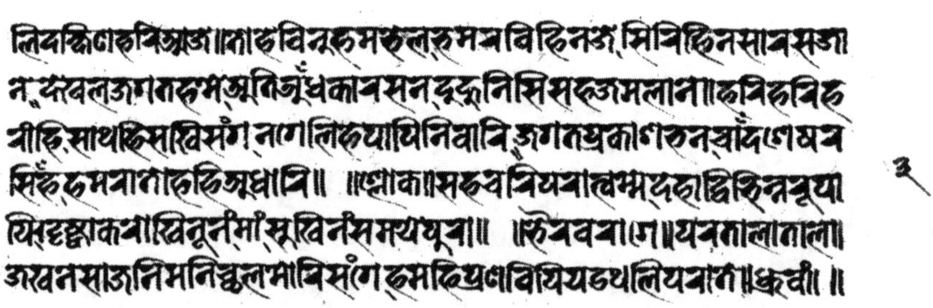

Folio 4R

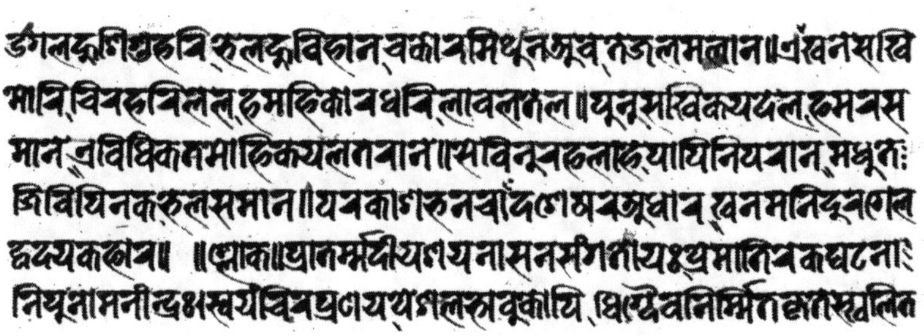

Folio 4V

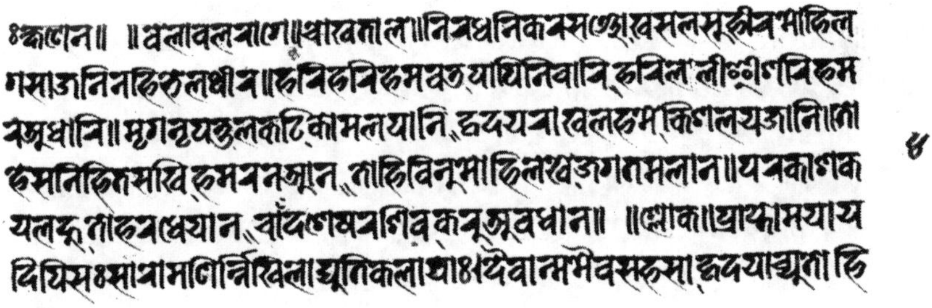

Folio 5R

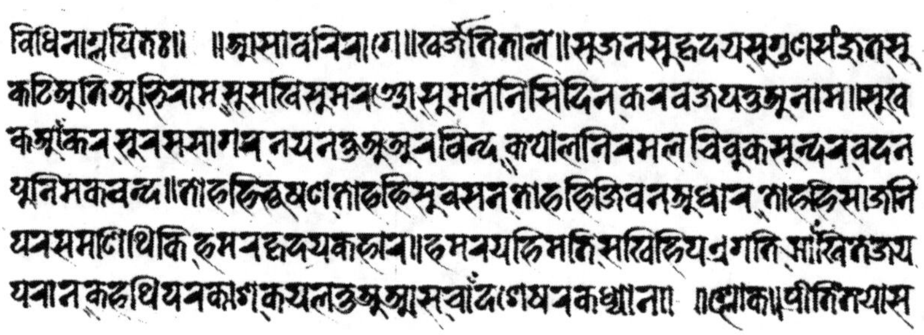

Folio 5V

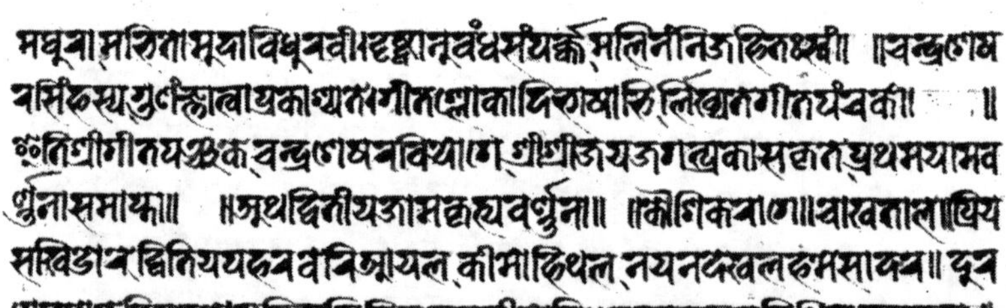

Folio 6R

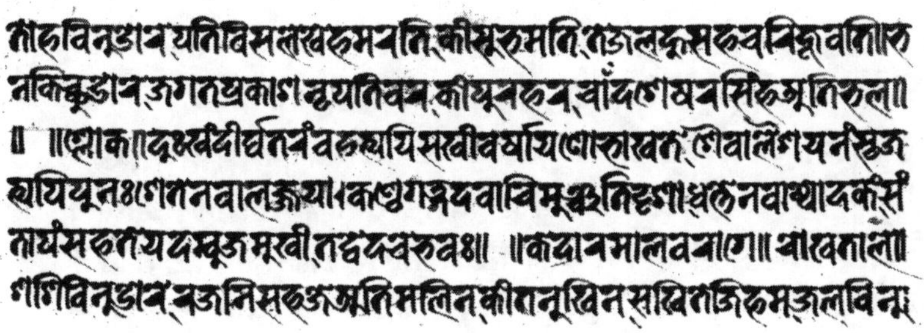

Folio 6V

Folio 7R

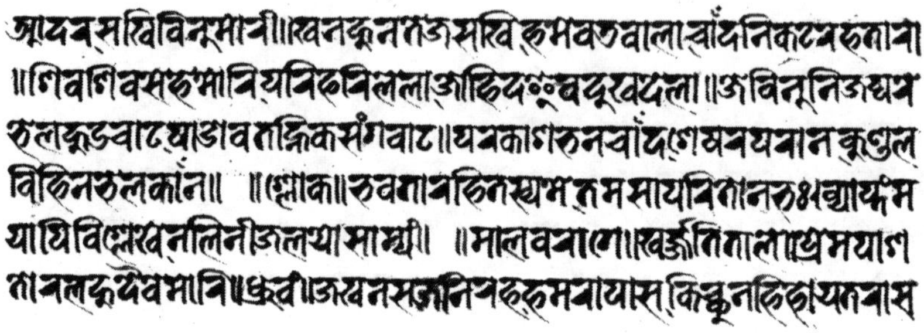

Folio 7V

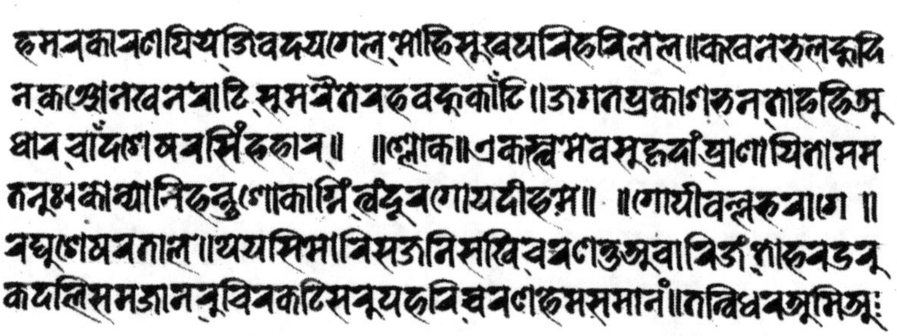

Folio 8R

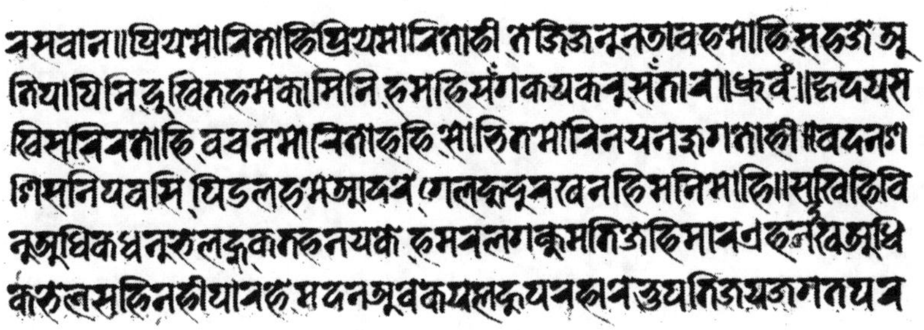

Folio 8V

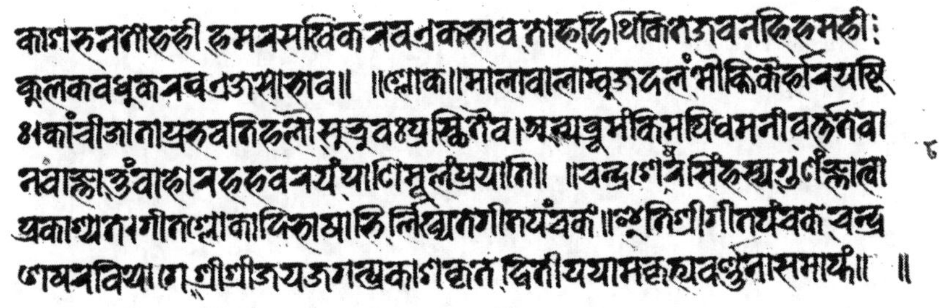

Folio 9R

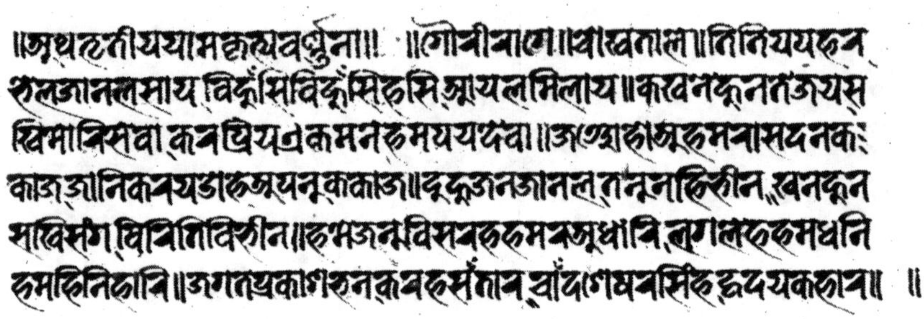

Folio 9V

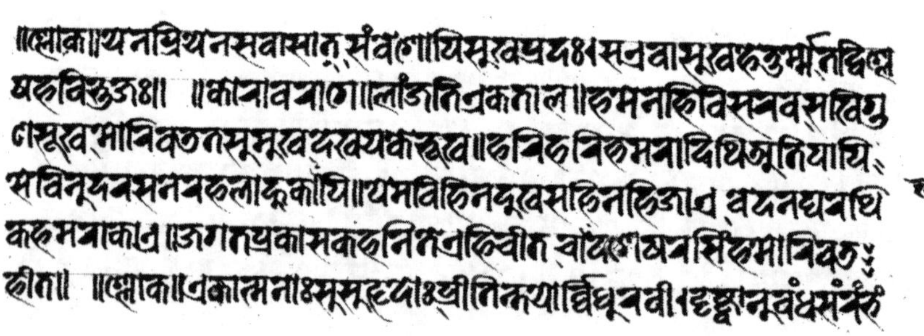

Folio 10R

Folio 10V

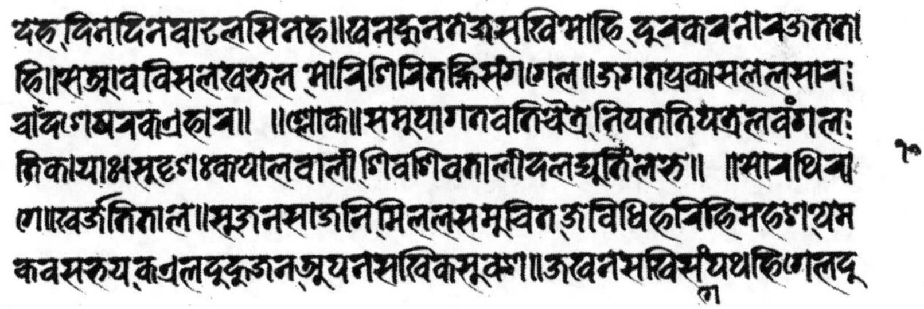

Folio 11R

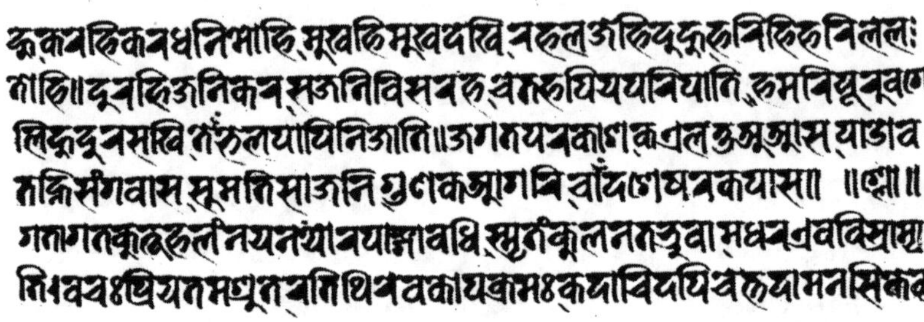

Folio 11V

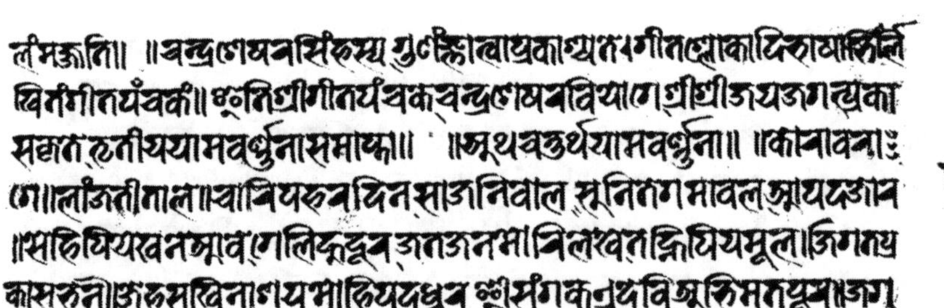

Folio 12R

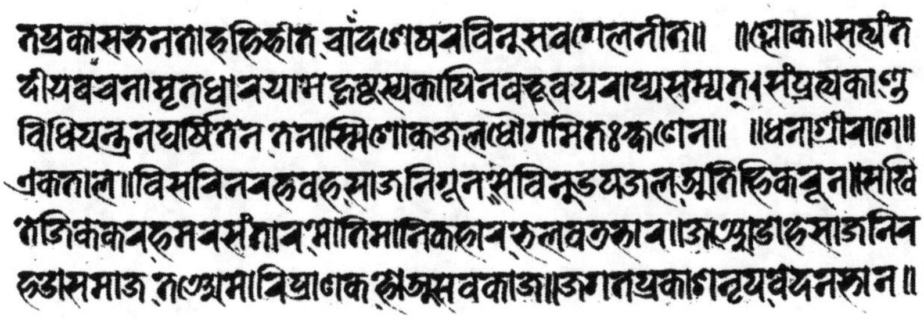

Folio 12V

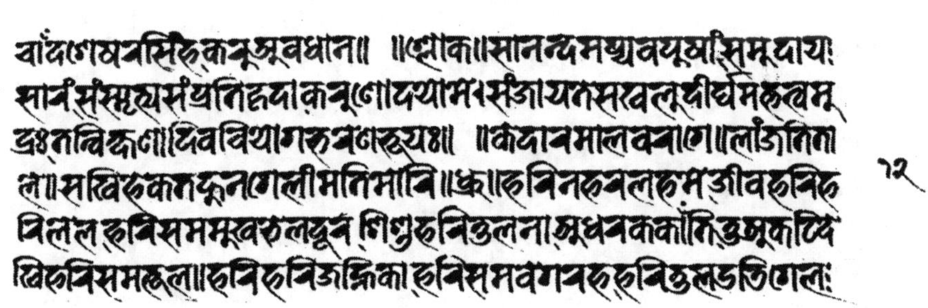

Folio 13R

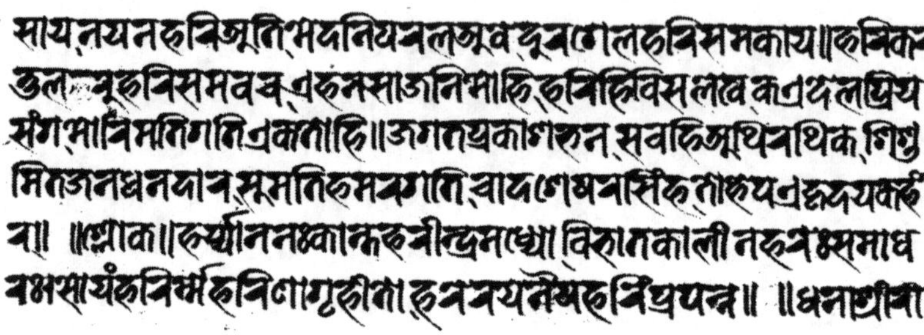

Folio 13V

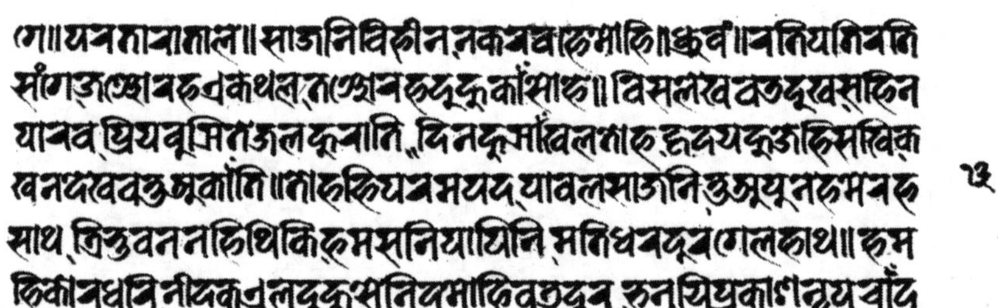

Folio 14R

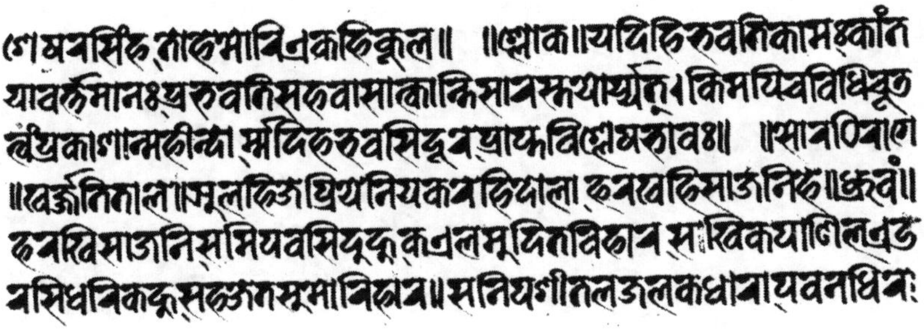

Folio 14V

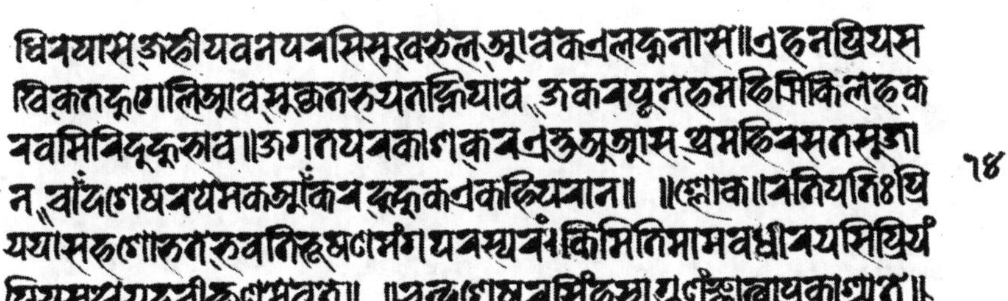

Folio 15R

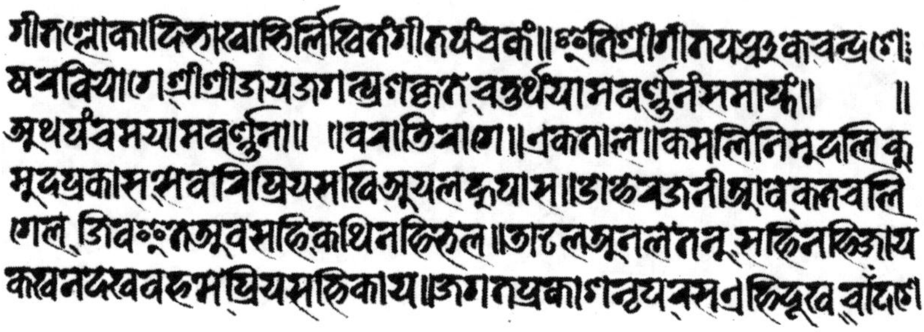

Folio 15V

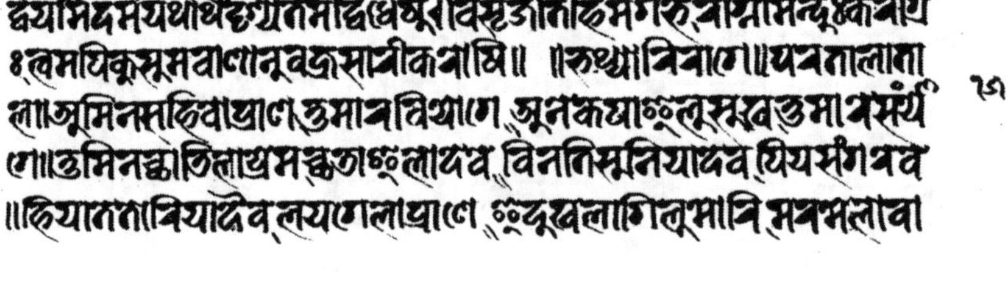

Folio 16R

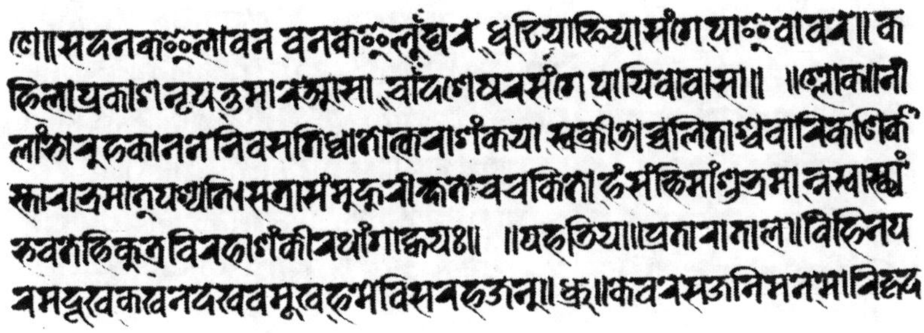

Folio 16V

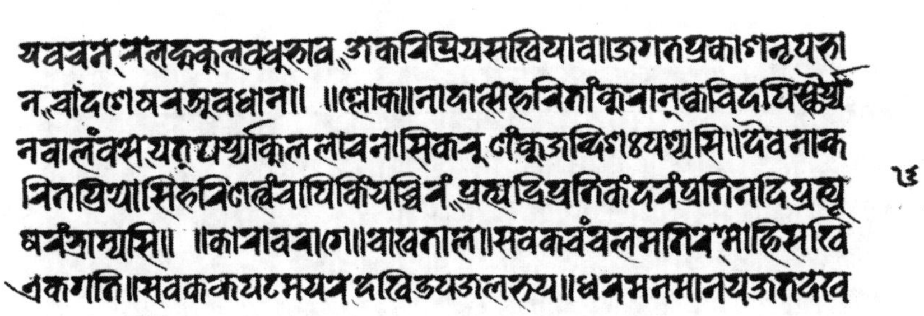

Folio 17R

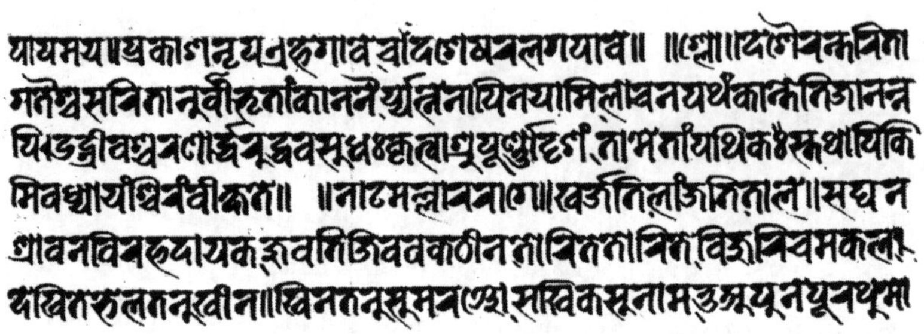

Folio 17V

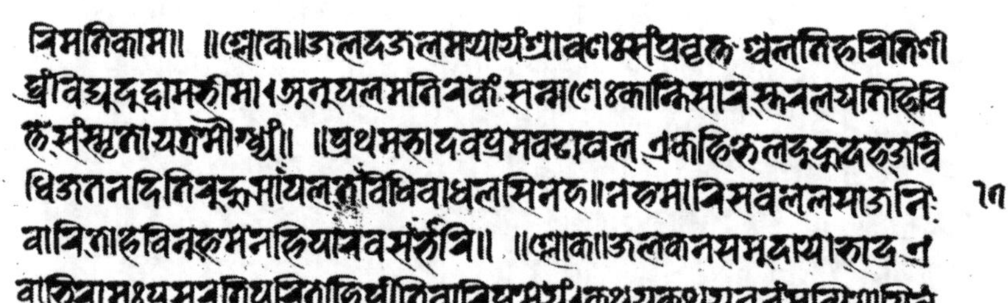

Folio 18R

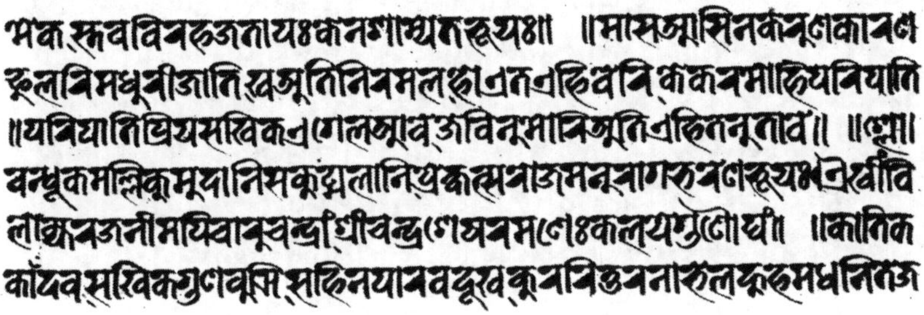

Folio 18V

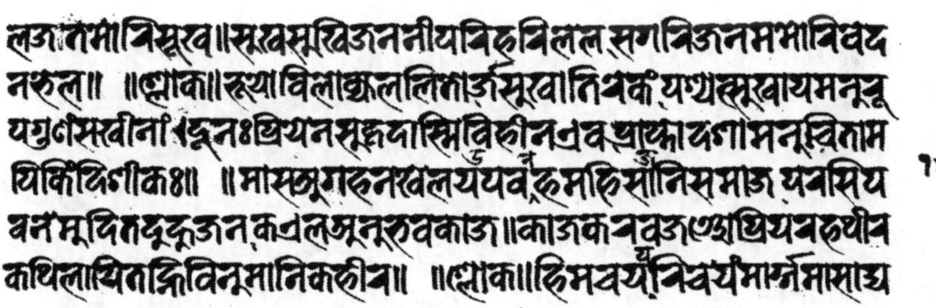

Folio 19R

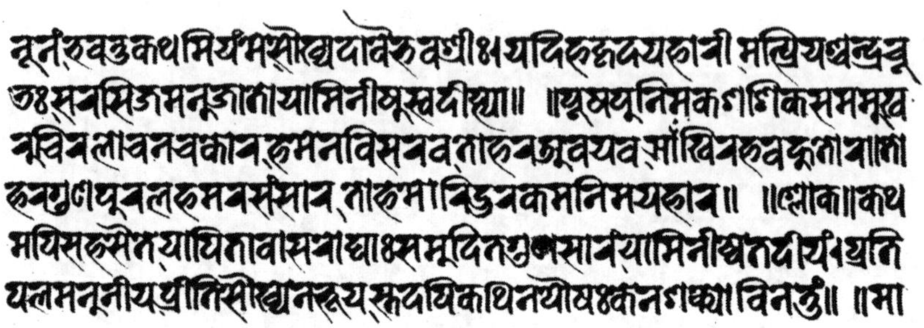

Folio 19V

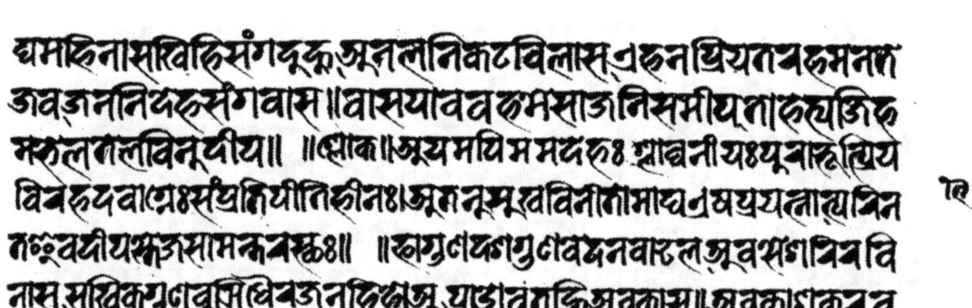

Folio 20R

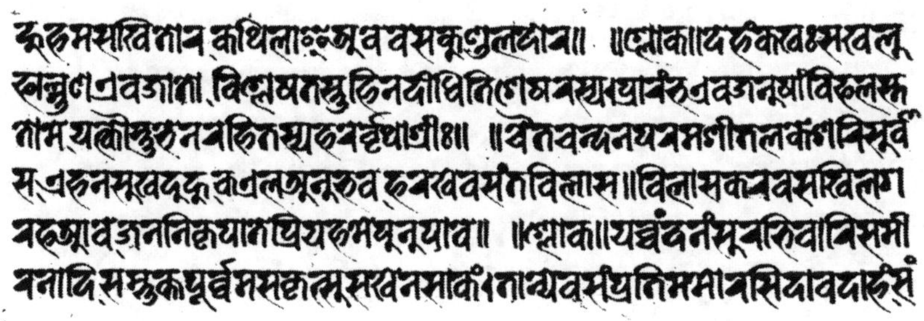

Folio 20V

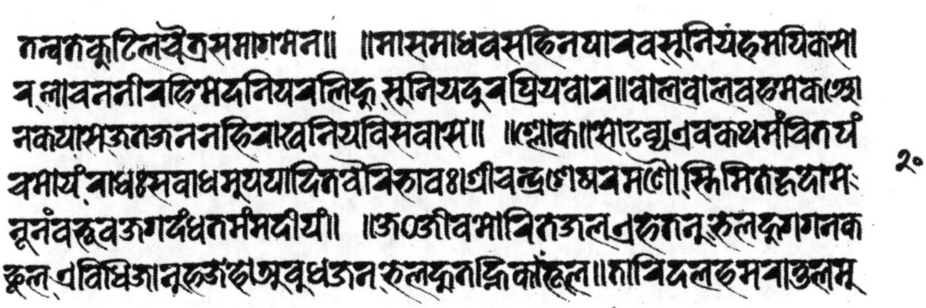

Folio 21R

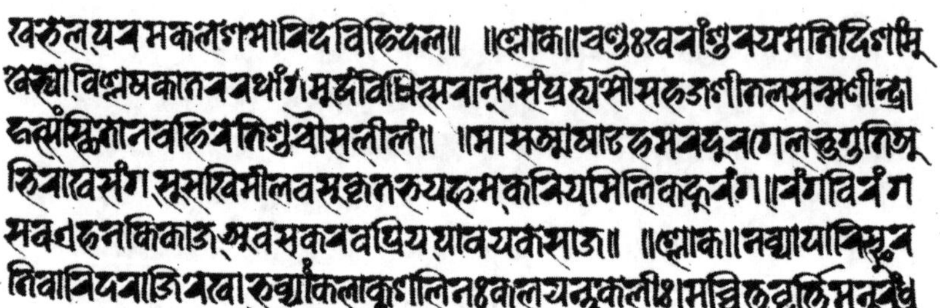

Folio 21V

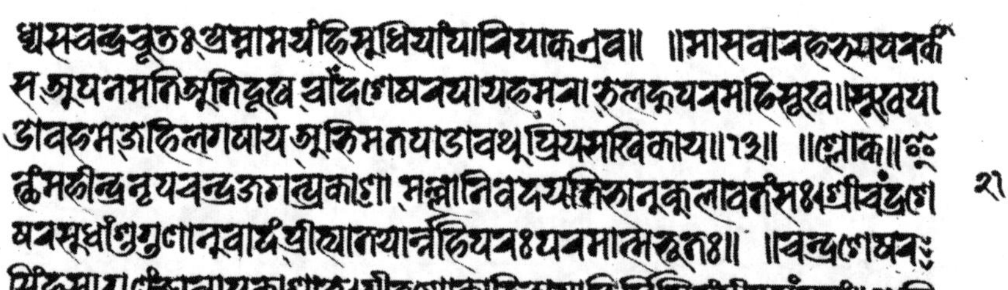

Folio 22R

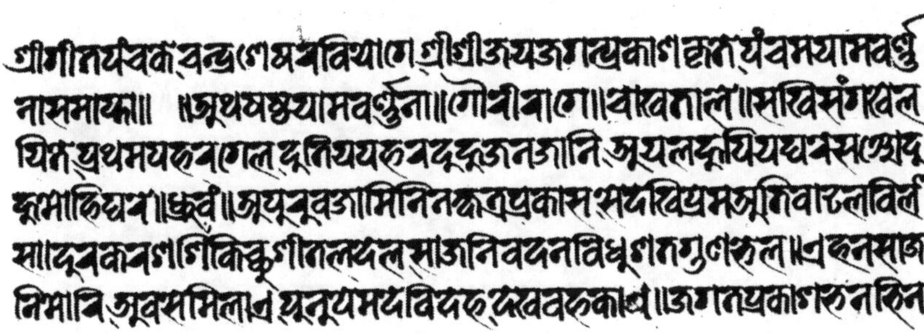

Folio 22V

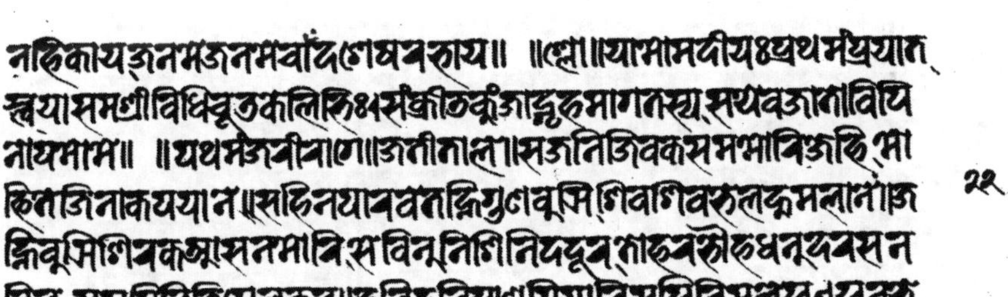

Folio 23R

Folio 23V

Folio 24R

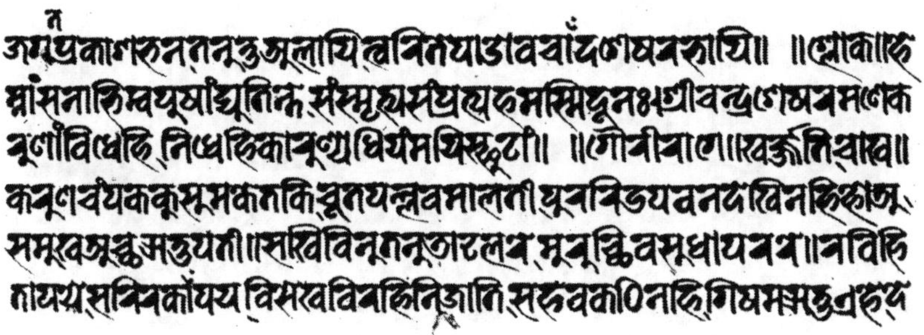

Folio 24V

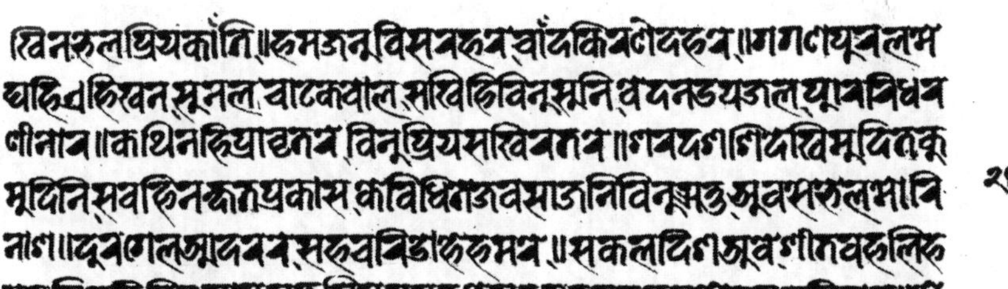

Folio 25R

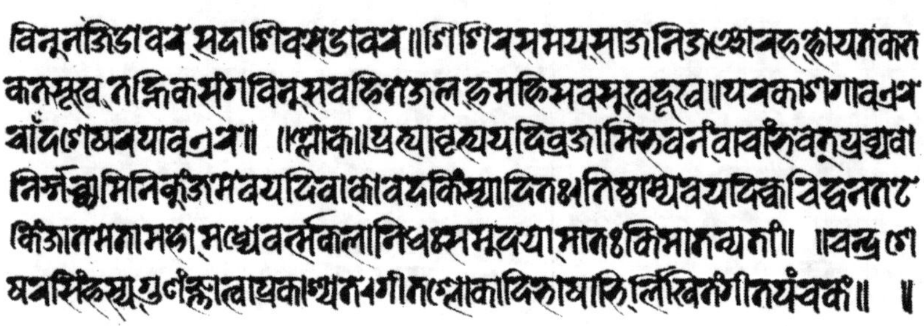

Folio 25V

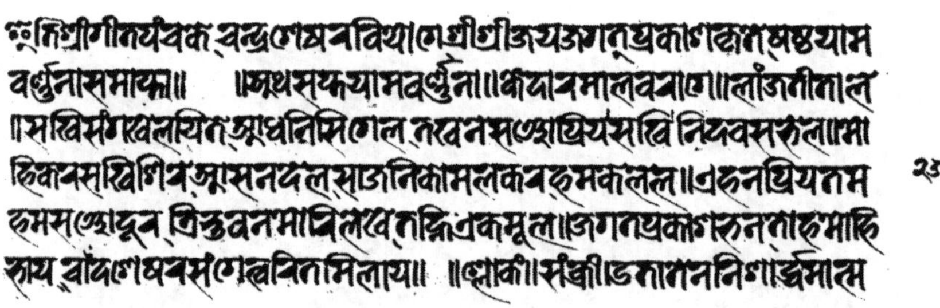

Folio 26R

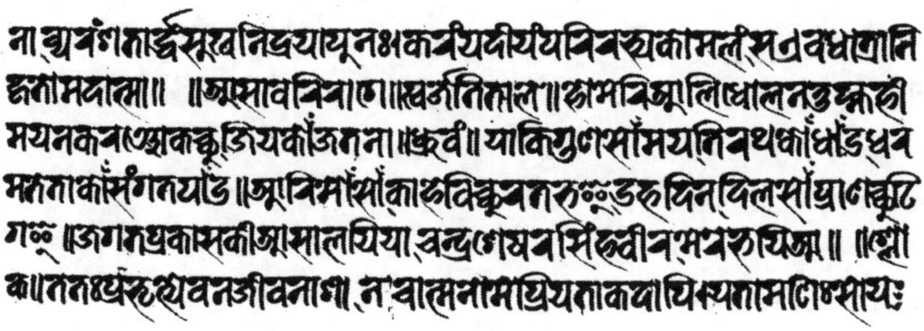

Folio 26V

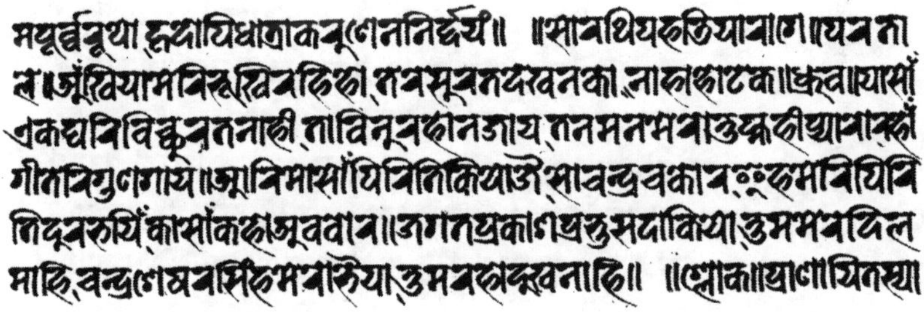

२६

Folio 27R

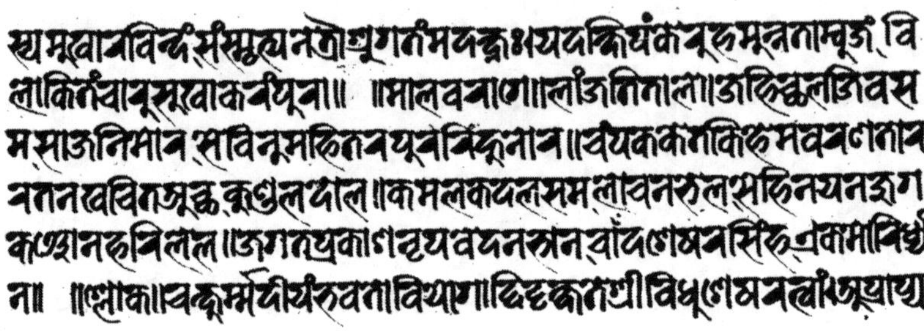

Folio 27V

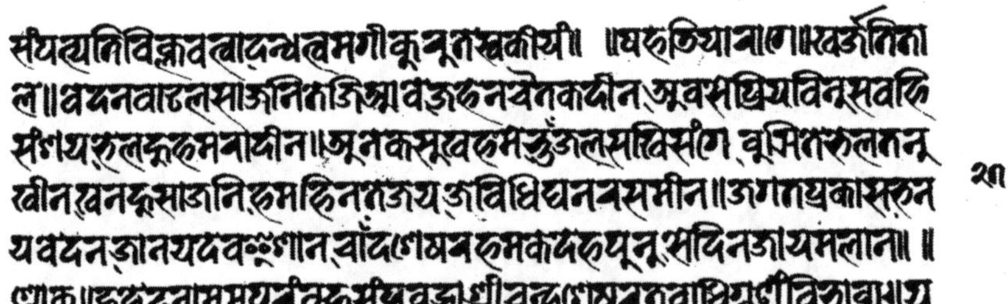

Folio 28R

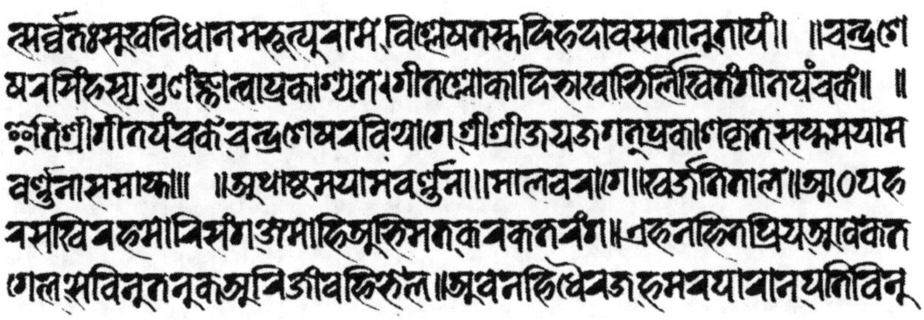

Folio 28V

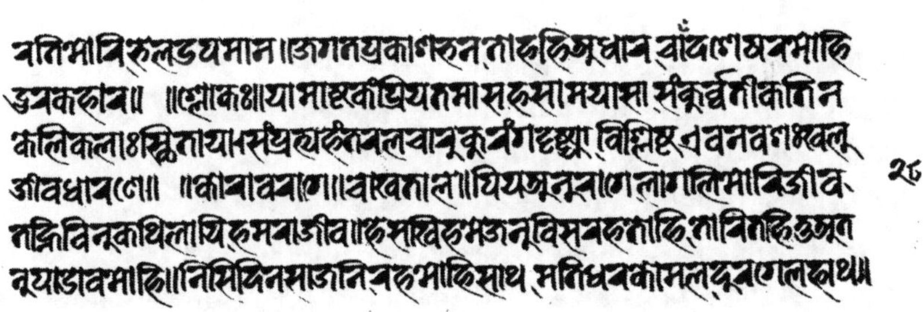

Folio 29R

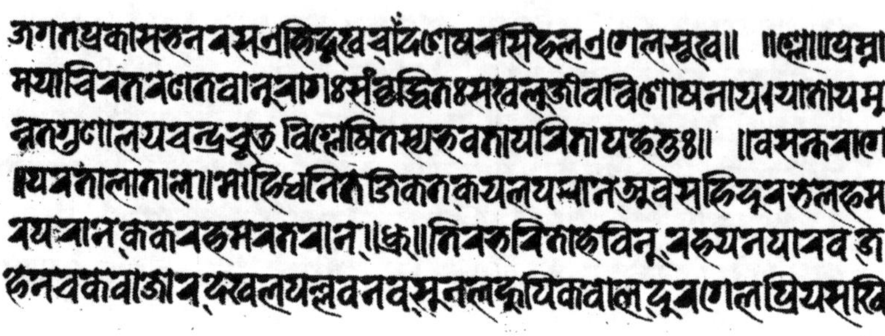

Folio 29V

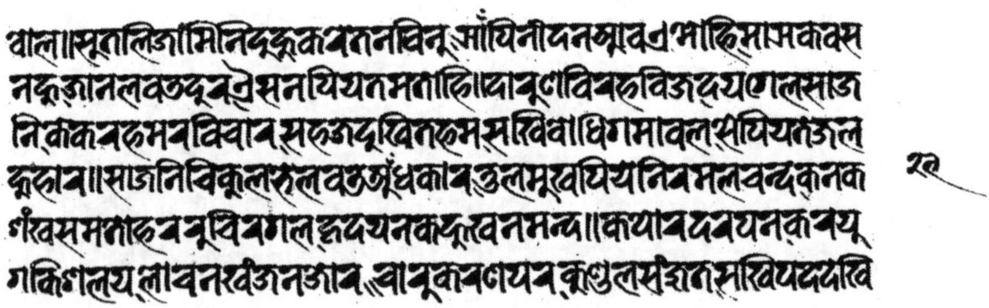

Folio 30R

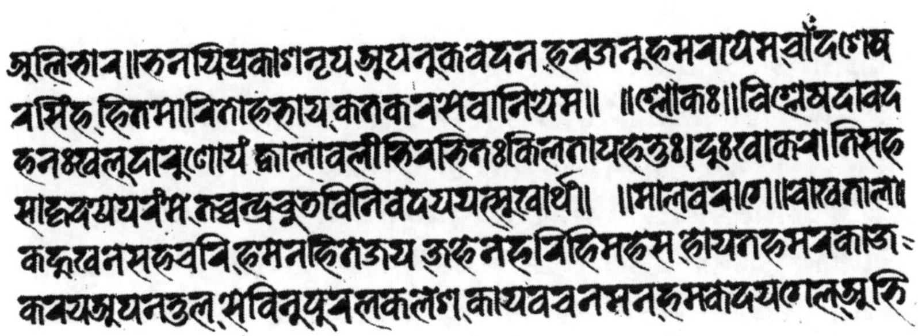

Folio 30V

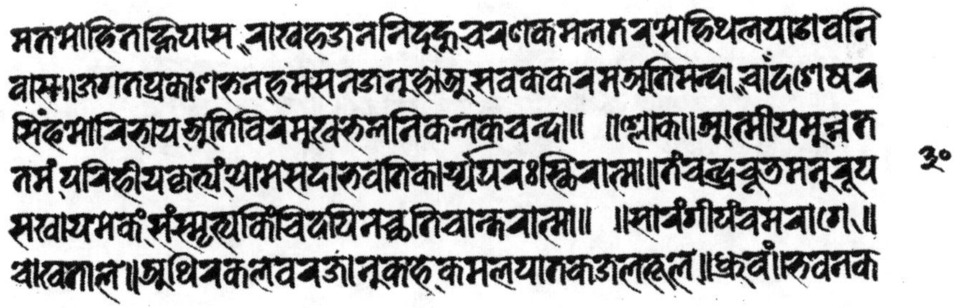

Folio 31R

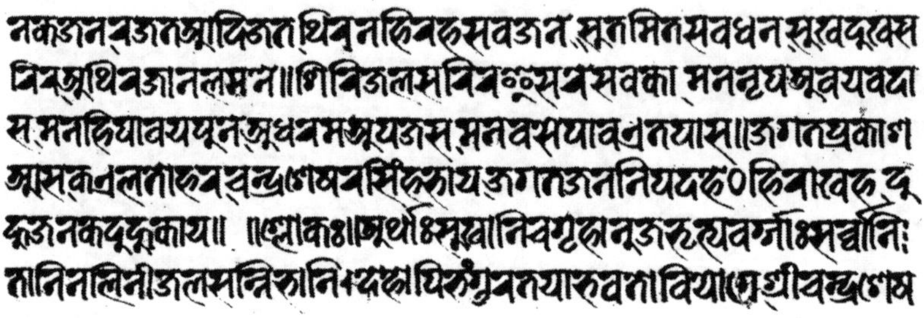

Folio 31V

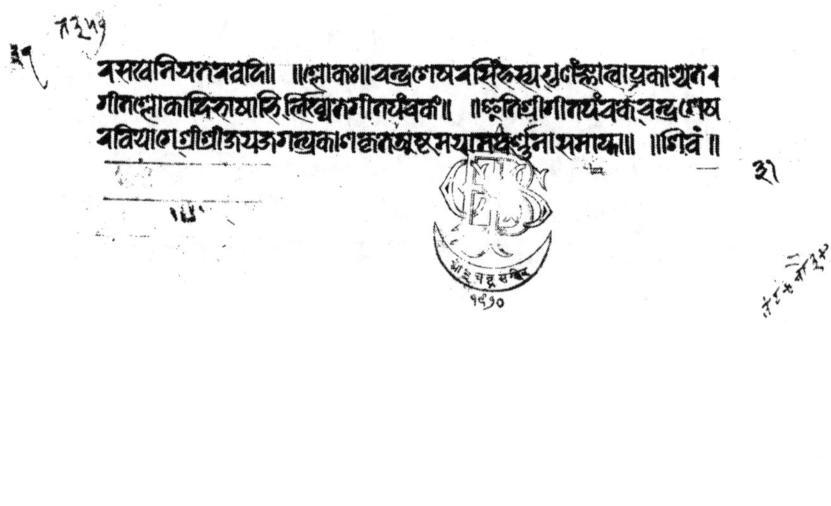

3

Transliteration into Devanāgarī Script

(१ प: १) औं [ॐ] नमो नाटेश्वराभ्यां ॥

ओतप्रोतं जगद्यत्र[जगद् यत्र], यो विश्वस्य हृदिस्थितः।
नमो आनन्दरू(२)पाय, तस्मै पूर्णाय शम्भवे॥

॥ *धनाछि रागे* ॥ *चोख ताले* ॥
विभुति भुषन अंगे, त्रिशूल (३) डमरु करे,
रह सङ्ग भूत गन, चाँद तिलक धरे ॥
गले मुण्ड माल, करण पर कुण्डल दो[डो](४)ल,
पहिरए बाघ छाल, चरण कमल जोर ॥
कर हर नित्य विहारे, नन्दिहि मुरुज ब(५)जाबे,
गणेश सेनापति नाचे, नारद आदिहि गित गाबे ॥
महेश्वर हे तोहे नाटक सो(६)हाबए,,
जगतप्रकाश नृप, कौतुके गाबए ॥

॥ *श्लोक* ॥
सानन्दं नन्दिहस्ता, हतमुरुज**(२ अ: १)**रवाहूतकौमारवर्हि,
त्रासान्नासाग्ररंध्रं विशति फणिपतौ भोगसंकोचभाजि ।
गं(२)डोड्डीनानिमालामुखरितककुभस्ताण्डवे शूलपाणे,
र्व्वैनायाक्यश्चिरं वो वदनवि(३)धुतयः पान्तु चीत्कारवत्यः ॥

॥ *इति नान्दिस्तुतिः* ॥

अथ प्रियसखीवियोगे, त(४)स्य वियोगव्याकुलेन तं प्रीत्यर्थं,
श्रीश्रीजयजगत्प्रकाशोहं, तस्य स्तुतिं करोमि ॥

॥ (५) ममाग्र यो मम प्राण, यथा प्राणसमाग्रजः ।
ममाग्रजो मम प्राण, सत्यमेव वचस्त्विदं (६) ॥

॥ *अहेराणी रागे* ॥ *चोख ताले* ॥
जेठ जिवन सखि, विसलेखे भेल मोरि, मिथुन पि**(२ प: १)**रिति सुक बारे,
नेपालक संमते नर दिठि वसु हय, से दिन दुर गेल हारे ॥

म(२)ति अति निरमल, सरुप गाँग जल,, मोहि सुख दायक प्राने,
लोल लोचन युग, ह(३)मे अनुरंजन, चारु दुहु खंजन जाने ॥
भौह कुटिल प्रिय, मनमथ धनु थिक, ऋ(४)जु देखि के नहि भूले,,
कर जुग किशलय, हृदयन धरि मोरि, रजनिहु निद (५) भेल दूरे ॥
जगतप्रकाश भन, चन्द्रशेखर शिव, कय देह मिलन जुगूति,
आन न मोर गति, तुअ पद पय मति, देथु सदा शिव मुगुति ॥

॥ *श्लोक* ॥
धिक् वारिसह**(३ अ: १)**संकीर्ण्णं, न गतं यदि हतेन ।
श्रीमत्प्रकाशनृपते, प्राणास एव मे नूनं ॥

॥ *विभा(२)स रागे* ॥ *खर्ज्जति ताले* ॥
तोहे वर सहचरि, जिवक दोसरि थिक[कि], अबे मुख दे(३)खिय न भेला,
जेहि नयन जुग, देखि हर मोहि दुख, से पिय खन दुर गेला ॥
ए(४)कहि तलप बसि, दुहु जन हँसि हँसि, बोललहु एक जिव जानि,,
हमहि रोदन (५) क[के]र दुर कर मोर सखि, आँचल किश[स]लय पानि ॥
दुहुक पिरिति देखि, शशधर (६) कुमुदिनि, कयलह मति अति लाजे,
खने विसलेख देखि, उगल कूर शशि, बह**(३ प १)**लि दछि[क्षि]ण हरि आजे ॥
तोह[हे] बिनु हम भेल, हमर विहिन जे, सिरि हिन सारस जा(२)ने,,
देखल जगत हमे, अति अँधकार सन, दुहु निसि सहज मलाने ॥
हरि हरि ह(३)रीहि, साथहि सखि संग, न गेलि हे पापिनि बारि,,
जगतप्रकाश भन, चाँदशेषर(४)सिँह, हमरा तोहहि अधारि ॥

॥ *श्लोक* ॥
सहचरि परोत्वम्मे, देहाद्विभिन्नरूपा(५)पि ।
दृष्ट्वां करोखि नूनं, मां, सुखिनं समये पुरा ॥

॥ *भैरव रागे* ॥ *परताला ताले* ॥
(६)जखने साजनि मनि छल मोरि संगे,
हमहि प्रणवि पिय उथ[ठ]लि पराते ॥ *ध्रुवं* ॥
(४ अ: १) उगलहु शिशु हरि, भेलहु विहान,
चकोर मिथुन अबे, तेजल मलान ॥
ए[हि] खने सखि (२) मोरि, चिर हरि लेल,
हमहि कोर धरि, लावल तेल ॥
पुनु सखि कय देल, हमर स(३)मा[ना]ने,
ए विधि कत मोहि कयल तराने ॥
से बिनु रहला हे, पापिनि परान,,
मधु ते(४)जि विपिनक, भेल समान ॥
परकाश भन चाँदशेषर अधार,,
खन मनि दुर गेल (५) हृदयक हार ॥

॥ *श्लोक* ॥
प्रातर्म्मदीयशयनासनसंगतो यः, प्रेमातिरेकघटना(६)निपुनो मनीन्द्रः ।
स्वयं चिरप्रणय,पेशलभावुकोपि, धिग्दैवनिर्म्मितकृते स्खलित**(४ पः १):** क्षणेन ॥

॥ *वेलावल रागे* ॥ *चोख ताले* ॥
निरधनि कर सञो खसल सुहीर,
मोहि ल(२)ग साजनि नहि भेल थीर ॥
हरि हरि हम बड, पापिनि बारि,
हरि लेली[लि], ईशरि हम(३)र अधारि ॥
मृग नृप तुल कटि, कोमल पानि,,
हृदय राखल हमे किश[स]लय जानि ॥
तो(४)हे सनि हित सखि, हमर न आन,,
तोहि बिनु मोहि लेखे, जगत मलान ॥
परकाश क(५)यलहु, तोहर धेयान,,
चाँदशेषर शिव, करु अवधान ॥

॥ *श्लोक* ॥
प्रोक्तो मया य(६)दिपि सः सारो मणिर्न्निखिलो द्युतिकलायाः ।
दैवान्ममैव सहसा, हृदयाच्युतो हि **(५ अः १)** विधिना ग्लपितः ॥

॥ *आसावरि रागे* ॥ *खर्ज्जति ताले* ॥
सुजन सुहृदय, सुगुण संजुत, सुक(२)टि अति अभिराम,,
सुसखि सुमरञो, सुमने निसि दिन, करब जप तुअ नाम ॥
सुखक (३) आँ[आ]कर, सुरस सागर, नयन तुअ अरविन्द,,
कपोल निरमल चिबुक सुन्दर, वदन (४) पुनिमक चन्द ॥
तोहहि भूषण तोहहि सुवसन, तोहहि जिवन अधार,,
तोहहि साजनि, (५) परसमणि थिकि, हमर हृदयक हार ॥
हमर यहि मति, सखिहि पए गति, झाँखि तेजय (६) परान,
कहथि परकाश, कयल तुअ आस, चाँदशेषरक ध्यान ॥

॥ *श्लोक* ॥
प्रीतिं तयो[:] स**(५ पः १)**मधुरा,मभितो मुदा विधुरवी ।
दृष्ट्वानुबंधसंपर्क्क, मलिनं निजहितः स्वं ॥

॥चन्द्रशेष(२)रसिंहस्य, गुणं ज्ञात्वा प्रकाश्यते ।
गीतश्लोकादिभाषाभि,र्लिख्यते गीतपंचकं ॥

॥ (३) इति श्रीगीतपञ्चके, चन्द्रशेषरवियोगे, श्रीश्रीजयजगत्प्रकासकृते, प्रथमयामव(४)र्ण्णना समाप्ता ॥

॥ *अथ द्वितीयजा[या]मकृत्यवर्ण्णना* ॥

॥ *कौशिक रागे* ॥ *चोख ताले* ॥
प्रिय (५) सखि ओरे, द्वितिय पहर बेरि आयल,
की मोहि थल, नयन देखल हमे सादर ॥
दुर (६) गेल ओरे, जिवक दोसरि, सखि किछु खन,
की मोहि धन, तुअ तुल नहि थिक जत जन ॥
(६ अ: १) तोह बिनु ओरे, पति विसलेखे हम रति,
की सुभ मति, तेजलहु सहचरि जूवति ॥
भ(२)न किछु ओरे, जगतप्रकाश नृपति वर,
की पुर हर, चाँदशेषरसिंह अति भल ॥

(३) ॥ ॥ *श्लोक* ॥
दुःखं दीर्घतरं वहत्यपि सखीवर्षा[र्ष्या]यणो भाखते,
शैवाले शयनं सृज(४)त्यपि पुनः शेते न वा लज्जया ।
कण्ठे गङ्गदवाचि मुञ्चति दृशा, धत्ते नवाप्योदकं,
सं(५)तापं सहते यदम्बुजमुखी, तद्वेद चे[तो]भवः ॥

॥ *केदार मालव रागे* ॥ *चोख ताले* ॥
(६) शशि बिनु ओरे, रजनि सहजे अति मलिन,
की तनु खिन, सखि तेजि हम, जल बिनु **(६ पः १)** मीन ॥
गुणमत ओरे गुपुतहि भेल मनि, हमर,
की अति भल, सहचरि दिथि कर क(२)मल ॥
जे बिनु ओरे, जिवक कलेस, अति वाध[ढ़]ल,
की जलधर, निवि ड[दु]हु देखि नहि (३) पारल ॥
दह दिश ओरे, मलिन देखल अबे जगत,
की गतागत, हरि लेल जेहि पि(४)य मोरि रत ॥
कहलहु ओरे, जगतप्रकाश नृपति यह दुख,
की शशि मुख, चाँदशे(५)षर, रह मोहि सुख ॥

॥ *श्लोक* ॥
तल्पे सहासमेकस्मिन्, वदता परप्राणत्वं ।
स प(६)रः सहसा शिव, स्तव वाप्य हि शिवः स ॥

॥ *धनाश्री रागे* ॥ *चोख ताले* ॥
आबे गेलि **(७ अ: १)** आदर, सखि बिनु मोरी ॥
खनहु न तेज सखि, हमे बड बाला, चाँद निकट रह तारा (२) ॥
शिव शिव सेहे मोरि, परि हरि लेला, जेहि दइवे दुख देला ॥
जे बिनु निज घरे (३) भेलहु उचाट, पाओब तह्निक संग बाट ॥
परकाश भन चाँदशेषर परान, कुण्डल (४) विहिन भेल काँन ॥

॥ *श्लोक* ॥
भवता रहितस्य मे, तमसा परितो नभः ।
व्याप्तं म(५)यापि विश्लेखे, नलिनीजलयो साम्यं ॥

॥ *मालव रागे* ॥ *खर्ज्जति ताले* ॥
प्रेम पाश (६) तोरलहु दैवे मोरि ॥ *ध्रुवं* ॥
जखने सजनि रह, हमरा पासे, किछु नहि होय तरासे (॥)
(७ प: १) हमर कारणे पिये, जिव दय गेल, मोहि सुख परि हरि लेल ॥
कखने भेलहु दि(२)न, कञोने खने राटि[ति], सुमरैत रहबहु काँटि[ति] ॥
जगतप्रकाश भन, तोहहि अ(३)धार, चाँदशेषरसिंह हार, ॥

॥ *श्लोक* ॥
एकस्त्वमेव सुहृदां प्राणायितो मम (४) तनुः ।
कोन्यो निहन्तु शोकाग्निं, त्वं दूरगो यदीह मे ॥

॥ *गोपीवल्लभ रागे* ॥ *रघुशेषर ताले* ॥
पेयसि मोरि सजनि सखि, चरण तुअ वारिजं, तोहर उरु (६) कदलि सम जाने,
रुचिर कटि सरुप हरि, वरण हेम समानं, तन्विधर अमिअ **(८ अ: १)** रस बाने ॥
प्रिये मोरि तोहि प्रिये मोरि तोही, तेजि जनु न डाबह मोहि, सहजे अ(२)ति पापिनि,
दुखित हमे कामिनि, हमहि सँग कय करु सँतारे ॥ *ध्रुवं* ॥
हृदय स(३)खि सरिर तोहि, बचन मोरि तोहहि[ही], सोभित मोरि नयन जुग तोही,
वदन श(४)शि सनि[मि]प बसि, पिउल हमे आदरे, गेलहु दुर खनहि मनि मोहि ॥
सखिहि बि(५)नु अधिक धनु भेलहु कतहु न यके, हमर लग कुमति जेहि मारे[,]
एहन दुख अधि(६)क भेल सहि नही पार हे, मदन अबे कयलहु परहारे [॥]
भुपति जय जगतपर**(८ प: १)**काश भन तोहही, हमर सखि करब एक भावे,
तोहहि थिकि तेजब नहि हमही, (२) कुलक वधु करबए जे सो भावे ॥

॥ *श्लोक* ॥
मालाबालाम्बुजदलं, मौक्तिकैर्हारयष्टि(३): । [,]
    कांचीजाता प्रभवति हलौ, सुभ्रुवः प्रस्थितैव ।
अन्य ब्रूमं किमपि धमनी वर्त्तते वा(४)नवाज्ञा,
    तुंबाहोरहह वरयं पाणिमूलं प्रयाति ॥

॥ *चन्द्रशेषरसिंहस्य, गुणं ज्ञात्वा (५) प्रकाश्यते ।*
गीतश्लोकादिभाषाभि,र्लिख्यते गीतपंचकं ॥

[॥] इति श्रीगीतपंचके, चन्द्र(६)शेषरवियोगे,, श्रीश्रीजयजगत्प्रकाशकृते, द्वितीययामकृत्यवर्ण्णना समाप्तं ॥

(९ अ: १) ॥ *अथ तृतीययामकृत्यवर्ण्णना* ॥

॥ *गौरी रागे* ॥ *चोख ताले* ॥
तितिय पहर, (२) भेल जानल साय, विहुँसि विहुँसि ह[हँ]सि, आयल मिलाय ॥
कखनेहु न तेजय, स(३)खि मोरि सेवा, कर प्रिय एक मने हम पय देवा ॥
जञो होअ हमरा सदनक (४) काज, जानि करय ओहे अपनुक काज ॥
दुहु जन जानल, तनु नहि भीन,, खनेहु न (५) सखि संग, पिरिति विहीन ॥
हमे जनु बिसरह हमर अधारि, लग लेह हमे धनि (६) हमहि निहारि ॥
जगतप्रकाश भन, करह सँतार, चाँदशेषरसिंह, हृदयक हार ॥ ॥

(९ प: १) ॥ *श्लोक* ॥
येन प्रियेन सवासात्, संवेशोपि सुखप्रदः ।
स एवासुखहेतुर्म्मे, तद्विश्ले(२)षहविभु[र्भु]जः ॥

॥ *कोराव रागे* ॥ *लांजति एक ताले* ॥
हमे नहि बिसरब, सखि गु(३)ण सूख, मोहि बड तसु मुख, देखयके भूख ॥
हरि हरि हमरा दिथि[ठि]अति पापि,, (४) से बिनु दरसने रहलाहु काँपि ॥
पेम विहिन दुख सहि नहि जाए, वेदन घर थि(५)क हमरा काए ॥
जगतप्रकास कह निते एहि चीत, चाँदशेषरसिंह मोरि बड (६) हीत ॥

॥ *श्लोक* ॥
एकात्मनोः सुसुहृदोः प्रीतिन्तयोर्व्विधुरवी ।
दृष्ट्वानुबंधसंरंभं **(१० अ: १)** प्रियया निजहितः स्वं ॥

॥ *विभास रागे* ॥ *एक ताले* ॥
विधु बिनु निसि हम भेल, (२) सुख सखि परि हरि रे[ले])ल ॥
नदि भेल नयनक नीर, सखि बिनु बाढ[ढ़]ल पीर ॥
भम(३)य भमर तसु लोभे, से बिनु हमे एहि सोभे ॥
परकास रस तुअ गाबे, चाँदशेषर (४) लग पाबे ॥

॥ *श्लोक* ॥
वेजनं वेजनं जरं[लं] जरं[लं], घनसारो घनसार इत्यपि ।
अबे(५)रोधपुरीखु कामिनीनां, कुररीमिव कातरध्वणिं ॥

॥ *गुज्जरी रागे* ॥ *परता(६)रा ताले* ॥
साय साय कुल वधु बारि, रस दय सुख लेल गारि ॥
समुचित दुहु जन **(१० प: १)** देह, दिने दिने वाढ[ढ़]ल सिनेह ॥
खनहु न तेज सखि मोहि, दुर कर नोर जत तो(२)हि ॥
से आबे विसलेख भेल, मोरि शिरि तह्नि संग गेल ॥
जगतप्रकास लेल सार, (३) चाँदशेषर कए[ल] हार ॥

॥ *श्लोक* ॥
समुपागतवति चैत्रे, निपतति[तितं]पत्रे लवंग(४)लतिकायाः ।
सुदृशः कपोलवाली, शिवशिवतालीदलद्युतिं लभे ॥

॥ *सोरथि[ठि] रा(५)गे* ॥ *खर्ज[ज्जं]ति ताले* ॥
सुजन साजनि, मिलल समुचित, जे विधि हरिहि महेश,
पेम(६)क बस भय, कएल दुहु जन, अपने सखिक सुवेश ॥
जखने सखि संगे पथहि गेल दु**(११ अ: १)**हु करहि कर धनि [धरि] मोहि,
मुखहि मुख देखि, रहल जेहि दुहु, हरिहि हरि लेल (२) तोहि ॥
दुरहि जनि कर,स[करह] जनि बिसरह, चेतह पिय परिपाति,,
हमरि पूरुब गे(३)लिहु दुर सखि, तैं भेल पापिनि जाति ॥
जगतपरकाश, कएल तुअ आस, पाओब (४) तह्नि संग बास,
सुमति साजनि, गुणक आगरि, चाँदशेषरक पास ॥

॥ *श्लो[क]* ॥
(५) गतागतकुतूहलं नयनयोरपाङ्गावधि, स्मृतं कुलनतभ्रुवा,मधर एव विस्राम्य(६)ति ।
वचः प्रियतमश्रुते,रतिथिरेव कोपक्रमः, कदाचिदपि चेत्तदा मनसि केव**(११ प १)**लं मज्जति ॥

॥ *चन्द्रशेषरसिंहस्य, गुणं ज्ञात्वा प्रकाश्यते* ।
गीतश्लोकादिभाषाभिर्लि(२)खितं गीतपंचकं ॥

[॥] इति श्रीगीतपंचके, चन्द्रशेषरवियोगे श्रीश्रीजयजगत्प्रका(३)सकृते, तृतीययामवर्ण्णना समाप्ता ॥

॥ *अथ चतुर्थयामवर्ण्णना* ॥

॥ *कोराव रा(४)गे* ॥ *लांजती ताले* ॥
चारि पहर दिन, साजनि बोल, सुनिते गमावल, आपद जोर (५) ॥
सेहि पिय खने आबे, गेलिहु दूर, जत जन मोरि लेखे, तह्नि पिय मूल ॥
जग(६)तप्रकास भने ॥ [sic]
जेह सखि नाशय, मोरि पद धूर, ई संग कए देवि, अभिमत पूर ॥
जग**(१२ अ: १)**तप्रकास भन तोहहि हीत, चाँदशेषर बिनु सब गेल नीत ॥

॥ *श्लोक* ॥
सत्यं त(२)दीयवचनामृतधारयाम, हृष्टस्य कापि नवभूवयराप्यसम्पत् ।
संप्रत्यकाण्ड(३)विधियन्त्रनघर्षितेन, तेनास्मि शोकजलधौ गमितः क्षणेन ॥

॥ *धनाश्री रागे* ॥ *(४) एक ताले* ॥
बिसरि न रहबह, साजनि गून,, से बिनु उपजल, अतिहि करून ॥
सखि (५) तेजि के कर, हमर संतार, मोति मानिक हार, भेल बड भार ॥
जत्रो ओहे साजनि र(६)हओ समाज, तत्रो मोरि प्राणक होअ सब काज ॥
जगतप्रकाश नृप, वेदन भान ॥ [,] **(१२ प: १)** चाँदशेषरसिंह, करु अवधान ॥

॥ *श्लोक* ॥
सानन्दमष्य[स्य] वपुषां, समुदाय(२)सारं, संस्मृत्य संप्रति हृदा करुणोदयो मे ।
संजायते स खलु दीर्घमहत्वमु(३)द्रः, तन्विक्षणादिव वियोगभरेण भूयः ॥

॥ *केदार मालव रागे* ॥ *लांजति ता(४)ले* ॥
सखि हे कतहु न गेली मति मोरि ॥ *ध्रु[वं]* ॥
हरि न हरल हमे, जीव हरि ह(५)रि लेल, हरि सम मुख भेल दूर,
शिशु हरि तुलना, अधरक काँति, तुअ कटि दे(६)खि हरि सम भूल ॥
हरि हरि जह्निका, हरि सम वेगे रह, हरि तुल उडि[ड़ि] गेल **(१३ अ: १)** साय,
नयन हरि अति, मेदनि परल अबे, दुर गेल हरि सम काय ॥
हरि कर (२) तुल उरु हरि सम वच[न], एहन[ने] साजनि मोहि,
हरिहि विसलेख, कए देल प्रिय (३) संग, मोरि मति गति एक तोहि ॥
जगतप्रकाश भन, सबहि अथिर थिक, शिशु (४) मित जन धन दार,
सुमति हमर गति, चा[चाँ]दशेषरसिंह, तोहे पए हृदयक हा(५)र ॥

॥ *श्लोक* ॥
हयर्यानन: कान्तहरीन्द्रमध्यो, विभातकालीनहरे: समाध(६)र: ।
सोयं हरिर्म्मे हरिणा गृहीतो, हरेरयेनैष हरिं प्रपन्न[:] ॥

॥ *धनाश्री रा* ***(१३ प: १)****गे* ॥ *परतारा ताले* ॥
साजनि विहीन, न करबाह मोहि ॥ *ध्रुवं* ॥
रति पति रति (२) संगे, जञो रह एक थल, तञो रह दुहुकाँ सोहे ॥
विसलेख बड दुख, सहि न (३) पारब, प्रिय बुझि तेजलहु राति,,
दिनहु झाँखल तोह, हृदयहु जेहि सखि, क(४)खन देखब तुअ काँति ॥
तोहहि परम पद, पावल साजनि, तुअ पुने हमे रह (५) साथ,
त्रिभुवन नहि थिकि, हम सनि पापिनि, मति धर दुर गेल हाथ ॥
हम(६)हि कोर धरि, नीद कएल दुहु, से निद मोहि बड दूर,,
भनयि प्रकाश नृप, चाँद**(१४ अ: १)**शेषरसिंह, तोहे मोरि एकहि कूल ॥

॥ *श्लोक* ॥
यदि हि भवति काम: कांत(२)या वर्त्तमान:, प्रभवति सहवासात्कान्तिसारस्तयोर्य्यत् ।
किमपि च विधिचूड(३)त्वं प्रकाशान्महीन्दो,र्म्मदिह भवसि दूरे, प्राप्तविश्लेषभाव: ॥

॥ *सोरठि रागे* (४) ॥ *खर्ज्जति ताले* ॥
झूलहि जे प्रिये निय करे हि[हिँ]दो[ड़ो]ला, हरखहि साजनि हे ॥ ध्रुवं ॥
(५) हरखि साजनि, समिप बसि दुहु, कएल मुदित विहार,
सखिक पाणि लए उ(६)रसि धरि कहु, सहजे तसु मोरि हार ॥
सनि[मि]प शीतल जलक धारा, पवन धिरे **(१४ प: १)** धिरे पासे,
जेही पवने परसि सुख भेल, आबे कएलहु नासे ॥
एहन प्रिय स(२)खि, कतहु गेलि आबे, सुकृत भय तह्नि पाबे,,
जकर पूने हमहि झिकि लेह, क(३)रब मिरि[लि] दुहु भावे ॥
जगतपरकाश, करए तुअ आस, प्रेमहि रस तसु जा(४)न,,
चाँदशेषर पेमक आँ[आ]कर, दुहुक एकहि परान ॥

॥ *श्लोक* ॥
रतिपतिः प्रि(५)यया सह शोभते, भवति भूषणमंगपरस्परं ।
किमिति मामवधीरयसि प्रियं[,] (६) प्रियसखे यदनीक्षणमेव ते ॥

॥ *चन्द्रशेषरसिंहस्य, गुणं ज्ञात्वा प्रकाश्यते* ॥
(१५ अः १) *गीतश्लोकादिभाखाभिर्लिखितं गीतपंचकं* ॥

[॥] इति श्रीगीतपंचके, चन्द्रशे(२)षरवियोगे, श्रीश्रीजयजगत्प्र[का]शकृते, चतुर्थयामवर्ण्णनं समाप्तं ॥

॥ *(३) अथ पंचमयामवर्ण्णना* ॥

॥ *वराडि रागे* ॥ *एक ताले* ॥
कमलिनि मुदलि कु(४)मुद प्रकास, से बेरि प्रिय सखि अयलहु पास ॥
ओहे रजनी आबे, कत चलि (५) गेल, जिबइते अबसहि, कथि[ठि]नहि भेल ॥
डाढ[ढ]ल अनले तनु, सहि नहि जाय[,] (६) कखने देखब हमे, (६) प्रिय सहि काय ॥
जगतप्रकाश नृप, रस एहि दूख,, चाँदशे**(१५ पः १)**षरसिंह, लए गेल सूख ॥

॥ *श्लोक* ॥
तव कुसुमशरत्वं, शीतरश्मित्वमिन्दो,,(२)र्द्वयमिदमयथार्थं दृश्यते मद्विधेषु ।
विसृजति हिमगर्भै,रग्निमिन्दुः कराग्रे(३):, त्वमपि कुसुमबाणान् वज्रसारी करोषि ॥

॥ *भथ्यारि रागे* ॥ *परताला ता (४)ले* ॥
अमि न सहिबो[लो] प्राण, तुमार वियोगे,, अनेक पाइलु[लुँ] सुख, तुमार संयो(५)गे ॥
तूमि न छाडिलो प्रेम, छडाइलो देबे,, विनति सुनिया देबे, पिय संग रेबे (६) ॥
हिया ते तोरिया दैबे, लय गेलो प्राणे,, इ दुख लागिलु[लुँ] मोरि मरमेलो[लुँ] बा**(१६ अः १)**णे ॥
सदन कइलो बन, बन कइलुँ घरे,, धु[धुँ]ढिया हिया संगे, पाइबो बरे ॥
क(२)हिलो प्रकाश नृप, तुमारे आसा,, चाँदशेषर संगे, पायिबो बासा ॥

॥ *श्लोक* ॥
नी(३)लांभोरुहकानने निवसति ध्वा[ध्वां]तोत्कराशंकया,
स्वकीडोच्चलिताश्च वारिकणिका(४)स्ताराभ्रमात् पश्यति ॥
सत्रासं मुहुरीक्षते च चकितो,हं संहिमांशुभ्रमा,न्न[,]
स्वास्थ्यं (५) भव[ज]ते हि कुत्र विरहाशंकीरथांगाह्वयः ॥

॥ *पहडिया [रागे]* ॥ *प्रतारा ताले* ॥
विहिन प(६)रम दूख, कखने देखब मूख, हमे विसरह जनु ॥ *ध्रु[वं]*॥
के वरे सजनि मने, मोरि हृद**(१६ पः १)**य वचने,,
रे[ले]लहु कुल वधु भाव,, जे करि प्रिय सखि पाव ॥
जगतप्रकाश नृप भा(२)न,, चाँदशेषर अवधान ॥

॥ *श्लोक* ॥
नादात्सेहरितां कुरा[ला]न् क्वचिदपि स्थैय्र्यं(३)न वा लंबसे,
यत् पय्र्याकुललोचनोसि करुणं कुजन्दिशः पश्यसि ॥
दैवेनान्त(४)रितप्रियोसि हरिण त्वं चापि किं यच्चिरं,,
प्रत्यद्रिप्रतिकं दरंप्रति नदि प्रत्यू(५)षरं भ्राम्यसि ॥

॥ *कोराव रागे* ॥ *चोख ताले* ॥
सबक चंचल मति रे, मोहि सखि (६) एक गति ॥
सबक कपट मय रे, देखि उपजल भय ॥
धरम न मानय [रे], जत देख **(१७ अः १)** पाप मय ॥
प्रकाश नृप एहे गाबे, चाँदशेषर लग पाबे ॥

॥ *श्लो[क]* ॥
देशैरन्तरिता(२)गतैश्च सरितानुर्वीभृतां काननै,
र्यत्नेनापि नयामि, लोचनपथं कान्तेति जानन्न(३)पि ।
उद्ग्रीवश्चरणार्द्धरुद्धवसुधः कृत्वाश्रुपूर्ण्णां दृशं,
तामेतां पथिकस्तथापि कि(४)मिव ध्यायंश्चिरं वीक्षते ॥

॥ *नाट मल्लार रागे* ॥ *खर्ज [र्ज्ज]ति लांजति ताले* ॥
सघन (५) श्रावन विरह दायक, जुवति जिबब कठीन,
तोरिते तोरिते, बिजुरि चमकल, (६) देखिते भेल तनु खीन ॥
खिन तनु सुमरञो, सखिक सुनाम,
तुअ पुने पूरथु मो**(१७ प १)**रि मति काम ॥

॥ *श्लोक* ॥
जलदजलमयोयं श्रावणः संप्रवृत्तश्चलति हरिति शी(२)घ्रं, विद्युदुद्दामभीमा ।
अनुपलमतिरेकं, सन्मणेः कान्तिसार,स्तरलयति हि चि(३)त्ते संस्मृतो यत्र मौग्ध्यं ॥ ॥

॥ प्रथम भादव प्रेम बढा[ढा]वल, एकहि भेल दुहु देह,
जे वि(४)धि जत नदि तिरुहु झाँपल, तैं विधि वाध[ढ]ल सिनेह ॥
नेह मोरि सब लेल साजनि (५) बारि,
तोहे बिनु हमे नहि पारब सँभारि ॥

॥ *श्लोक* ॥
जलकनसमुदायो भाद्र ए(६)वाभिरामः, प्रसरति परितो हि प्रीतिवारिप्रमेयं ।
कथय कथय नूनं मत्प्रियोसि त्व**(१८ अः १)**मेक,स्तव विरहजतापः केन शाम्येत भूयः ॥

॥ मास आसिन करुण कारण (२) फुलरि[लि] मधुरी जाति,
ख अति निरमल, होएत एहि बेरि, के कर मोहि परिपाति (३) ॥
परिपाति प्रिय सखि कए गेल आबे,
जे बिनु मोरि अति एहि तनु ताबे ॥

॥ *श्लो[क]* ॥
(४) बन्धूकमल्लिकुमुदानि सकृद्मलानि, प्रेक्षेत्सरोजमनुरागभरेण भूयः ॥
ऐखीं वि(५)लोक्य रजनीमपि चारुचन्द्रां, श्रीचन्द्रशेषरमणेः कलये गुणौघं ॥ ॥

॥ कातिक (६) काँदब, सखिक गुण बुझि, सहि न पारब दूख,
कुररि तुर[ल]ना भेलहु हम धनि, तेज**(१८ पः १)**ल जति मोरि सूख ॥
सुख सुखि[सखि] जननी परि हरि लेल,
सगरि जनम मोरि वेद(२)न भेल ॥

॥ *श्लोक* ॥
भूयो विलोक्य ललितो,र्जसुखातिरेकं, पश्यत्सुखायमनुरू(३)पगुणं सखीनां ।
दूनः प्रियेन सुहृदास्मि विहीन एव, प्राप्तो दशामनुचिताम(४)पि किं दिशीकः ॥

॥ मास अगहन खेलय उपवन, हमहि साजनि समाज,
परसि प(५)वने मुदित दुहु जन, कएल अनुभव काज ॥
काज करब जञो प्रिय रह थीर[,]
(६) कथि लायि तह्नि बिनु मानिक हीर ॥

॥ *श्लोक* ॥
हिमचयपरिचेयं मार्ग्गमासाद्य **(१९ अः १)** नूनं, भवतु कथमियं मे, सौख्यदा वैभवश्रीः ।
यदिह हृदयहारी, मत्प्रियश्चन्द्रचू(२)डः, सरसिजमनुजातो यामिनीषु स्वदीप्त्या ॥

॥ पूष पुनिमक शशिक सम मुख[,] (३) रुचिर लोचन चकोर,
हमे न बिसरब, तोहर अवयव, झाँखि रहबहु तोर ॥
तो(४)हर गुणे पुरल हमर संसार,
तोहे मोरि ऊरक मनि मय हार ॥

॥ *श्लोक* ॥
कथम(५)पि सहसैते, यापिता वासरोघाः समुदितगुणसारं, यामिनीष्वेतदीयं ।
प्रति(६)पलमनुनीय[यं], प्रीतिसौख्येन भूय,स्तदपि कथिनपौषः केन शक्यो विनेतुं ॥

॥ ॥ मा**(१९ पः १)**घ महिना सखिहि संग दुहु, अनल निकट विलास,
एहन प्रियतर हमे न ते(२)जब, जननि देह संग बास ॥
बास पावब हमे साजनि समीप,
तोहे त्यजि ह(३)म भेल तेल बिनु दीप ॥

॥ *श्लोक* ॥
अयमपि मम देहः श्लाघनीयः पुराभूत्प्रिय (४) विरहदवाग्नेः संप्रति पी[प्री]तिहीनः ।
अननुसुखविनीतो माघ एष प्रयत्ना,त्परिन(५)त इव दीपस्तेजसामन्तरस्थः ॥

॥ फागुण दश गुण वेदन बाढ[द]ल, अबसे शरिर वि(६)नास,
सखिक गुण बुझि, धैरज नहि होअ, पाओब तह्नि अवकास ॥

अवकाश करब(**२० अ: १**)हु हम सखि तोर,
कथि लाइ अबे बेस (२) कुण्डल दोर [डोल] ॥

॥ *श्लोक* ॥
देहं कखः स खलु (२) फाल्गुण एव जातो, विश्लेषतस्तुहिनदीधितिशेषरस्य ।
प्रारंभ एव जनुषां विफलस्त(३)तो मे, यत्कौस्तुभेन रहितस्य हरेर्वृथा श्रीः ॥

॥ चैत चन्दन परम शीतल[,] [कोमल] केशरि सुवा(४)स,
एहन सुख दुहु, कएल अनुभव, हरखे वसंत विलास ॥
विलास करब सखि लग (५) रह आबे,
जननि कृपा ते प्रिय हमे पुनु पाबे ॥

॥ *श्लोक* ॥
यच्चंदनं सुरभिवारिसमी(६)रनादि, सम्भुक्तपूर्व्वमसकृत्सुसखेन साकं ।
तान्येव संप्रति ममोरसि दावदाहं, सं(**२० प: १**)तत्वते कुटिलचैत्रसमागमेन ॥

॥ मास माधव सहि न पारब, सुनिय हम पिक सो(२)र,
लोचन नीरहि मेदनि परलिहु सुनिय दुर प्रिय बोर[ल] ॥
बोल बोलव हमे कञो(३)नक पासे,
जत जन नहि राख निय विसवासे ॥

॥ *श्लोक* ॥
सोढव्य एव कथमंचितपं(४)चमोयं, राधः स वाधमुपपादितवैरिभावः ।
श्रीचन्द्रशेषरमणौ, स्तिमिते हृदो मे (५) नूनं बभूव जगदंधतमं मदीयं ॥

॥ जेठ जीव मोरि तेजल एहे तनु, भेलहु गगनक (६) फूल,
ए विधि जानुह जे होअ बुध जन, भेलहु तह्निकाँ भूल ॥
तारि दल हमरा तुल मु(**२१ अ: १**)ख भेल,
परम कलेश मोरि देविहि देल ॥

॥ *श्लोक* ॥
चण्डः खरांशुरयमेति दिशां मु(२)खेभ्यो, विश्लेषकातररथांगमुदं विधित्सरान् ।
संप्रत्यसौ सहजशीतलसन्मणीन्द्रो[,] (३) हृत्संस्थितो नवहिरेति शुचौ सलीलं ॥

॥ मास आषाढ हमर दुर गेल, भुगुति अ(४)भिराख संग,
सुसखि मीलब सुकृत भय हमे, करिय मिलि कहु रंग ॥
रंग विरंग (५) सब एहन कि काज,
अबसे करब प्रिय, पाबय के साज ॥

॥ *श्लोक* ॥
नव्या पारिस्फुर[रं](६)ति वारिदराजिरेखा, भव्याः कलाकुशलिनः कलयन्तु केलीः ।
मच्चित्तवृर्त्तिमनुरंध्र(**२१ प: १**)ध्यसचन्द्रचूडः, प्रेम्नामयं हि सुधियां पा[प]रिपाक एव ॥

॥ मास बारह भ[न]य परका(२)स, अपने मति अति दूख,
चाँदशेषर पाय हमरा, भेलहु परमहि सूख ॥
सुख पा(३)ओब हमे, जेहि लग पाय,
अभिमत पाओबथु प्रिय सखि काय ॥ १३ ॥

॥ *श्लोक* ॥
इ(४)त्थं महीन्द्रनृपचन्द्रजगत्प्रकाशो, मल्लो निवेदयति भानुकुलावतंसः ।
श्रीचंद्रशे(५)षरसुधांशुगुणानुवादं, प्रीत्या तयोर्न्नहि परः परमात्मभूतः ॥

॥ *चन्द्रशेषर(६)सिंहस्य, गुणं ज्ञात्वा प्रकाश्यते ।*
गीतश्लोकादिभाषाभि,र्लिखितं गीतपंचकं ॥

इति (२२ अः १) श्रीगीतपंचके, चन्द्रशेषरवियोगे, श्रीश्रीजयजगत्प्रकाशकृते, पंचमयामवर्ण्ण(२)ना समाप्ता ॥

॥*अथ षष्ठयामवर्ण्णना* ॥

[॥] *गौरी रागे* ॥ *चोख ताले* ॥
सखि संग खेल(३)यिते, प्रथम पहर गेल, दुतिय पहर दुहु जन जानि,
अयलहु पिय घरे सञो दु(४)हु मोहि घरे ॥ *ध्रुवं* ॥
अपुरुब जामिनि नक्षत्र प्रकास, से देखि प्रेम अति बाढ[ढ]ल विला(५)स ॥
दुर क[के]र शशि किछु शीतल देल, साजनि वदन विधु शत गुण भेल ॥
एहन साज(६)नि मोरि, अबसे मिलाए, पुनु पेम देवि देह, देखबह काए ॥
जगतप्रकाश भन भिन **(२२ पः १)** नहि काय, जनमे जनमे चाँदशेषर भाय ॥

॥ *श्लो[क]* ॥
यामो मदीयः प्रथमं प्रयात(२)स्त्वया सम श्रीविधिचूडकेलिभिः ।
संक्रीडकुंजाद्गृहमागतस्य, स येव जातो विपि(३)नोपमो मे ॥

॥ *पथमंजरी रागे* ॥ *जती ताले* ॥
सजनि जिवक सम मोरि जेहि, मो(४)हि तेजि नाक पयाने,
सहि न पारबे तह्नि गुण बुझि, शिव शिव भेलहु मलाने ॥
ज(५)ह्नि बुझि शिरक आसन मोरि, से बिनु निशि निद दूर,
तोहर भौह धनु दरसन (६) बिनु, सुख पिरिति गेल कूर[ल] ॥
हरि हरि प्राण पियारि, सखि विसलेख एखन भे**(२३ अः १)**ल,
कथि लायि एह तनु कलेवर, साजनि बिनु संशय गेल ॥
जगतप्रकाश गाबए (२) निय मति परम दूख,
चाँदशेषर बर सुन्दर, तोहे त्यजि दुर गेल सूख ॥

॥ *श्लोक* (३) ॥
सखे मम त्वं हृदये द्वितीयः, किमित्यकाण्डे रहितः क्षणेन ।
विश्लेषतस्तेन हि जी(४)वधारणे, क्षमो भवामीति[त्य]वधार्य्य तां मुहुः ॥

॥ *कामोद रागे* ॥ *चोख ताले* ॥
सज(५)नि ल[अ]पन हमे, शशि सम जान, से बिनु तिमिर निसि मोरि उपमान ॥
सहि नहि होअ(६)य प्रेम विहीन, आबे भेल मोहि बड, परम कुदीन ॥
कखने सुनब हमे, अमृत बानि **(२३ पः १)** देखब लोचन भरि साजनि मानि ॥
परकास भन मोरि दुर गेलि हार, चाँदशेष(२)र मोरि जिबक अधार ॥

॥ *श्लोक* ॥
सखे मुखन्ते शशिनः समं मम, स्फुटं मनः तस्य (३) रुचा प्रकाशितं ।
यतस्तमो मां परितः प्रवाधते, त्वदीयमुद्रेकलसत्स्वरूपं ॥

॥ *(४) नाट रागे* ॥ *चोख ताले* ॥
साजनि वदन भेल, परम सुहेम, कखनेहु नहि तेज (५) सेवा नियेम ॥
से सखि बिनु हमे, जिओब कि काज, निसि दिन मोरि मति, साजनि स(६)माज ॥
लोचन देखल जत, पिय्र सखि जानि, तोहे बिनु मोरि भेल, धन जन हानि ॥
(२४ अः १) जगतप्रकाश भन, तनु तुअ लायि, त्वरित पाओब चाँदशेषर भायि ॥

॥ *श्लोक* ॥
हे(२)म्नां सनाभिम्बपुषां द्युतिस्ते, संस्मृत्य संप्रत्यहमस्मिदूनः ॥
श्रीचन्द्रशेषरमणे करु(३)णां विधेहि, निधेहि कारुण्यधियं मयि स्फुटां ॥

॥ *गौरी रागे* ॥ *खर्ज्जति, चोख* [*ताले*] ॥
(४) करुण चंपक कुसुम केतकि[की], चूत पल्लव मालती,
पुररि[लि] उपवन देखि नहि होअ, (५) स[सं]मुख अछ ऋतु पती ॥
सखि बिनु तनु डाढ[ढ]ल रे, मुरुछि वसुधा पर रे ॥
रविहि (६) तापय, सरिर काँपय, विसेष विरहिनि जाति,
सहब कठिनहि गिषम ऋतु एहे, दे**(२४ पः १)**खि न भेल प्रिय काँति ॥
हम[मे] जनु बिसरह रे, चाँद किरणे देह रे, ॥
गगण पुरल मे(२)घहि एहि खन, सुनल चाट[त]क बोल,
सखिहि बिनु सुनि, वेदन उपजल, पु[sic]ररि[पुरलि] धर(३)णी नोर ॥
कथि नहि प्रावृत रे, बिनु प्रिय सखि रत रे ॥
शरद शशि देखि मुदित कु(४)मुदिनि, सबहि नक्षत प्रकास,
के विधि तेजब साजनि बिनु ऋतु, अबसे भेल मोरि (५) नाश ॥
दुर गेल आदर रे, सहचरि ओहे हम रे ॥
सकल दिश अबे, शीत बहलिह (६) पुरलि महिहि तुसार,
सजनि रस मत, हेम[मं]त ऋतु पर, हरखे कयल विहार ॥
से **(२५ अः १)** बिनु न जिओब रे, सदा शिव सेओब रे ॥
शिशिर समय, साजनि जञो रह, होयत कत (२) कत सूख,
तह्निक संग बिनु, सबहि तेजल, हमहि सब सुख दूख ॥
परकाश गाबए रे (३) चाँदशेषर पाबए रे ॥

॥ **श्लोक** ॥
प्रत्यावृत्य यदि व्रजामि भवनं, वाचां भवेत् प्रच्यवो[,]
(४)निर्गच्छामि निकुंजमेव यदि वा, को वेद किं स्यादितः ।
तिष्ठाम्येव यदि क्वचिद्वनतटे, (५) किं जातमेतामहो,
मध्ये वर्त्मकलानिधः[धेः] समुदयो, मातः किमातन्यतां ॥

॥ *चन्द्रशे(६)षरसिंहस्य, गुणं ज्ञात्वा प्रकाश्यते ।*
गीतश्लोकादिभाषाभि,र्लिखितं गीतपंचकं ॥

॥ (२५ पः १) इति श्रीगीतपंचके, चन्द्रशेषरवियोगे, श्रीश्रीजयजगत्प्रकाशकृते, षष्ठयाम(२)वर्ण्णना समाप्ता ॥

॥ *अथ सप्तयामवर्ण्णना* ॥

[॥] *केदार मालव रागे* ॥ *लांजती ताले* ॥
(३) ॥ सखि संग खेलयिते, आध निसि गेल, तखने सञो प्रिय सखि निद बस भेल ॥
मो(४)हि कर सखि शिरे, आसन देल, साजनि कोमल कर, हमके लेल ॥
एहन प्रियतम (५) हम सञो दूर, त्रिभुवन मोरि लेखे, तह्नि एक मूल ॥
जगतप्रकाश भन, तोह मोहि (६) भाय,, चाँदशेषर संगे त्वरित मिलाय ॥ ॥

॥ *श्लोकं* ॥
संकीडता तेन निशार्द्धमात्म(२६ अः १)ना, व्यरं शतार्द्धं सुखनिद्रया पुनः ।
करं यदीयं परिरभ्य कोमलं, स एव धात्रा नि(२)हृतो मदात्मा ॥

॥ *आसावरि रागे* ॥ *खर्जति ताले* ॥
हो मेरि आलि धोल न तुज्झ ही (३) मय न करञो कछु, जिय कौं जतनो ॥ *ध्रुवं* ॥
या कि गुण सौं मय, तिरथ कौं धाँउ, धर(४)म तेता कौं संगत पाँउ ॥
आरि[लि] मौं साँ, काहे बिछुरत भई, उह दिन, दिल सौं प्राण छुटि (५) गई ॥
जगतप्रकास की आसा लयिया, चन्द्रशेषरसिंह वीर, मेरे भयिआ ॥

॥ *श्लो(६)क* ॥
ततः प्रभृत्येव न जीवनाशा, न चात्मनो मे प्रियता कदापि ।
यता[तो] मणिः सोय**(२६ प १)**मपूर्व्वरूपो, हृदोपि धात्रा करुणेन निर्दयं ॥

॥ *सोरथि[ठि] पहडिया रागे* ॥ *पर ता(२)ले* ॥
अँखिया मेरि भूखि रहि हो, तेरे सुरत देखन को,, ना हा हो टेक ॥ *ध्रुवं* ॥
या सौं (३) एक घरि विछुरत नाही, ता बिनु रहो न जाय,
तन मन मेरो तुझ ही प्यारो, रहौं(४)गी तेरि गुण गाय ॥
आरि[लि] मो सौं पिरिति कियो जै,सो चन्द्र चकोर,
इह मेरि पिरि(५)ति दुर भयिँ, को सौं कहो अब बोर[ल] ॥
जगतप्रकाश प्रभु सदा कियो, तुम मेरे दिल (६) माहि,
चन्द्रशेषरसिंह मेरो भैया, तुम रहो दुख नाहि ॥

॥ *श्लोक* ॥
प्राणायितस्या(**२७ अ: १**)स्य मुखारविन्दं, संस्मृत्य नेत्रो[त्रा]श्रुगतं मदक्ष्नः ।
यदक्षिपं केरुहमुन्नताम्बुजं, वि(२)लोकितं चारुसुखाकरं पुरा ॥

॥ *मालव रागे* ॥ *लांजति ताले* ॥
जेहि छल[लि] जिव स(३)म, साजनि मोर, से बिनु महि तर[ल] पुररि[लि]हु नोर ॥
चंपक केतकि हेम वरण तोर[,] (४) रतन खचित अछ, कुण्डल दो[डो]ल ॥
कमलक दल सम, लोचन भेल, सेहि नयन जुग (५) कओोन हरि लेल ॥
जगतप्रकाश नृप वेदन भान, चाँदशेषरसिंह, एक मोरि ध्या(६)न ॥

॥ *श्लोक* ॥
चक्षुर्म्मदीयं भवतो वियोगाद्दिदृक्षते श्रीविधुशेषर त्वां ।
अप्राप्य (**२७ प: १**) संप[प्र]त्यतिविक्लवत्वा,दन्धत्वमगी कुरु ते स्वकीयं ॥

॥ *पहडिया रागे* ॥ *खर्जति ता (२)ले* ॥
वेदन बाढ[ढ]ल साजनि तेजि आबे, जहेन चैतक दीन,
अबसे प्रिय बिनु सबहि (३) संशय, भेलहु हमरा दी[ही]न ॥
अनेक सुख हमे भुँजल सखि संगे, बुझिते भेल तनु (४) खीन,
खनहु साजनि, हमहि न तेजय, जे विधि घन रस मीन ॥
जगतप्रकास, भन(५)य वेदन, जानय देव ईशान,
चाँदशेषर हमके देह पुनु, से दिन जाय मलान ॥

॥ *(६) श्लोक* ॥
हृद्वेदना मम परं बहुसं[शः] पबृद्धा, श्रीचन्द्रशेषर तवाधिगुणं विभाव्य ।
य(**२८ अ: १**)त्सर्व्वतः सुखनिधानमभूत्पुरा मे, विश्लेषतस्तदिह दावसतानुतापं ॥

॥ *चन्द्रशे(२)षरसिंहस्य, गुणं ज्ञात्वा प्रकाश्यते* ।
गीतश्लोकादिभाखाभिर्लिखितं गीतपंचकं ॥

॥ (३) इति श्रीगीतपंचके, चन्द्रशेषरवियोगे, श्रीश्रीजयजगत्प्रकाशकृते, सप्तमयाम४)वर्ण्णना समाप्ता ॥

॥ *अथाष्टमयामवर्ण्णना* ॥

[॥] *मालव रागे* ॥ *खर्जति ताले* ॥
आठ पह(५)र सखि रह मोरि संग, जे मोहि अभिमत, कर कत रंग ॥
एहन हित प्रिय, आबे कत (६) गेल, से बिनु तनुक अरि जीवहि भेल ॥
अबे नहि धैरज, हमर पा[प]रान, पति बिनु (**२८ प: १**) रति मोरि, भेल उपमान ॥
जगतप्रकाश भन, तोहहि अधार, चाँदशेषर मोहि (२) ऊरक हार ॥

॥ *श्लोकः* ॥
यामाष्टकं प्रियतमा सहसा मया सा, संकुर्व्वती कति न (२) केलि कलाः स्थिताया ।
संप्रत्यहं तरलचारुकुरंगदृष्ट्या, विश्लिष्ट एव नवशः खलु (४) जीवधारणे ॥

॥ *कोराव रागे* ॥ *चोख ताले* ॥
पिय अनुरागे, लागलि मोरि जीव, (५) तह्नि बिनु, कथि लायि, हमरा जीव ॥
हे सखि हमे जनु बिसरह तोहि, तोरितहि तुअ त(६)नु पाओब मोहि ॥
निसि दिन साजनि, रह मोहि साथ, मति धर कोमल, दुर गेल हाथ ॥
(२९ अ: १) जगतप्रकास भन रस एहि दूख, चाँदशेषरसिंह लए गेल सूख ॥

॥ *श्लो[क]* ॥
प्रेम्ना (२) मया चिरतरेण तवानुरागः संवृद्धितः स खलु जीवविशोषनाय ।
यातो यमु(३)न्नतगुणालयचन्द्रचूड, विश्लेषितस्य भवता परितापहेतुः ॥

॥ *वसन्त रागे (४)* ॥ *परताला ताले* ॥
मोहि धनि तेजि कत, कयल पयाने, अबसहि दुर भेल हम(५)र पराने,
के कर हमर तराने, ॥ *ध्रु[वं]* ॥
तिर[ल] भरि तोहे बिनु, रहय न पारब, ज(६)हेन चकेवा जोर,
देखल पल्लव नव, सुनलहु पिक बोल, दुर गेल प्रिय सखि **(२९ प: १)** बोल ॥
सुतलि जामिनि दुहु करे तन बिनु, झाँपि नीद न आबए मोहि,
माझक वस(२)नहु, जानल बड दुर, ऐसन पियतम तोहि ॥
दारुण विरह बिज, दय गेल साज(३)नि, के कर हमर विचार,
सहजे दुखित हम, सखि बोधि गमावल, से पिय तेजल(४)हु हार ॥
साजनि चिकुल[र] भेल बड अँधकार, तुल मुख पिये निरमल चन्द,
कनक (५) शंख सम तोहर रुचिर गल, हृदय न कहु खन मन्द ॥
कपोर दरपन, कर यु(६)ग किशलय, लोचन खंजन जोर,,
चारु करण पर, कुण्डल संजुत, सखि पद देखि **(३० अ: १)** अ[भे]लि भोर ॥
भनयि प्रकाश नृप, अपनुक वेदन, हर जनु हमरा पेम,
चाँदशेष(२)रसिंह, हित मोरि तोह भाय, कत कर सेवा नियेम ॥

॥ *श्लोकः* ॥
विश्लेषदावद(३)हनः खलु दारुणोयं ज्वालावलीभिरभितः किल तापहेतुः ।
दुःखा करोति सह(४)सा हृदये परं मे, तच्चन्द्रचूड विनिवेदय यत्सुखार्थं ॥

॥ *मालव रागे* ॥ *चोख ताले* ॥
(५) कहु खने सहचरि, हमे नहि तेजय, जहेने हरिहि महेस,
होयत हमर काज,, (६) करय अपन तुल, से बिनु पुरल कलेश ॥
काय वचन मन, हमके दय गेल, अभि**(३० प: १)**मत मोहि तह्नि पास,,
राखह जननि दुहु, चरण कमल तर, सेहि थल पाओब नि(२)वास ॥
जगतप्रकाश भन, हम सन जनु होअ, सबक करम अति मन्दा,,
चाँदशेषर(३)सिंह मोरि भाय, अति विर मुख भेल निकन्तक चन्दा ॥

॥ *श्लोक* ॥
आत्मीयमुन्नत(४)तमं परिहीय कृत्यं, यो मे सदा भवति कार्य्यपरः स्थिरात्मा ।
तं चन्द्रचूडमनुरूप(५)सखायमेकं, संस्मृत्य किंचिदपि नेच्छति चान्तरात्मा ॥

॥ *सारंगी पंचम रागे,* ॥ *(६) चोख ताले* ॥
अथिर कलेवर जानुक[जानु] हे, कमल पातक जल तूले ॥ *ध्रुवं* ॥
भवन क**(३१ अ: १)**नक जन, रजत आदि जत, थिर नहि रह सब जने,
सुत मित सब धन सुख दुख स(२)रिर, अथिर जानल मने ॥
शिरि जल सरिर इसरे सबका, मन नृप अवयव दा(३)स,
मनहि पाबय पुने, अधरम अपजस, मन बसे पाव एत पास ॥
जगतप्रकाश (४) आस, कएल तोहर, चन्द्रशेषरसिंह भाय,
जगत जननि पद हेठहि राखह, दु(५)हु जनक दुहु काय ॥

॥ *श्लोकः* ॥
अर्थाः सुखानि च गृहानुजभृत्यवर्ग्गाः[,] सर्व्वानि (६) तानि नलिनीजलसन्निभानि ।
देहोपि भंगुरतया भवतो वियोगे, श्रीचन्द्रशेष**(३१ प: १)**र सखे नियतेरवेदि ॥

॥ *श्लोकः* ॥
चन्द्रशेषरसिंहस्य, गुणं ज्ञात्वा प्रकाश्यते ।
(२)गीतश्लोकादिभाषाभि,र्लिख्यते गीतपंचकं ॥

॥ इति श्रीगीतपंचके, चन्द्रशेष(३)रवियोगे, श्रीश्रीजयजगत्प्रकाशकृते अष्टमयामवर्ण्णना समाप्ता ॥ शिवं ॥

4

Transliteration into Roman Script

Prior to presenting the text of *Gītapañcaka* into the Roman script, it is considered worthwhile to pinpoint and explain the use of a number of diacritic marks that are conventionally used to faithfully and consistently represent the Devanāgarī orthography. A few of the prominent diacrics are described below in brief.

1. In the present work. a diacritical mark such as a tilde placed above a vowel grapheme, e.g. (< *ã* >), represents a feature of what is generally called the spontaneous vowel nasalization: in the Devanāgarī script, this feature is indicated by means of a *candravindu*. In the phonetic literature, such vowels are described as phonemically nasal vowels.
2. A dot underneath the bilabial nasal consonant grapheme <*m*> (e.g. <*ṃ*>) represents what is called an *anuśvāra* in the Devanāgarī script.
3. A dot underneath a consonant grapheme (e.g. < *ṭ ḍ ṇ ṛ ṣ*> represents a retroflex consonant.
4. A dot above the dental nasal grapheme <*n*> (e.g. <*ṅ*> represents a velar nasal consonant.
5. A horizontal bar above a vowel grapheme (e.g. *ā, ī, ū*) represents the long vowel graphemes written as <*ā*>, <*ī*>, <*ū*> or as <*kā*>, <*kī*>, <*kū*>, etc. in the Roman script.
6. A combination of two vowel graphemes written as <aï> and <aü> represents the diphthongs [əĭ, əŭ], respectively as distinct from and in contradistinction to the non–diphthongal vowel cluster <*ai*> [əi] and <*au*> [əu].
7. The symbol <*ś*> represents the Devanāgarī <श> grapheme, while the symbol <*ṣ*> represents the Devanāgarī <ष> grapheme.

8. Finally, in order to indicate the Folio and Line number in the Roman text given below, the letter **V** represents the Latin word *Verso* 'back' while the letter **R** represents the Latin word R*ecto* 'front'. Thus, Folio 1 V: 1 would mean "Folio 1 Verso Line number 1", while Folio 5 R: 5 would mean "Folio 5 Recto Line number 5."

Text: Roman Transliteration

(1 V: 1) õ [oṃ] namo nāṭeśvarābhyāṃ ||

otaprotaṃ jagadyatra[jagad yatra] yo viśvasya hṛdisthitaḥ |
namo ānandarū(2)pāya, tasmaï pūrṇṇāya śambhave ||

|| dhanāchi rāge || cokha tāle ||
vibhuti bhuṣana aṃge, triśūla (3) ḍamaru kare,
raha saṅga bhūta gana, cā̃da tilaka dhare ||
gale muṇḍa māla, karaṇa para kuṇḍala d[ḍ]o(4)la,
pahirae bāgha chāla, caraṇa kamala jora ||
kara hara nitya vihāre, nandihi muruja ba(5)jābe,
gaṇeśa senāpati nāce, nārada ādihi gita gābe ||
maheśvara he tohe, nāṭaka so(6)hābae,,
jagataprakāśa nṛpa, kaütuke gābae ||

|| śloka ||
sānandaṃ nandihastā, hatamuruja**(2R:1)**ravāhūtakaümāravarhi,
trāsānnāsāgraraṃdhraṃ viśati phaṇipataü bhogasaṃkocabhāji ||
gaṃ(2)ḍoḍḍīnānimālāmukharitakakubhastāṇḍave śūlapāṇe,
rvvaïnāyākyaściraṃ vo vadanavi(3)dhutayah pāntu cītkāravatyaḥ ||

|| iti nāndistutiḥ ||
atha priyasakhīviyoge, ta(4)sya viyogavyākulena taṃ prītyarthaṃ,
śrīśrījayajagatprakāśohaṃ, tasya stutiṃ karomi ||

(5) mamāgra yo mama prāṇa, yathā prāṇasamāgrajaḥ |
mamāgrajo mama pṛāṇa, satyameva vacastvidaṃ (6) ||

|| aherāṇī rāge || cokha tāle ||
jeṭha jivana sakhi, visalekhe bhela mori, mithuna pi**(2 V: 1)**riti suka bāre,
nepālaka saṃmate nara diṭhi vasu haya, se dina dura gela hāre ||
ma(2)ti ati niramala, sarupa gā̃ga jala,, mohi sukha dāyaka prāne,

lola locana yuga, ha(3)me anuraṃjana, cāru duhu khaṃjana jāne ||
bhaüha kuṭila priya, manamatha dhanu thika, ṛ(4)ju dekhi ke nahi bhūle,,
kara juga kiśalaya, hṛdayana dhari mori, rajanihu nida (5) bhela dūre ||
jagataprakāśa bhana, candraśekhara śiva, kaya deha milana jugūti,
āna na (6) mora gati, tua pada paya mati, dethu sadā śiva muguti ||

|| śloka ||
dhik vārisaha**(3 R: 1)**saṃkīrṇṇaṃ, na gataṃ yadi hatena |
śrīmatprakāśanṛpate, prāṇāsa eva me nūnaṃ ||

|| vibhā(2)sa rāge || kharjjati tāle ||
tohe vara sahacari, jivaka dosari thika[i], abe mukha de(3)khiya na bhelā,
jehi nayana juga, dekhi hara mohi dukha, se piya khana dura gelā ||
e(4)kahi talapa basi, duhu jana hãsi hãsi, bolalahu eka jiva jāni,
hamahi rodana (5) ka[ke]ra dura kara mora sakhi, ā̃cala kiś[s]alaya pāni ||
duhuka piriti dekhi, śaśadhara (6) kumudini, kayalaha mati ati lāje,
khane visalekha dekhi, ugala krūra śaśi, baha**(3 V: 1)**li dachiṇa hari āje ||
toha[he] binu hama bhela, hamara vihina je, siri hina sārasa jā(2)ne,
dekhala jagata hame, ati ãdhakāra sana, duhu nisi sahaja malāne ||
hari hari ha(3)rīhi, sāthahi sakhi saṃga, na geli he pāpini bāri,,
jagataprakāśa bhana, cā̃daśeṣara(4)sīha, hamarā tohahi adhāri ||

|| śloka ||
sahacari parotvamme, dehādvibhinnarūpā(5)pi |
dṛṣṭvāṃkarokhi nūnaṃ, māṃ, sukhinaṃ samaye purā ||

|| bhaïrava rāge || paratālā tāle ||
(6) jakhane sājani mani chala mori saṃge,
hamahi praṇavi piya uth[ṭh]ali parāte *|| dhruvaṃ ||*
(4 R: 1) ugalahu śiśu hari, bhelahu vihāna,
cakora mithuna abe, tejala malāna ||
e[hi] khane sakhi (2) mori, cira hari lela,
hamahi kora dhari, lāvala tela ||
punu sakhi kaya dela, hamara sa(3)m[n]āne,

e vidhi kata mohi kayala tarāne ||
se binu rahalā he, pāpini parāna,,
madhu te(4)ji vipinaka, bhela samāna ||
parakāśa bhana cā̃daśeṣara adhāra,,
khana mani dura gela (5) hṛdayaka hāra ||

|| śloka ||
prātarmmadīyaśayanāsanasaṃgato yaḥ, premātirekaghaṭanā(6) nipuno manīndraḥ |
svayam ciraprаṇaya,peśalabhāvukopi, dhigdaïvanirmmitakṛte skhalita**(4 V:1)**ḥ kṣaṇena ||

|| velāvala rāge || cokha tāle ||
niradhani kara saño, khasala suhīra,
mohi la(2)ga sājani nahi bhela thīra ||
hari hari hama baḍa, pāpini bāri,
hari lelī[i] īśari hama(3)ra adhāri ||
mṛga nṛpa tula kaṭi, komala pāni,
hṛdaya rākhala hame kiśalaya jāni ||
to(4)he sani hita sakhi, hamara na āna,
tohe binu mohi lekhe, jagata malāna ||
parakāśa ka(5)yalahu, tohara dheyāna,
cā̃daśeṣara śiva, karu avadhāna ||

|| śloka ||
prokto mayā ya(6)dipi saḥ sāro maṇirnnikhilo dyutikalāyāḥ |
daïvānmamaïva sahasā, hṛdayācyuto hi **(5 R: 1)** vidhinā glapitaḥ ||

|| āsāvari rāge || kharjjati tāle ||
sujana suhṛdaya, suguṇa saṃjuta, suka(2)ṭi ati abhirāma,
susakhi sumarаño, sumane nisi dina, karaba japa tua nāma ||
sukha(3)ka ā̃[ā]kara, surasa sāgara, nayana tua aravinda,
kapola niramala, cibuka sundara, vadana (4) punimaka canda ||
tohahi bhūṣaṇa tohahi suvasana, tohahi jivana adhāra,
tohahi sājani, (5) parasamaṇi thiki, hamara hṛdayaka hāra ||
hamara yahi mati, sakhihi pae gati, jhā̃khi tejaya (6) parāna,
kahathi parakāśa, kayala tua āsa, cā̃daśeṣaraka dhyāna ||

।। śloka ।।
prītiṃ tayo[ḥ] sa**(5 V: 1)**madhurā, mabhito mudā vidhuravī ।
dṛṣṭvānubaṃdhasaṃparkka, malinaṃ nijahitaḥ svaṃ ।।

।। candraśeṣa(2)rasiṃhasya, guṇaṃ jñātvā prakāśyate ।
gītaślokādibhāṣābhi,rlikhyate gītapaṃcakaṃ ।।

।। (3) iti śri gītapañcake, candraśeṣaraviyoge,
śrīśrījayajagatprakāsakṛte, prathamayāmava(4)rṇṇanā samāptā ।।

।। atha dvitīyaj[y]āmakṛtyavarṇṇanā ।।

।। kaüśika rāge ।। cokha tāle ।।
priya (5) sakhi ore, dvitiya pahara beri āyala,
kī mohi thala, nayana dekhala hame sādara ।।
dura (6) gela ore, jivaka dosari, sakhi kichu khana,
kī mohi dhana, tuva tula nahi thika jata jana ।।
(6 R: 1) toha binu ore, pati visalekhe hama rati,
kī subha mati, tejalahu sahacari jūvati ।।
bha(2)na kichu ore, jagataprakāśa nṛpati vara,
kī pura hara, c̃ādaśeṣarasiṃha ati bhala ।।

(3) *।। śloka ।।*
duḥkhaṃ dīrghataraṃ vahatyapi sakhīvarṣ[ṣ]āyaṇo bhākhate,
śaïvālaï śayanaṃ sṛja(4)tyapi punaḥ śete na vā lajjayā ।
kaṇṭhe gaṅgadavāci muñcati dṛśā, dhatte navāpyodakaṃ,
saṃ(5)tāpaṃ sahate yadambujamukhī, tadveda ce[to]bhavaḥ ।।

।। kedāra mālava rāge ।। cokha tāle ।।
(6) śaśi binu ore, rajani sahaje ati malina,
kī tanu khina, sakhi teji hama, jala binu **(6 V: 1)** mīna ।।
guṇamata ore guputahi bhela mani, hamara,
kī ati bhala, sahacari dithi kara ka(2)mala ।।
je binu ore, jivaka kalesa, ati bādh[ḍh]ala,
kī jaladhara, nivi ḍa[du]hu dekhi nahi (3) pārala ।।
daha diśa ore, malina dekhala abe jagata,
kī gatāgata, hari lela jehi pi(4)ya mori rata ।।
kahalahu ore, jagataprakāśa nṛpati yaha dukha,
kī śaśi mukha, c̃ādaśe(5)ṣara, raha mohi sukha ।।

|| śloka ||
talpe sahāsamekasmin, vadatā paraprāṇatvaṃ |
sa pa(6)raḥ sahasā śiva, stava vāpya hi śivaḥ sa ||

|| dhanāśrī rāge || cokha tāle ||
ābe geli **(7 R: 1)** ādara, sakhi binu morī ||
khanahu na teja sakhi, hame baḍa bālā, cā̃da nikaṭa raha tārā (2) ||
śiva śiva sehe mori, pari hari lelā, jehi daive dukha delā ||
je binu nija ghare (3) bhelahu ucāṭa, pāoba tahnika saṅga bāṭa ||
parakāśa bhana cā̃daśeṣara parāna, kuṇḍala (4) vihina bhela kā̃na ||

|| śloka ||
bhavatā rahitasya me, tamasā parito nabhaḥ |
vyāptaṃ ma(5)yāpi viślekhe, nalinījalayo sāmyaṃ ||

|| mālava rāge || kharjjati tāle ||
prem pāśa (6) toralahu daïve mori || *dhruvaṃ* ||
jakhane sajani raha, hamarā pāse, kichu nahi hoya tarāse ||
(7 V: 1) hamara kāraṇe piye, jiva daya gela, mohi sukha pari hari lela ||
kakhane bhelahu di(2)na, kañone khane rāṭ[t]i, sumaraïta rahabahu kā̃ṭ[t]i ||
jagataprakāśa bhana, tohahi a(3)dhāra, cā̃daśeṣarasiṃha hāra, ||

|| śloka ||
ekastvameva suhṛdāṃ, prāṇāyito mama (4) tanuḥ |
konyo nihantu śokāgniṃ, tvaṃ durago yadīha me ||

|| gopīvallabha rāge || (5) *raghuśeṣara tāle ||*
peyasi mori sajani sakhi, caraṇa tua vārijaṃ, tohara uru (6) kadali sama jāne,
rucira kaṭi sarupa hari, varaṇa hema samānaṃ, tanvidhara amia **(8 R: 1)** rasa bāne ||
priye mori tohi priye mori tohī, teji janu na ḍābaha mohi, sahaje a(2) ti pāpini,
dukhita hame kāmini, hamahi sā̃ga kaya karu sātāre || *dhruvaṃ* ||
hṛdaya sa(3)khi sarira tohi, vacana mori tohahi[ī], sobhita mori nayana juga tohī,

vadana śa(4)śi san[m]ipa basi, piula hame ādare, gelahu dura khanahi mani mohi ||
sakhihi bi(5)nu adhika dhanu bhelahu katahu na yake, hamara laga kumati jehi māre[,]
ehana dukha adhi(6)ka bhela sahi nahī pāra he, madana abe kayalahu parahāre [||]
bhupati jaya jagatapara(**8 V: 1**)kāśa bhana tohahī, hamara sakhi karaba eka bhāve,
tohahi thiki tejaba nahi hamahī, (2) kulaka vadhu karabae je so bhāve ||

|| śloka ||
mālābālāmbujadalaṃ, maüktikaïrhārayaṣṭi(3)ḥ |[,]
kāṃcījātā prabhavati halaü, subhruvaḥ prasthitaïva |
anya brūmaṃ kimapi dhamanī varttate vā(4)navājñā,
tuṃbāhorahaha varayaṃ, pāṇimūlaṃ prayāti ||

|| candraśeṣarasiṃhasya, guṇaṃ jñātvā (5) prakāśyate |
gītaślokādibhāṣābhi,rlikhyate gītapṃcakaṃ ||

[||] iti śrīgītapaṃcake, candra(6)śeṣaraviyoge, śrīsrījayajagatprakāśakṛte, dvitīyayāmakṛtyavarṇṇanā samāptaṃ||

(9 R: 1) *atha tṛtīyayāmakṛtyavarṇṇanā ||*

|| gaürī rāge || cokha tāle ||
titiya pahara, (2) bhela jānala sāya, vihũsi vihũsi ha[hã]si, āyala milāya ||
kakhanehu na tejaya, sa(3)khi mori sevā, kara priya eka mane hama paya devā ||
jaño hoa hamarā sadanaka (4) kāja, jāni karaya ohe apanuka kāja ||
duhu jana jānala, tanu nahi bhīna,, khanehu na (5) sakhi saṃga, piriti vihīna ||
hame janu bisaraha hamara adhāri, laga leha hame dhani (6) hamahi nihāri ||
jagataprakāśa bhana, karaha sãtāra, cãdaśeṣarasiṃha, hṛdayaka hāra ||

(9 V: 1) *|| śloka ||*
yena priyena savāsāt, saṃveśopi sukhapradaḥ |
sa evāsukhaheturmme, tadviśle(2)ṣahavi[r]bhujaḥ ||

// korāva rāge // lāṃjati eka tāle //

hame nahi bisaraba, sakhi gu(3)ṇa sūkha, mori baḍa tasu mukha, dekhayake bhūkha ||

hari hari hamarā dith[ṭh]i ati pāpi,, (4) se binu darasane rahalāhu kā̃pi ||

pema vihina dukha sahi nahi jāe, vedana ghara thi(5)ka hamarā kāe ||

jagataprakāsa kaha nite ehi cīta, cā̃daśeṣarasiṃha mori baḍa (6) hīta ||

// śloka //

ekātmanoḥ susuhṛdoḥ prītintayorvvidhuravī ||

dṛṣṭvānubaṃdhasaṃraṃbhaṃ **(10 R: 1)** priyayā nijahitaḥ svaṃ ||

// vibhāsa rāge // eka tāle //

vidhu binu nisi hama[e] bhela, (2) sukha sakhi pari hari re[le]la ||

nadi bhela nayanaka nīra, sakhi binu bāḍhala pīra ||

bhama(3)ya bhamara tasu lobhe, se binu hame ehi sobhe ||

parakāsa rasa tua gābe, cā̃daśeṣara (4) laga pābe ||

// śloka //

vejanaṃ vejanaṃ jara[la]ṃ jara[la]ṃ, ghanasāro ghanasāra ityapi ||

abe(5)rodhapurīkhu kāminīnāṃ, kurarīmiva kātaradhvaṇiṃ ||

// gujjarī rāge // paratā(6)rā tāle //

sāya sāya kula vadhu bāri, rasa daya sukha lela gāri ||

samucita duhu jana **(10 V: 1)** deha, dine dine bāḍhala sineha ||

khanahu na teja sakhi mohi, dura kara nora jata to(2)hi ||

se ābe visalekha bhela, mori śiri tahni saṃga gela ||

jagataprakāsa lela sāra, (3) cā̃daśeṣara kae[la] hāra ||

// śloka //

samupāgatavati caïtre, nipatati[titaṃ]patre lavaṃgala(4)tikāyāḥ ||

sudṛśaḥ kapolavālī, śivaśivatālīdaladyutiṃ labhe ||

// sorath[ṭh]i rā(5)ge // kharj[j]ati tāle //

sujana sājani, milala samucita, je vidhi harihi maheśa,

pema(6)ka basa bhaya, kaela duhu jana, apane sakhika suveśa ||

jakhane sakhi saṃge pathahi gela du**(11 R: 1)**hu, karahi kara dhani[dhari] mohi,

mukhahi mukha dekhi, rahala jehi duhu, harihi hari lela (2) tohi ||

durahi jani kara,sa[ha] jani bisarah, cetaha piya paripāti,,

hamari pūruba ge(3)lihu dura sakhi, tẽ bhela pāpini jāti ||
jagataparakāśa, kaela tua āsa, pāoba (4) tahni saṃga bāsa,
sumati sājani, guṇaka āgari, cā̃daśeṣaraka pāsa ||

|| ślo[ka] ||
(5)gatāgatakutūhalaṃ nayanayorapāṅgāvadhi, smṛtaṃ
kulanatabhruvā,madhara eva visrāmya(6)ti |
vacaḥ priyatamaśrute,ratithireva kopakramaḥ, kadācidapi cettadā manasi
keva**(11 V: 1)**laṃ majjati ||

|| candraśeṣarasiṃhasya, guṇaṃ jñātvā prakāśyate |
gītaślokādibhāṣābhirli(2)khitaṃ gītapaṃcakaṃ ||

[||] iti śrīgītapaṃcake, candraśeṣaraviyoge, śrīśrījayajagatprakā(3) sakṛte, tṛtīyayāmavarṇṇanā samāptā ||

|| atha caturthayāmavarṇṇanā ||

|| korāva rā(4)ge || lāṃjatī tāle ||
cāri pahara dina, sājani bola, sunite gamāvala, āpada jora (5) ||
sehi piya khane ābe, gelihu dūra, jata jana mori lekhe (6) tahni piya mūla||
jaga(6)taprakāsa bhane || [*sic*]

jeha sakhi nāśaya, mohi pada dhūra, ī saṃga kae devi, abhimata pūra ||
jaga**(12 R: 1)**taprakāsa bhana tohahi hīta, cā̃daśeṣara binu saba gela nīta ||

|| śloka ||
satyaṃ ta(2)dīyavacanāmṛtadhārayāma, hṛṣṭasya kāpi navabhūvayarāpyasampat |
saṃpratyakāṇḍa(3)vidhiyantranagharṣitena, tenāsmi śokajaladhaü gamitaḥ kṣaṇena ||

||dhanāśrī rāge || (4) *eka tāle ||*
bisari na rahabaha, sājani gūna,, se binu upajala, atihi karūna ||
sakhi (5) teji ke kara, hamara saṃtāra, moti mānika hāra, bhela baḍa bhāra ||
jaño ohe sājani ra(6)hao samāja, taño mori prāṇaka hoa saba kāja ||
jagataprakāśa nṛpa, vedana bhāna ||[,] **(12 V: 1)** cā̃daśeṣarasiṃha, karu avadhāna ||

|| śloka ||

sānandamaṣ[s]ya vapuṣāṃ, samudāya(2)sāraṃ, saṃsmṛtya saṃprati hṛdā karuṇodayo me |
saṃjāyate sa khalu dīrghamahatvamu(3)draḥ, tanvikṣaṇādiva viyogabhareṇa bhūyaḥ ||

|| kedāra mālava rāge || lāṃjati tā(4)le ||
sakhi he katahu na gelī mati mori *|| dhru[vaṃ] ||*
hari na harala hame, jīva hari ha(5)ri lela, hari sama mukha bhela dūra,
śiśu hari tulanā, adharaka kā̃ti, tua kaṭi de(6)khi hari sama bhūla ||
hari hari jahnikā, hari sama vege raha, hari tula uḍi gela **(13 R: 1)** sāya,
nayana hari ati, medani parala abe, dura gela hari sama kāya ||
hari kara (2) tula uru hari sama vaca[na], ehana[ne] sājani mohi,
harihi visalekha, kae dela priya (3) saṃga, mori mati gati eka tohi ||
jagataprakāśa bhana, sabahi athira thika, śiśu (4) mita jana dhana dāra,
sumati hamara gati, cā[cā̃]daśeṣarasiṃha, tohe pae hṛdayaka hā(5)ra ||

|| śloka ||
haryyānanaḥ kāntaharīndramadhyo, vibhātakālīnahareḥ samādha(6)raḥ |
soyaṃ harirmme hariṇā gṛhīto, harerayenaïṣa hariṃ prapanna[ḥ]) ||

*|| dhanāśrī rā(***13 V: 1)***ge || paratārā tāle ||*
sājani vihīna, na karabāha mohi *|| dhruvaṃ ||*
rati pati rati (2) saṃge, jaño raha eka thala, taño raha duhukā̃ sohe ||
visalekha baḍa dukha, sahi na (3) pāraba, priya bujhi tejalahu rāti,,
dinahu jhā̃khala toha, hṛdayahu jehi sakhi, ka(4)khana dekhaba tua kā̃ti ||
tohahi parama pada, pāvala sājani, tua pune hame raha (5) sātha,
tribhuvana nahi thiki, hama sani pāpini, mati dhara dura gela hātha ||
hama(6)hi kora dhari, nīda kaela duhu, se nida mohi baḍa dūra,,
bhanayi prakāśa nṛpa, cā̃da**(14 R: 1)**śeṣarasiṃha, tohe mori ekahi kūla ||

|| śloka ||
yadi hi bhavati kāmaḥ, kāṃta(2)yā varttamānaḥ, prabhavati sahavāsātkāntisārastayoryyat |

kimapi ca vidhicūḍa(3)tvaṃ prakāśānmahīndo,rmmadiha bhavasi dūre, prāptavisleṣabhāvaḥ ।।

।। *soraṭhi rāge* (4) ।। *kharjjati tāle* ।।
jhūlahi je priye niya kare hidolā [hĩḍolā], harakhahi sājani he ।। *dhruvaṃ*।।
(5) harakhi sājani, samipa basi duhu, kaela mudita vihāra,
sakhika pāṇi lae u(6)rasi dhari kahu sahaje tasu mori hāra ।।
sani[mi]pa śītala jalaka dhārā, pavana dhire **(14 V: 1)** dhire pāse,
jehī pavane parasi sukha bhela, ābe kaelahu nāse ।।
ehana priya sa(2)khi, katahu geli ābe, sukṛta bhaya tahni pābe,,
jakara pūne hamahi jhiki leha, ka(3)raba miri[li] duhu bhāve ।।
jagataparakāśa, karae tua āsa, premahi rasa tasu jā(4)na,
cā̃daśeṣara pemaka ā̃[ā]kara, duhuka ekahi parāna ।।

।। *śloka* ।।
ratipatiḥ pri(5)yayā saha śobhate, bhavati bhūṣaṇamaṃgaparasparaṃ ।
kimiti māmavadhīrayasi priyaṃ[,] (6) priyasakhe yadanīkṣaṇameva te ।।

।। *candraśeṣarasiṃhasya, guṇaṃ jñātvā prakāśyate* ।।
(15 R: 1) *gītaślokādibhākhābhirlikhitaṃ gītapaṃcakaṃ*

।। **iti śrīgītapaṃcake, candraśe(2)ṣaraviyoge, śrīśrījayajagatpra[kā] śakṛte, caturthayāmavarṇṇanaṃ samāptaṃ** ।।

।। (3) *atha paṃcamayāmavarṇṇanā* ।।

।। *varāḍi rāge* ।। *eka tāle* ।।
kamalini mudali ku(4)muda prakāsa, se beri priya sakhi, ayalahu pāsa ।।
ohe rajanī ābe, kata cali (5) gela, jibaite abasahi, kath[th]inahi bhela ।।
ḍāḍhala anale tanu, sahi nahi jāya[,] (6) kakhane dekhaba hame, priya sahi kāya ।।
jagataprakāśa nṛpa, rasa ehi dūkha,, cā̃daśe**(15 V: 1)**ṣarasiṃha, lae gela sūkha।।

।। *śloka* ।।
tava kusumaśaratvaṃ, śītaraśmitvamindo,,(2)
rdvayamidamayathārthaṃ dṛśyate madvidheṣu ।

visṛjati himagarbhaï,ragniminduḥ karāgre(3)ḥ, tvamapi kusumabāṇān vajrasārī karoṣi ||

|| bhathyāri rāge || paratālā tā(4)le ||

ami na sahibo[lo] prāṇa, tumāra viyoge,, aneka pāilu[ũ] sukha, tumāra saṃyo(5)ge ||

tumī na chāḍilo prema, chaḍāilo debe,, vinati suniyā debe, piya saṃga rebe (6) ||

hiyā te toriyā daïbe, laya gelo prāṇe,, i dukha lāgilu[ũ] mori, maramelo bā**(16 R: 1)**ṇe ||

sadana kailo bana, bana kailũ ghare,, dhu[ḍhũ]ḍhiyā hiyā saṃge, pāibo bare ||

ka(2)hilo prakāśa nṛpa, tumāre āsā,, cā̃daśeṣara saṃge, pāyibo bāsā ||

|| śloka ||

nī(3)lāṃbhoruhakānane nivasati dhvā[ṃ]totkarāśaṃkayā,
svakrīḍoccalitāśca vārikaṇikā(4)stārābhramāt paśyati |
satrāsaṃ muhurīkṣate ca cakito,haṃ saṃhimāṃśubhramā,nna[,]
svāsthyaṃ (5) bhava[ja]te hi kutra virahāśaṃkīrathāṃgāhvayaḥ ||

|| pahaḍiyā [rāge] || pratārā tāle ||

vihina pa(6)rama dūkha, kakhane dekhaba mūkha, hame bisaraha janu || *dhru[vaṃ] ||*

ke vare sajani mane, mori hṛda**(16 V: 1)**ya vacane,,

r[l]elahu kula vadhu bhāva,, je kari priya sakhi pāva ||

jagataprakāśa nṛpa bhā(2)na,, cā̃daśeṣara avadhāna||

|| śloka ||

nādātseharitāṃ kur[l]ān kvacidapi sthaïryyaṃ(3)na vā laṃbase,
yat paryyākulalocanosi karuṇaṃ kujandiśaḥ paśyasi ||
daïvenānta(4)ritapriyosi hariṇa tvaṃ cāpi kiṃ yacciraṃ,
pratyadripratikaṃ daraṃprati nadi pratyū(5)ṣaraṃ bhrāmyasi ||

|| korāva rāge || cokha tāle ||

sabaka caṃcala mati re, mohi sakhi (6) eka gati ||

sabaka kapaṭa maya re, dekhi upajala bhaya ||

dharama na mānaya [re], jata dekha **(17 R: 1)** pāpa maya ||

prakāśa nṛpa ehe gābe, cā̃daśeṣara laga pābe ||

// ślo[ka] //

deśaïrantaritā(2)gataïśca saritānurvībhṛtāṃ kānanaï,
ryyatnenāpi nayāmi locanapathaṃ kānteti jānanna(3)pi ।
uḍgrīvaścaraṇārddharuddhavasudhaḥ kṛtvāśrupūrṇṇā[ṃ] dṛśaṃ,
tāmetāṃ pathikastathāpi ki(4)miva dhyāyaṃściraṃ vīkṣate ॥

// nāṭa mallāra rāge // kharjati lāṃjati tāle //

saghana (5) śrāvana viraha dāyaka, jubati jibaba kaṭhīna,
torite torite, bijuri camakala, (6) dekhite bhela tanu khīna ॥
khina tanu sumaraño, sakhika sunāma,
tua pune pūrathu mo**(17 V: 1)**ri mati kāma ॥

// śloka //

jaladajalamayoyaṃ śrāvaṇaḥ saṃpravṛttaścalati hariti śī(2)ghraṃ,
vidyududdāmabhīmā ।
anupalamatirekaṃ, sanmaṇeḥ kāntisāra,staralayati hi ci(3)tte, saṃsmṛto
yatra maügdhyaṃ ॥

॥ prathama bhādava prema baḍhāvala, ekahi bhela duhu deha,
je vi(4)dhi jata nadi tiruhu jhā̃pala, tẽ vidhi bādh[ḍh]ala sineha ॥
neha mori saba lela sājani (5) bāri,
tohe binu hame nahi pāraba saṃbhāri ।

// śloka //

jalakanasamudāyo bhādra e(6)vābhirāmaḥ, prasarati parito hi
prītivāriprameyaṃ ।
kathaya kathaya nūnaṃ matpriyosi tva**(18 R: 1)**meka, stava virahajatāpaḥ
kena śāmyeta bhūyaḥ ॥

॥ māsa āsina karuṇa kāraṇa (2) phular[l]i madhurī jāti,
kha ati niramala, hoeta ehi beri, ke kara mohi paripāti (3) ॥
paripāti priya sakhi kae gela ābe,
je binu mori ati ehi tanu tābe ॥

// ślo[ka] //

(4) bandhūkamallikumudāni sakṛdmalāni, prekṣetsarojamanurāga-
bhareṇa bhūyaḥ ॥
aïkhīṃ vi(5)lokya rajanīmapi cārucandrāṃ, śrīcandraśeṣaramaṇeḥ kalaye
guṇaüdhaṃ ॥

|| kātika (6) kā̃daba, sakhika guṇa bujhi, sahi na pāraba dūkha,
kurari tur[l]anā bhelahu hama dhani, teja**(18 V: 1)**la jati mori sūkha ||
sukha su[sa]khi jananī pari hari lela,
sagari janama mori veda(2)na bhela ||

|| śloka ||
bhūyo vilokya lalito, rjasukhātirekaṃ, paśyatsukhāyamanurū(3) paguṇaṃ sakhīnāṃ |
dūnaḥ priyena suhṛdāsmi vihīna eva, prāpto daśāmanucitāma(4)pi kiṃ diśīkaḥ||

|| māsa agahana khelaya upavana, hamahi sājani samāja,
parasi pa(5)vane mudita duhu jana, kaela anubhava kāja ||
kāja karaba jaño priya raha thīra[,]
(6) kathi lāyi tahni binu mānika hīra ||

|| śloka ||
himacayapariceyaṃ mārggamāsādya **(19 R: 1)** nūnaṃ, bhavatu kathamiyaṃ me, saükhyadā vaïbhavaśṛīḥ |
yadiha hṛdayahārī, matpriyaścandracū(2)ḍaḥ, sarasijamanujāto yāminīṣu svadīptyā ||

|| pūṣa punimaka śaśika sama mukha[,] (3) rucira locana cakora,
hame na bisaraba, tohara avayava, jhā̃khi rahabahu tora ||
to(4)hara guṇe pūrala hamara sāsāra,
tohe mori ūraka mani maya hāra ||

|| śloka ||
katha(5)mapi sahasaïte, yāpitā vāsarodhāḥ samuditaguṇasāraṃ, yāminīṣvetadīyaṃ |
prati(6)palamanunīya[ṃ], prītisaükhyena bhūya, stadapi kathinapaüṣaḥ kena śakyo vinetuṃ ||

|| mā**(19 V: 1)**gha mahinā sakhihi saṃga duhu, anala nikaṭa vilāsa,
ehana priyatara hame na te(2)jaba, janani deha saṃga bāsa ||
bāsa pāvaba hame sājani samīpa,
tohe tyaji ha(3)ma bhela tela binu dīpa ||

ıı śloka ıı

ayamapi mama dehaḥ ślāghanīyaḥ purābhūtpriya (4) virahadavāgneḥ
saṃprati pī[prī]tihīnaḥ ı
ananusukhavinīto māgha eṣa prayatnā,tparina(5)ta iva
dīpastejasāmantarasthaḥ ıı

ıı phāguṇa daśa guṇa vedana bāḍhala, abase śarira vi(6)nāsa,
sakhika guṇa bujhi, dhaïraja nahi hoa, pāoba tahni avakāsa ıı
avakāśa karaba**(20 R: 1)**hu hama sakhi tora,
kathi lāi abe besa kuṇḍala dora[ḍola] ıı

ıı śloka ıı

dehaṃ kakhaḥ sa khalu (2) phālguṇa eva jāto,
viśleṣatastuhinadīdhitiśeṣarasya ı
prāraṃbha eva januṣāṃ viphalasta(3)to me, yatkaüstubhena rahitasya
harervṛthā śrīḥ ıı

caïta candana parama śītala[,] [komala] keśari suvā(4)sa,
ehana sukha duhu, kaela anubhava, harakhe vasaṃta vilāsa ıı
vilāsa karaba sakhi laga (5) raha ābe,
janani kṛpā te priya hame punu pābe ıı

ıı śloka ıı

yaccaṃdanaṃ surabhivārisamī(6)ranādi,
sambhuktapūrvvamasakṛtsusakhena sākaṃ ı
tānyeva saṃprati mamorasi dāvadāhaṃ, saṃ**(20 V: 1)**tatvate
kuṭilacaïtrasamāgamena ıı

ıı māsa mādhava sahi na pāraba, suniya hama pika so(2)ra,
locana nīrahi medani paralihu, suniya dura priya bor[l]a ıı
bola bolaba hame kaño(3)naka pāse,
jata jana nahi rākha niya visavāse ıı

ıı śloka ıı

soḍhavya eva kathamaṃcitapaṃ(4)camoyaṃ, rādhaḥ sa
vādhamupapāditavaïribhāvaḥ ı
śrīcandraśeṣaramaṇaü,stimite hṛdo me (5) nūnaṃ babhūva jaga-
daṃdhatamaṃ madīyaṃ ıı

|| jeṭha jīva mori tejala ehe tanu, bhelahu gaganaka (6) phūla,
e vidhi jānuha je hoa budha jana, bhelahu tahnikā̃ bhūla ||
tāri dala hamarā tula mu**(21 R: 1)**kha bhela,
parama kaleśa mori devihi dela ||

|| śloka ||

caṇḍaḥ kharāṃśurayameti diśāṃ mu(2)khebhyo,
viśleṣakātararathāṃgamudaṃ vidhitsarān ।
saṃpratyasaü sahajaśītalasanmaṇīndro[,] (3) hṛtsaṃsthito navahireti śucaü salīlaṃ ||

|| māsa āṣāḍha hamara dura gela, bhuguti a(4)bhirākha saṃga,
susakhi mīlaba sukṛta bhaya hame, kariya mili kahu raṃga ।
raṃga viraṃga (5) saba ehana ki kāja,
abase karaba priya, pābaya ke sāja ||

|| śloka ||

navyā pārisphura[ṃ](6)ti vāridarājirekhā, bhavyāḥ kalākuśalinaḥ kalayantu kelīḥ ।
maccittavṛrttimanuraṃdhra**(21 V: 1)**dhyasacandracūḍaḥ premnāmayaṃ hi sudhiyāṃ pā[pa]ripāka eva ||

|| māsa bāraha bha[na]ya parakā(2)sa, apane mati ati dūkha,
cā̃daśeṣara pāya hamarā, bhelahu paramahi sūkha ||
sukha pā(3)oba hame, jehi laga pāya,
abhimata pāobathu priya sakhi kāya ||

|| śloka ||

i(4)tthaṃ mahīndranṛpacandrajagatprakāśo, mallo nivedayati bhānukulāvataṃsaḥ ।
śrīcaṃdraśe(5)ṣarasudhāṃśuguṇānuvādaṃ, prītyā tayornnahi paraḥ paramātmabhūtaḥ ||

|| candraśeṣara(6)siṃhasya, gunaṃ jñātvā prakāśyate ।
gītaślokādibhāṣābhi,rlikhitaṃ gītapaṃcakaṃ ||

iti (22 R: 1) śrīgītapaṃcake, candraśeṣaraviyoge, śrīśrījayajagatprakāśakṛte, paṃcamayāmavarṇṇa(2)nā samāptā ||

|| atha ṣaṣṭhayāma varṇṇanā ||

II gaüṛī rāge II cokha tāle II
sakhi saṃga khela(3)yite, prathama pahara gela, dutiya pahara duhu jana jāni,
ayalahu piya ghare saño du(4)hu mohi ghare II *dhruvaṃ* II
apuruba jāmini nakṣatra prakāsa, se dekhi prema ati bāḍhala vilā(5) sa II
dura ka[e]ra śaśi kichu śītala dela, sājani vadana vidhu śata guṇa bhela II
ehana sāja(6)ni mori, abase milāe, punu pema devi deha, dekhabaha kāe II
jagataprakāśa bhana bhina **(22 V: 1)** nahi kāya, janame janame cā̃daśeṣara bhāya II

II ślo[ka] II
yāmo madīyaḥ prathamaṃ prayāta(2)stvayā sama śrīvidhicūḍakelibhiḥ I
saṃkrīḍakuṃjādgṛhamāgatasya, sa yeva jāto vipi(3)nopamo me II

II pathamaṃjari rāge II jatī tāle II
sajani jivaka sama mori jehi, mo(4)hi teji nāka payāne,
sahi na pārabe tahni guṇa bujhi, śiva śiva bhelahu malāne II
ja(5)hni bujhi śiraka āsana mori, se binu niśi nida dūra,
tohara bhaüha dhanu darasana (6) binu, sukha piriti gela kūr[l]a II
hari hari prāṇa piyāri, sakhi visalekha ekhana bhe**(23 R: 1)**la,
kathi lāyi eha tanu kalevara, sājani binu saṃśaya gela II
jagataprakāśa gābae (2) niya mati parama dūkha,
cā̃daśeṣara bara sundara, tohe tyaji dūra gela sūkha II

II śloka (3) *II*
sakhe mama tvaṃ hṛdaye dvitīyah, kimityakāṇḍe rahitaḥ kṣaṇena I
viśleṣatastena hi jīva(4)dhāraṇe, kṣamo bhavāmīti[tya]vadhāryya tāṃ muhuḥII

II kāmoda rāge II cokha tāle II
saja(5)ni lapana[apana] hame, śaśi sama jāna, se binu timira nisi mori upamāna II
sahi nahi hoa(6)ya prema vihīna, ābe bhela mohi baḍa, parama kudīna II

kakhane sunaba hame, amṛta bāni **(23 V: 1)** dekhaba locana bhari sājani māni ||

parakāsa bhana mori dura geli hāra, cā̃daśeṣa(2)ra mori jivaka adhāra ||

|| śloka ||

sakhe mukhante śaśinaḥ samaṃ mama, sphuṭaṃ manaḥ tasya (3) rucā prakāśitaṃ ||

yatastamo māṃ paritaḥ pravādhate, tvadīyamudrekalasatsvarūpaṃ ||

(4) *nāṭa rāge || cokha tāle ||*

sājani vadana bhela, parama suhema, kakhanehu nahi teja (5) sevā niyema||

se sakhi binu hame, jioba ki kāja, nisi dina mori mati, sājani sa(6) māja ||

locana dekhala jata, priya sakhi jāni, tohe binu mori bhela, dhana, jana hāni ||

(24 R: 1) jagataprakāśa bhana, tanu tua lāyi, tvarita pāoba cā̃daśeṣara bhāyi ||

|| śloka ||

he(2)mnāṃ sanābhimbapuṣāṃ dyutiste, saṃsmṛtya saṃpratyahamasmidūnaḥ |

śrīcandraśeṣaramaṇe ka(3)ruṇāṃ vidhehi, nidhehi kāruṇyadhiyaṃ mayi sphuṭāṃ||

|| gaürī rāge || kharjjati, cokha [*tāle*] *||*

(4) karuṇa caṃpaka kusuma ketaki[ī], cūta pallava mālatī,

purar[l]i upavana dekhi nahi hoa, (5) sa[ṃ]mukha acha ṛtu patī ||

sakhi binu tanu ḍāḍhala re, muruchi vasudhā para re ||

ravihi (6) tāpaya, sarira kā̃paya, viseṣa virahini jāti,

sahaba kaṭhinahi, giṣama ṛtu ehe, de**(24 V: 1)**khi na bhela priya kā̃ti ||

hama[e] janu bisaraha re, cā̃dakiraṇe deha re, ||

gagaṇa purala me(2)ghahi ehi khana, sunala cāṭ[t]aka bola,

sakhihi binu suni, vedana upajala, pu | [*sic*]rari[purali] dhara(3)ṇī nora ||

kathi nahi prāvṛta re, binu priya sakhi rata re ||

śarada śaśi dekhi mudita ku(4)mudini, sabahi nakṣata prakāsa,

ke vidhi tejaba sājani binu ṛtu, abase bhela mori (5) nāśa ||

dura gela ādara re sahacari ohe hama re ||
sakala diśa abe, śīta bahaliha (6) purali mahihi tusāra,
sajani rasa mata, hema[ṃ]ta ṛtu para, harakhe kayala vihāra ||
se **(25 R: 1)** binu na jioba re, sadā śiva seoba re ||
śiśira samaya, sājani jaño raha, hoyata kata (2) kata sūkha,
tahnika saṃga binu, sabahi tejala, hamahi saba sukha dūkha ||
parakāśa gābae re (3) cā̃daśeṣara pābae re ||

|| śloka ||
pratyāvṛtya yadi vrajāmi bhavanaṃ, vācāṃ bhavet pracyavo [,]
(4) nirggacchāmi nikuṃjameva yadi vā, ko veda kiṃ syāditaḥ |
tisṭhāmyeva yadi kvacidvanataṭe (5) kiṃ jātametāmaho,
madhye vartmakalānidha[e]ḥ samudayo, mātaḥ kimātanyatāṃ ||

|| candraśe(6)ṣarasiṃhasya, guṇaṃ jñātvā prakāśyate |
gītaślokādibhāṣābhir,likhitaṃ gītapaṃcakaṃ ||

||(25 V: 1) iti śrīgītapaṃcake, candraśeṣaraviyoge, śrīśrījayajagatprakāśakṛte, ṣaṣṯhayāma(2)varṇṇanā samāptā ||

|| atha saptayāmavarṇṇanā||

[||] *kedāra mālava rāge || lāṃjatī tāle* (3) ||
sakhi saṃga khelayite, ādha nisi gela, takhane saño priya sakhi nida basa bhela ||
mo(4)hi kara sakhi śire, āsana dela, sājani komala kara, hamake lela ||
ehana priyatama (5) hama saño dūra, tribhuvana mori lekhe, tahni eka mūla ||
jagataprakāśa bhana, toha mohi (6) bhāya,, cā̃daśeṣara saṃge tvarita milāya ||

|| slokaṃ ||
saṃkrīḍatā tena niśārddhamātma**(26 R: 1)**nā, vyaraṃ śatārddhaṃ sukhanidrayā punaḥ |
karaṃ yadīyaṃ parirabhya komalaṃ, sa eva dhātrā ni(2)hṛto madātmā ||

|| āsāvari rāge || kharjati tāle ||
ho meri āli dhola na tujjha hī (3) maya na karaño kachu, jiya kõ jatano
|| dhruvaṃ ||

yā ki guṇa sõ maya, tiratha kõ dhā̃u, dhara(4)ma tetā kō̧ saṃgat pā̃u ||
ār[l]i mõ sõ, kāhe bichurata bhạī, uha dina, dila sō̧ prāṇa chuṭi (5) gaī ||
jagataprakāsa kī āsā layiyā, candraśeṣarasiṃha vīra, mere bhayiā ||

// *ślo(*6)*ka* //
tataḥ prabhṛtyeva na jīvanāśā, na cātmano me priyatā kadāpi |
yatā[to] maṇiḥ soya**(26V:1)**mapūrvvarūpo, hṛdopi dhātrā karuṇena nirddayaṃ ||

// *sorath[ṭh]i pahaḍiyā rāge* // *para tā*(2)*le* //
ãkhiyā meri bhūkhi rahi ho, tere surata dekhana ko,, nā hā ho ṭeka || *dhruvaṃ* ||
yā sõ (3) eka ghari vichurata nāhī, tā binu raho na jāya,
tana mana mero tujha hī pyāro, rahõ(4)gī teri guṇa gāya ||
ār[l]i mo sõ piriti kiyo jaï,so candra cakora,
iha meri piri(5)ti dura bhayī̃, ko sõ kaho aba bor[l]a ||
jagataprakāśa prabhu sadā kiyo, tuma mere dila (6) māhi,
candraśeṣarasiṃha mero bhaïyā, tuma raho dukha nāhi ||

// *śloka* //
prāṇāyitasyā**(27R:1)**sya mukhāravindaṃ, saṃsmṛtya netro[ā] śrugataṃ madakṣanaḥ |
yadakṣipaṃ keruhamunnatāmbujaṃ, vi(2)lokitaṃ cārusukhākaraṃ purā ||

// *mālava rāge* // *lāṃjati tāle* //
jehi chala[li] jiva sa(3)ma, sājani mora, se binu mahi tar[l]a purar[l]ihu nora ||
caṃpaka ketaki hema varaṇa tora[,] (4) ratana khacita acha, kuṇḍala d[ḍ]ola ||
kamalaka dala sama, locana bhela, sehi nayana juga (5) kañona hari lela ||
jagataprakāśa nṛpa vedana bhāna, cā̃daśeṣarasiṃha, eka mori dhyā(6)na ||

// *śloka* //
cakṣurmmadīyaṃ bhavato viyogāddidṛkṣate śrīvidhuśeṣara tvāṃ |
aprāpya **(27 V: 1)** saṃpa[pra]tyativiklavatvā,dandhatvamagī kuru te svakīyaṃ||

// pahaḍiyā rāge // kharjati tā(2)le //
vedana bāḍhala sājani, teji ābe, jahena caïtaka dīna,
abase priya binu sabahi (3) saṃśaya, bhelahu hamarā dī[hī]na ||
aneka sukha hame bhũjala sakhi saṃge, bujhite bhela tanu (4) khīna ||
khanahu sājani, hamahi na tejaya, je vidhi ghana rasa mīna ||
jagataprakāsa, bhana(5)ya vedana, jānaya deva īśāna,
cā̃daśeṣara hamake deha punu, se dina jāya malāna ||

// (6) *śloka* //
hṛdvedanā mama paraṃ bahusaṃ[śaḥ] prabṛddhā, śrīcandraśeṣara tavādhiguṇaṃ vibhāvya ||
ya**(28 R: 1)**tsarvvataḥ sukhanidhānamabhūtpurā me, viśleṣatastadiha dāvasatānutāpaṃ ||

// candraśe(2)ṣarasiṃhasya, guṇaṃ jñātvā prakāśyate /
gītaślokādibhākhābhirlikhitaṃ gītapaṃcakaṃ //

|| (3) iti śrīgītapaṃcake, candraśeṣaraviyoge, śrīśrījayajagatprakāśakṛte, saptamayāma(4)varṇṇanā samāptā ||

// athāṣṭamayāma varṇṇanā //

mālava rāge // kharjati tāle //
āṭha paha(5)ra sakhi raha mori saṃga, je mohi abhimata, kara kata raṃga ||
ehana hita priya, ābe kata (6) gela, se binu tanuka ari jīvahi bhela ||
abe nahi dhaïraja, hamara pā[a]rāna, pati binu **(28 V: 1)** rati mori, bhela upamāna ||
jagataprakāśa bhana, tohahi adhāra, cā̃daśeṣara mohi (2) ūraka hāra ||

// śloka //
yāmāṣṭakaṃ priyatamā sahasā mayā sā, saṃkurvvatī kati na (3) keli kalāḥ sthitāyā |
saṃpratyahaṃ taralacārukuraṃgadṛṣṭyā, viśliṣṭa eva navaśaḥ khalu (4) jīvadhāraṇe ||

// korāva rāge // cokha tāle //
priya anurāge, lāgali mori jīva, (5) tahni binu, kathi lāyi, hamarā jīva,
he sakhi hame janu bisaraha tohi, toritahi tua ta(6)nu pāoba mohi ||
nisi dina sājani, raha mohi sātha, mati dhara komala, dura gela hātha,

(29 R: 1) jagataprakāsa bhana rasa ehi dūkha, cā̃daśeṣarasiṃha lae gela sūkha।।

।। ślo[ka] ।।

premnā (2) mayā ciratareṇa tavānurāgaḥ saṃvṛddhitaḥ sa khalu jīvaviśoṣanāya ।
yāto yamu(3)nnataguṇālayacandracūḍa, viśleṣitasya bhavatā paritāpahetuḥ ।।

।। vasanta rāge (4) ।। paratālā tāle ।।
mohi dhani teji kata, kayala payāne, abasahi dura bhela hama(5)ra parāne, ke kara hamara tarāne, *।। dhru[vaṃ] ।।*
tir(l)a bhari tohe binu, rahaya na pāraba, ja(6)hena cakevā jora,
dekhala pallava nava, sunalahu pika bola, dura gela priya sakhi **(29 V: 1)** bola ।।
sutali jāmini duhu kare tana binu, jhā̃pi nīda na ābae mohi,
mājhaka vasa(2)nahu, jānala baḍa dura, aïsana piyatama tohi ।।
dāruṇa viraha bija, daya gela sāja(3)ni, ke kara hamara vicāra,
sahaje dukhita hama, sakhi bodhi gamāvala, se piya tejala(4)hu hāra ।।
sājani cikul[r]a bhela baḍa ā̃dhakāra, tula mukha piye niramala canda,
kanaka (5) śaṃkha sama tohara rucira gala, hṛdaya na kahu khana manda।।
kapora darapana, kara yu(6)ga kiśalaya, locana khaṃjana jora,,
cāru karaṇa para, kuṇḍala saṃjuta, sakhi pada dekhi **(30 R; 1)** ali[bheli] bhora ।।
bhanayi prakāśa nṛpa, apanuka vedana, hara janu hamarā pema,
cā̃daśeṣa(2)rasiṃha, hita mori toha bhāya, kata kara sevā niyema ।।

।। ślokaḥ ।।
viśleṣadāvada(3)hanaḥ khalu dāruṇoyaṃ, jvālāvalībhirabhitaḥ kila tāpahetuḥ ।
duḥkhā karoti saha(4)sā hṛdaye paraṃ me, taccandracūḍa vinivedaya yatsukhārthaṃ ।।

।। mālava rāge ।। cokha tāle ।।
(5) kahu khane sahacari, hame nahi tejaya, jahene harihi mahesa,
hoyata hamara kāja,, (6) karaya apana tula, se binu purala kaleśa ।।

kāya vacana mana, hamake daya gela, abhi**(30 V: 1)**mata mohi tahni pāsa,,
rākhaha janani duhu, caraṇa kamala tara, sehi thala pāoba ni(2)vāsa ।।
jagataprakāśa bhana, hama sana janu hoa, sabaka karama ati mandā,,
cā̃daśeṣara(3)siṃha mori bhāya, ati vira mukha bhela nikantaka candā ।।

।। śloka ।।
ātmīyamunnata(4)tamaṃ parihīya kṛtyaṃ, yo me sadā bhavati kāryyaparaḥ sthirātmā ।
taṃ candracūḍamanurūpa(5)sakhāyamekaṃ, saṃsmṛtya kiṃcidapi necchati cāntarātmā ।।

।। sāraṃgī paṃcama rāge, ।। (6) *cokha tāle ।।*
athira kalevara jānuka [jānu] he, kamala pātaka jala tūle *।। dhruvaṃ।।*
bhavana ka**(31 R: 1)**naka jana, rajata ādi jata, thira nahi raha saba jane,
suta mita saba dhana sukha dukha sa(2)rira, athira jānala mane ।।
śiri jala sarira isare sabakā, mana nṛpa avayava dā(3)sa,
manahi pābaya pune, adharama apajasa, mana base pāva eta pāsa ।
jagataprakāśa (4) āsa, kaela tohara, candraśeṣarasiṃha bhāya,
jagata janani pada heṭhahi rākhaha, du(5)hu janaka duhu kāya ।।

।। ślokaḥ ।।
arthāḥ sukhāni ca gṛhānujabhṛtyavarggāḥ[,] sarvvāni (6) tāni nalinījalasannibhāni ।
dehopi bhaṃguratayā bhavato viyoge, śrīcandraśeṣa**(31 V: 1)**ra sakhe niyateravedi ।।

।। ślokaḥ ।।
candraśeṣarasiṃhasya, guṇaṃ jñātvā prakāśyate ।
(2) *gītaślokādibhāṣābhi,rlikhyate gītapaṃcakaṃ ।।*

।। iti śrīgītapaṃcake, candraśeṣa(3)raviyoge,
śrīśrījayajagatprakāśakṛte aṣṭamayāmavarṇṇanā samāptā ।।
।। śivaṃ ।।

5

Translation into English

(Fol. 1 Verso)

Homage to Lords of dance – Śiva and Pārvatī.

To them who encompass the Universe and who reside in the heart of Universe;

To them who are embodiments of happiness and who are complete, I offer my obeisance.

(...) (...)

Ashes are ornaments in (his) body, a trident and a tambourine in his hands;
Spirits accompany him, moon is the forehead mark.
A string of human skulls in his neck, ear–rings dangle in ears;
He wears a tiger–hide, his two feet are lotuses.
Daily does the lord rejoice and Nandī plays the *mṛdaṅga*–drum;
Gaṇeśa – the lord of votaries – dances; Nārada and others sing a song.
O Maheśvara! The dance becomes you so;
King Jagatprakāśa sings out of sheer curiosity.

Sanskrit Verse

(Fol. 2 Recto)

Nandī–the Bull plays the *mṛdaṅga*–drum by his hands with glee and delight,

Serpent–King wriggles and squeezes his entire body in his own nostrils out of sheer fear, nay *angst*, of Kārtikeya's mount–the–Peacock;

Nandī–the Bull shakes his *kakubha* (i.e. the lump of fatty meat forming a hump on his neck) and his *gaṇḍoḍḍi* (i.e. the long leathery fan–like cartilage dangling in front of his face and temple of the throat) in quick rhythmic succession in sheer delight during Śiva's frantic dance (with violent gesticulation);

In sheer ecstasy, Nandī–the Bull billows out shrieks of joy and offers a blessing of protection: May the moon protect you all for long!

Thus ends the Song of Blessing.

Now, in sad and loving memory of my dear friend, and feeling intensely poignant pain of separation, and in a bid to offer him delight, I, *śrīśrījaya* Jagatprakāśa, commemorate him (through this verse–song).
He (i.e. Candraśeṣarasiṃha) is my elder brother, my life; as an elder brother he is as dear to me as my life.
He is my elder brother, my life; this is the truth, nothing but the truth.

(...) (...)

(Folio 2 Verso)

My life–like and dear friend parted from me (i.e. left for the heavenly abode) in the month of *Jeṭha* (May–June) on Friday;
It was in the Nepāla Saṃvat 782 (1662 CE); on that day my necklace went far away.
His mind was very pure, as pure as the water from the Ganges, (he was) pleasure–giving to my life;
His two eyes were crimson–red and pleasing to me, they were well–known to be as pretty and agile as those of a wagtail.
His eyebrows had a beautiful curvature; they were like the arrows of Kāmadeva (Hindu Eros); who would not be oblivious of themselves (after a cast of even a cursory glance at him)?
His two hands were lotus–like, he (always) kept them on my heart; Alas, my sleep at night is (now) gone for good!
Jagatprakāśa says; O lord Śiva with a moon on forehead! Kindly arrange for us to be re–united again;
None else can offer me deliverance; O lord Śiva! May my mind be ever devoted to your feet and may you offer me deliverance!

Sanskrit Verse

(Folio 3 Recto)

If, by ill luck, I, honorable king Jagatprakāśa, am unable to retrieve my life–like lotus (i.e. Candraśeṣarasiṃha), then fie upon me!

(...) (...)

You are my best friend, a second embodiment of my life; alas I can no longer (continue to) look at your face!

Looking at those two eyes of yours bereft me of my woes; the dear friend is suddenly gone far.

Sitting together on the same bed, laughingly we spoke to each other and treated each other as but one life;

My friend! Wipe away my tears of sorrows with the hem–like tender hands of yours.

Seeing our love and affection, the moon and the water–lily felt deeply abashed in their minds;

Seeing our sad separation, suddenly the moon rose brilliantly, the southern wind blew harder today.

(Folio 3 Verso)

Without you I am bereft of my self; the moon, when bereft of its beams, knows it well;

The world looked very dark–like to me, both the day and the night felt visibly dull.

Oh lord! You took him away from me, a sinner as I was, I was selectively left out and I could not accompany him;

Jagatprakāśa says: O Candraśekhara! You alone are the axis (of my existence).

Sanskrit Verse

You are my greatest friend, even if we have two separate entities; you are still my best friend;

How happy I used to be earlier to catch even a glimpse of your beautiful face!

(...) (...)

As soon as my best friend came to me, I woke up in the morning and offered my obeisance to him. *Refrain*

(Folio 4 Recto)

The baby–sun rose, the morning dawned;

Soon the *cakora*[1] couple parted with a heavy heart.

Right then my friend took off my garment;
Caressing me into his lap, he anointed my body with bath oil.
Then my friend bathed me (a younger brother as I was);
In this manner he did many such favors to me.
Alas, now I have to live my sinful life without him!
It was as if I missed the honey for the woods.
Prakāśa says: C̃ādaśeṣara is the axis of my existence;
All of a sudden my best friend and the necklace of my heart went away.

Sanskrit Verse

He who was full of deep love, he who used to share my bed with me until late in the morning, he who was adept in possessing knowledge of all on–goings, and he who was both tender and sensitive to softer feelings, was all of a sudden perished by God; Fie upon such a God who did that!

(Folio 4 Verso)

(...) *(...)*
The benevolent friend fell out of my poor (cursed) hands;
My friend could not remain steady with me (for long).
O God! A great sinner as I was;
The Goddess abducted the axis of my life.
Waist as thin as that of a lion and hands tender;
Knowing them to be lotuses I put those tender hands on my heart.
None else is my benefactor as you were, my friend!
Without you the world is gloomy to me.
Prakāśa has remembered you;
May lord Śiva and C̃ādaśeṣara take a heed!

Sanskrit Verse

I was extremely fortunate to receive the brightest jewel (in the form of my dear friend Candraśeṣarasiṃha); unfortunately, all of a sudden God snatched him away from my heart and perished him for ever.

(Folio 5 Recto)

(...) *(...)*
Benevolent, good–hearted, endowed with good virtues, very handsome and with a suitable waist;

I rehearse the name of my best friend day and night with a pure heart; I will recite your name (again and again).
A repository of happiness, an ocean of pure love, your eyes are lotus–like;
Pure cheeks, shapely chin; your face is like a full moon.
You are my ornament, my best attire, the axis of my life;
You, my friend, are a touchstone, a necklace of my heart.
In my view my deliverance depends on (my) friend, I wish to die after catching a glimpse (of my friend);
Says Prakāśa: I held hopes on him (lit. you) and thought of Cā̃daśeṣara.

Sanskrit Verse

(Folio 5 Verso)

Our love between the two of us is being appreciated from all corners; in spite of having become a widower, seeing the close contact and attachment between the two of us, and in spite of having caused loss or even harm to my own good, and knowing the qualities of Candraśeṣarasiṃha, I have chosen to publish the *Gītapañcaka* containing songs composed in the medium of Maithili and *śloka* in the medium of Sanskrit.

Thus ends the first *yāma* 'canto' of *Gītapañcaka* written by śrīśrījaya Jagatprakāśamalla in sad and loving memory of Candraśeṣara.

Now the second yāma 'canto' begins describing the (good) deeds (of Candraśeṣarasiṃha).

(...) *(...)*
O dear friend! The second 'watch' of the day arrived;
Then at my place I devoutly caught a glimpse of you.
All of a sudden, my friend – the embodiment of my life – went away;
Of all my wealth and of all my men, no one is equal to you.

(Folio 6 Recto)

Without you, I am likened to a husband suffering from the pain of separation from his beloved;
It cannot be a good augury that I lost a friend at his prime youth.
Say something O greater king Jagatprakāśa!
That the lord may do great good to Candraśeṣara!

Sanskrit Verse

The lotus–faced lady–friend named Varṣṣāyaṇa says: in a bid to endure the burning pain of separation she made a bed of (wet and cool) moss; nonetheless she could not sleep on that bed due to modesty and bashfulness. Due to her infirm frame, feeble and inscrutable moaning wails of woe come out of her throat intermittently; she doesn't even get to wash her ever–tearing eyes with the water of a small well and continues to endure the bereavement of separation. Make up (your) mind as to realize this grim pain!

(...) (...)
Without the moon, the night is naturally awfully dull;
Just as forsaking my friend at the moment I am like a fish without water.

(Folio 6 Verso)

My wise and jewel–like friend disappeared all of a sudden;
How soothing it used to be to behold the friend's lotus–hands!
Without whom my life's misery grew in great measure;
Or was it that the king of cloud, Indra, could not bear to see the two of us (so very happy)?
Presently in (all) ten directions the world looked gloomy to me;
What had I after all done that God took away my dear friend from me?
King Jagatprakāśa said the woeful tale;
Will moon-faced Cā̃daśeṣara remain (the source of) my happiness?

Sanskrit Verse

While sitting together on a nice bed and viewing each other's life as one's own and singing the praise of Śiva i.e. Candraśeṣara, alas, all of a sudden he turned into Śiva-the-Benefactor, i.e. he passed away.

(...) (...)

(Folio 7 Recto)

Presently (all my) pride is vanished in absence of my friend. *Refrain*
Do not forsake me, my friend, even for a moment; I am but very tender–aged; stay near me just as a star is close to the moon.
Alas, the Lord took away my friend; the Lord gave me sorrows!

Without whom I felt utterly lonesome in my house; hopefully I will find a way to be in his company.
Prakāśa says: C̃ādaśeṣara is (his) life; (he is now) without ear–rings in (his) ears.

Sanskrit Verse

In absence of you, I see mere darkness all around the firmament. Just as the lily and the water look alike, similarly, due to pain of separation, there is no difference between me and the darkness around.

(...) *(...)*
God tore my love–knots into pieces. *Refrain*
When my friend is near, I know not fear.

(Folio 7 Verso)

It was due to me that I was left to live, but my happiness was taken away. (Irrespective of) when the day dawned and when the night arrived, I will keep on rehearsing your beauty and splendour.
Jagatprakāśa says: You alone are the axis of my existence; C̃ādaśeṣara is (my) necklace.

Sanskrit Verse

I am alive only due to the virtue of a good–hearted friend like you. Only by your grace can I cross over the fiery river of separation i.e. *bhavasāgara* ‘the Worldly River’.

(...) *(...)*
My dear friend! Your feet are lotuses; your thighs (as shapely as) the banana tree trunk;
Your waist is suitably slim, your beauty is divine, your complexion has the glow of gold, and your lips have the sweet juice of ambrosia.

(Folio 8 Recto)

My dear! You are dearest to me; do not forsake me and do not leave me all of a sudden; I am naturally the greatest sinning person, I am but a sorrowful person; by keeping me in your company, offer me deliverance. *Refrain*
Friend! (It is) my heart in your body, my speech is but yours and my two eyes suit you so;

Sitting near your moon–face, I drank deep (from my eyes) with regard, but all of a sudden my gem was gone far away (from me).
Without (my) friend I became the poorer, nowhere could I be together as I was struck with ill thoughts.
The agony increased more and more, I couldn't bear it any longer now that Kāmadeva (Hindu Eros) has smitten me hard.

(Folio 8 Verso)

King Jayajagatprakāśa says: You alone, my friend, can make us feel alike. You alone are (my real friend), I will not forsake you, even if the daughter–in–law of the (royal) progeny makes one do as she pleases. [Note: The meaning of the last *caraṇa* of this song remains somewhat unclear.]

Sanskrit Verse

A slender damsel, who has such beauteously curved eyebrows and who wears a garland of lotus flowers and a long necklace of pearls intertwined together, has such a narrow waist – rendered so due to the acute pain of separation – that her waistband ornament cannot hold and pulls lower and lower and that it is hard to tell if her pulses continue to beat at all. Such a slender damsel, soaked as she is in deep sorrow, has positioned herself to let her calabash vessel–like oval jaw lean pensively on the palm of her hand. What a piteous sight! This is indeed a matter of great sorrow.

Knowing the qualities of Candraśeṣarasiṃha, I have chosen to publish the Gītapañcaka containing songs in Maithili and śloka in Sanskrit.

Thus ends the description of the second *yāma* 'canto' of śrīgītapañcaka composed by śrīśrījaya Jagatprakāśa in sad and loving memory of Candraśeṣara.

(Folio 9 Recto)

Now the third yāma 'canto' describing the (good) deeds (of Candraśeṣarasiṃha) begins.

(...) (...)
Realizing that it was the third 'watch' i.e. close to the evening and smiling sparingly (my friend) came to meet me.
My friend never ceased to serve me; Single–mindedly he did favors to me.

If I ever felt the need of his company, he used to offer me company considering it as his own duty.
Both of us knew that (our) bodies were but inseparable and that together we were never short of love and affection even for a brief while.
Forget me not, O my axis of hope! Look at me and keep me close to you, O friend!
Jagatprakāśa says: offer me deliverance; Cā̃daśeṣarasiṃha is the necklace of (my) heart.

(Folio 9 Verso)
Sanskrit Verse

The dear friend's company offers me great joy and happiness; the pain of separation from him is the sole cause of my sorrow.

(...) (...)
I will never forget the merit and the pleasure of the company of my friend; I have a great desire to see his beautiful face (once again).
O lord! I have a sinner's eyesight; no wonder that I was deprived of catching even a glimpse of him.
The sorrow of loveless–ness is unbearable; my body is home to pain.
Jagatprakāśa says: I should bear it in mind daily; Cā̃daśeṣarasiṃha is my great benefactor.

Sanskrit Verse

Viewing the benevolent and deep love subsisting between the Moon and the Sun – who have but one single soul – it appears that a similar type of deep love exists between the two (of us) i.e. between king Jagatprakāśa and Candraśeṣara.

(Folio 10 Recto)

(...) (...)
I have become (like) a night without moon; my happiness was snatched away by my friend.
Tears from my eyes filled a river; without my friend, my pain grew more.
A bee roams in greed of honey; I am likened to that (bee) without him.
Prakāśa sings this song for you; I may find Cā̃daśeṣara near me.

Sanskrit Verse

The hand fan (that used to provide cool breeze against the fiery heat of separation from Candraśeṣara) has turned totally useless. The cold water, having lost its cooling power, has failed to provide coolness. The (cool) camphor has turned into the ironsmith's fiery hand–bellows. Strangely enough, the city–abode of comely lasses, soaked in sorrow as it is, reverberates with woeful shrill wails like those of a separated *kurarī*[2]–bird.

(...) (...)

During the evening, the friend (lit. the respectable lady) [the meaning remains unclear] singled me out with all the water (of tears) and squeezed all happiness out (of me).

(Folio 10 Verso)

Both of us were in good health; day by day our affection grew.

Do not forsake me even for a moment, O friend! Wipe away all my tears (of sorrow).

Now that sad separation has occurred, my pride, my real self, went along with him.

Jagatprakāśa knew the essence of it; he made Candraśeṣara (his) necklace.

Sanskrit Verse

With the advent of the month of *Caïtra* (i.e. the spring season), the fallen leaves of a clove tree have turned as yellow as the yellow (and dried) leaves of a palm tree; in a similar way the colorful flush of the cheeks of the damsel in distress of separation too has turned yellow – which is indeed a matter of great sorrow.

(...) (...)

I happened to meet my benevolent friend just as Maheśa (and his consort Pārvatī);

Out of sheer love and affection we dressed each other up with suitable clothes.

As soon as I took to the road together with my friend, he held me with his hands;

(Folio 11 Recto)

While we were both gazing at each other's face, God abducted him (lit. you) away.
Do not render us apart, never forget your friend, and be warned about it.
My friend died ahead of me; that's why I have become but a sinning person.
Jagatprakāśa held high hopes on you; I will receive his company.
(My) friend is good–natured and a repository of virtues; (I will remain) near Candraśeṣara.

Sanskrit Verse

His (i.e. Candraśeṣara's) visits (lit. coming and going) gave us constant delight until our eyelids remained open – the pleasant memory of which is still remnant on the lips of the comely ladies. His occasional acts of speech were received like the visit of a casual guest; his words of anger, if ever he uttered them, have been consigned to memory.

(Folio 11 Verso)

Knowing the merits of Candraśeṣarasiṃha, I have chosen to publish the Gītapañcaka containing songs in Maithili and śloka in Sanskrit.

Thus ends the description of the third *yāma* 'canto' of *Gītapañcaka* composed by śrīśrījaya Jagatprakāśa in sad and loving memory of Candraśeṣara.

Now the description of the fourth yāma 'canto' begins.

(...) (...)
Up until the fourth 'watch' (i.e. the end of the day) my friend kept talking; as soon as I heard that I had lost him, my sorrow knew no bounds.
Now the same friend has suddenly gone far away; of all my men he was for me the pivot.
O Goddess! Fulfill my wish and get me re–united with the friend who removed the dust off my feet.

(Folio 12 Recto)

Jagatprakāśa says: You alone are (my) benefactor; without Candaśeṣara all is gone for good.

Sanskrit Verse

It is true that I constantly listened to his nectar–like sweet words, i.e. I always obeyed his words. He, who had obtained youthful good health, was all of a sudden dragged away by the divine Providence ahead of time – as a result of which I have been drowned in the Ocean of Sorrow by Time.

(...) (...)

Without reminiscing about the virtues of my friend I will not survive; without him compassion grew aplenty.

Who else but my friend can offer me deliverance? The necklace of pearls and gems lies very heavy (on my chest now).

If I could re–live in the company of my friend, then all the wishes of my life would be fulfilled.

King Jagatprakāśa says (this) in sorrow:

(Folio 12 Verso) May Cā̃daśeṣara take a heed!

Sanskrit Verse

His body was once a repository of the very essence of happiness; reminiscing about the sad separation (i.e. death) from Candraśeṣarasiṃha, compassion grew aplenty in my heart. By catching even the faintest glimpse of him and feeling an intense pain of separation from him, my countenance is for sure contorted.

(...) (...)

O friend! Nowhere is my mind wandered off. *Refrain.*

God did not abduct me, God indeed took away my life; the moon–faced friend went far away.

Your red lips compare to the red light of the newly–risen baby–sun; seeing your suitably thin waist one may even forget the lion (the King of the Forest is famously known for its narrow waist).

What a pity! The friend who was blessed to walk with the gait of an elephant all of a sudden vanished in thin air like a God.

(Folio 13 Recto)

With eyes very pretty and lotus–like, the friend is now lying unconscious (i.e. dead) on the ground; his body – once as heavy and healthy as an elephant – is now reduced to thinness.

His hand was like the trunk of an elephant, his heart as large as an elephant and his speech was like the sweet voice of a cuckoo–bird; such indeed was my friend!
It was God who separated me from the company of my friend; you alone are my mind and life.
Jagatprakāśa says: all is unsteady, including child, friend, people, wealth, and (even) wife;
O benevolent Cā̃daśeṣarasiṃha! My deliverance rests on you; I lay the necklace of my heart on you.

Sanskrit Verse

He, who resided among the beautifully–brave lions with a face as bold as that of a lion, and he, who had lips red like the redness of the early morning baby–sun, is all of a sudden turned into a piteously crying deer that is miserably held in the cruel clutches of a fierce lion. The very same friend of mine with a beauteous figure is now (reduced to) a supplicant to lord Viṣṇu, i.e. he is no more.

(Folio 13 Verso)

(...) (...)
(O Lord!) Do not render me alone without my friend. *Refrain*
If Lord Kāmadeva (Hindu Eros) gets to live with his consort Rati at one place, then that suits them both so.
Separation is very painful, I cannot bear it; reminiscing about (the sweet memory of) my friend, I managed to spend the night (somehow or other).
The friend whom I looked at daily inside my heart; when shall I get a glimpse of his good looks?
O Goddess! It was due to the grace of your supreme feet that I received my friend, and it was due to your kind blessing that we were able to live together.
No one is more sinful than me in Three Worlds, bear in mind that I lost him out of my hand.
Embracing me in his lap we (he and I) used to sleep together; now the same sleep is far from me.
King Prakāśa says: O Cā̃daśeṣarasiṃha! You and I are of the same ancestry.

(Folio 14 Recto)

Sanskrit Verse

You are for sure born of illustrious parents as beautiful as Kāmadeva and Rati; you – the Moon of the Earth – are suddenly gone far away to the heavenly abode. Such are the ways of God.

(...) (...)

My friend frolicks (on a swing) unaided and derives supreme delight.
Refrain
Feeling happy and sitting close to each other, my friend and I enjoyed it so very much.
Holding the hands of my friend and placing them on my heart, I naturally made a necklace of them.
Nearby was a sprout of cold water and a gentle breeze passed by us.

(Folio 14 Verso)

The touch of the very–same gentle breeze that gave us happiness has now ruined everything.
Such a dear friend suddenly vanished into thin air; by performing good deeds I will be re–united with him.
By virtue of those (good deeds), I will be able to snatch him back and together we will offer prayers with devotion.
Jagatprakāśa expects this of you – he who knows about the sentiment of love.
C̃ādaśeṣara is a repository of love; we both have but one life.

Sanskrit Verse

As Kāmadeva suits well in the company of his beloved consort Rati, and as ornaments suit well on limbs in different parts of the (human) body, similarly, I would have looked more and more beautiful had you (i.e. Candraśeṣara) lived longer with me. But, you disappeared all of a sudden; why on earth do you (continue to) give me false assurances!

Knowing the merits of Candraśeṣarasiṃha and in a bid to extol and highlight them, I have chosen to publish Gītapañcaka containing songs in Maithili and śloka in Sanskrit.

(Folio 15 Recto)

Thus ends the description of the fourth *yāma* 'canto' of *Gītapañcaka* composed by śrīśrījaya Jagatprakāśa in sad and loving memory of Candraśeṣara.

Now the description of the fifth yāma 'canto' begins.

(...) (...)

The lotus flower squeezed itself in and the moon light was well spread out; it was at that time that my friend came to me.

Where is the very–same night gone now? Suddenly it has become difficult to bear (this) life.

I can no longer bear my body which is being burnt by the fire (of pangs of separation); when after all would I be able to catch a glimpse of the figure of my dear friend?

King Jagatprakāśa suffers this sentiment of sorrow; Cāṃdaśeṣarasiṃha took away (all) the happiness.

(Folio 15 Verso)

Sanskrit Verse

As I am grievously smitten by the pain of separation from my friend, the flower–like soft arrows of Kāmadeva and the soothingly cool beams of the Moon have both proven totally ineffective to me because the Moon, which possesses ice in its embryo, is (presently) showering the rain of fire on me. O Kāmadeva! Your flower–like arrows (of love) too have turned into life–consuming thunder–bolts.

(...) (...)

I cannot bear (my) life any longer due to pangs of separation from you.

In your (good) company I found much happiness.

It was not you who quit loving me; it was indeed God who caused it to be so.

Lord! Listen to my entreaty; I want to live with my friend.

God broke my heart and he took away (his) life.

I am anguished by it and it pierced me like arrows.

(Folio 16 Recto)

I looked for him from one grove to another; I also looked for him inside the house.

If I (continue to) look for him with devotion, I am sure to ultimately find him.
Said king Prakāśa: You alone are my hope; I may eventually get to live in the company of Cā̃daśeṣara.

Sanskrit Verse

As the *cakavā* bird – for fear of separation and on suspicion of lest it might be dark – happens to reside in blue lotus–woods and mistakes the perturbed wavy water used for play for clusters of stars and again mistakes a (white) goose for a (bright) moon at night and is constantly on nerves – no matter where or when –, similarly, I, Jagatprakāśa, too am never and nowhere and under no circumstances happy (due to separation from my dear friend).

(...) (...)
Without (you), (I experience) great sorrow; when shall I (get to) see (your) face? Forget me not. *Refrain*

(I know not) what went through the mind of my friend, or in my heart and speech.

(Folio 16 Verso)

Finally I sensed the feelings of the friend (lit. the respectable lady); (now) I will do whatever it takes to get my dear friend back.
King Jagatprakāśa says: May Cā̃daśeṣara take a heed!

Sanskrit Verse

Since God abducted your dear friend from you for long, you no longer wear green *kuśa* (*Poa Cynosuroides*) on your fingers (i.e. do not perform any propitious acts of worship during the period of impurity); you do not quite stay steadfastly in one place, and in a plaintive voice you continue to stare all around with swift and compassionate eyes. Not only this, in utter helplessness, you mistake a mountain for a low flat land and a full–flowing river for a dry and barren sandy river–bed.

(...) (...)
Every one is fickle–minded; my friend (alone) is single–minded.
Every one is deceitful; seeing it (my) fear grew.
Duty is discarded; wherever one casts an eye it is sinful.

(Folio 17 Recto)

King Jagatprakāśa sings this (song); May he find Cā̃daśeṣara near (him)!

Sanskrit Verse

O wayfarer! In spite of knowing the above–stated fact that my most intimate friend was forcibly sent into exile by the river–like (i.e. illustrious) king – the king of the strongest kings of all –, and in spite of knowing that he had been far and far away, I continue to strive hard to bring him (i.e. Candraśeṣarasiṃha) to my mind's eye. I raise my neck skyward and raise one of my feet knee–high in the air and I keep gazing intently with tearful eyes in all directions for long but know not why. In other words, I ought not to strive to look around for him any more; after all, he is dead.

(...)   (...)

The densely cloudy (month of) *Śrāvana* (Sanskrit *Śrāvaṇa*; July–August) offers acute pangs of separation; it is all the more difficult for a young damsel to survive (in this rainy month).

The lightning kept shining in quick succession; the sight of it made my body weak and frail.

It is with a sad heart that I repeatedly recite and remember the name of my friend.

By your grace, may my wishes be fulfilled!

(Folio 17 Verso)

Sanskrit Verse

With the advent of the month of *Śrāvaṇa* (July–August), the clouds are loaded with rain–water. Dreadfully frightful lightnings flicker in quick succession. At a time like this, reminiscing about the essence of the beautifully–glowing gem, i.e. my intimate friend Candraśeṣarasiṃha, I am totally at a loss and know not what to do.

To begin with, (the month of) *Bhādava* (Sanskrit *Bhādra*; August–September) heightened love; the two bodies became but one.

Just as (in the rainy season) a full–flowing river engulfs its banks as well, so has our love overpowered (us).

All my love was selectively snatched away by my friend.

Without you, I cannot control myself.

Sanskrit Verse

The wonderful month of *Bhādra* (August–September) is heavily clouded with rain–water; in this month the water of love is spread all around. O my only dear friend! Kindly illumine me on who will quell the fiery pangs of separation from you again.

(Folio 18 Recto)

The month of *Āsina* (Sanskrit *Āśvina*; September–October) causes compassion as many kinds of fragrant flowers are in bloom.

The sky is very clear at this time (of the year); who will take care of me (now)?

True, my dear friend had taken good care of me earlier; but now without him my body burns grievously.

Sanskrit Verse

In the month of *Āśvina* (September–October), during noon *camelī*, *kumuda*, and *kamala* flower–plants are laden with buds – the sight of which fills the heart with deep affection. Presently, while witnessing the clear and beaming moonlit night it appears as if one is witnessing Candraśeṣara – the ensemble of gem–like glowing virtues and attributes.

In (the month of) *Kātika* (Sanskrit *Kārtika*; October–November), I cry reminiscing about the good virtues of my friend; I will no longer be able to bear the sorrow.

O friend! I became lonesome like a *kurari*; I forsook all my happiness.

(Folio 18 Verso)

The Goddess took away all the pleasures I had with my best friend; my entire life became sorrowful.

Sanskrit Verse

Hark! The month of *Kārtika* (October–Novenber), full of glee and gaiety and studded with appropriate virtues befitting dear friends, is here. But, alas, I am deeply saddened in absence of my good friend; I am indeed encircled from all directions with adversely inopportune conditions.

In the month of *Agahana* (Sanskrit *Mārgaśīrṣa*; November–December), I played out into the garden in the company of my friend.

The two of us were very happy to feel the gentle brush of a breeze of wind; we had a nice experience thereof.
One can experience love only when the dear friend is steady;
Of what use are the gems and diamonds without him (any way)?

(Folio 19 Recto)

Sanskrit Verse

The month of *Mārga* (November–December) – the harbinger of cold snow – has arrived. How can worldly possessions offer me comfort and solace in a grim month like this? Had my dear friend Candraśeṣara – the necklace of my heart and beauteously beaming like a lotus – been here with me during the night of the month of *Mārga*, the worldly possessions may have offered me comfort and happiness. But, alas, that is not to be so.
In the month of *Pūsa* (Sanskrit *Paüṣa*; December–January), your face beamed like the full moon and your eyes were as lovely as those of a *cakora*.
I will never forget your face; I will keep on gazing at your (face).
My world is filled with the virtue of your merits;
You are indeed the gem–studded necklace of my heart.

Sanskrit Verse

Suddenly, the month of *Paüṣa* (December–January) – the obstructer of the broad sunlight of the day, the enhancer of nightly pleasures, and the provider of happiness of love – has arrived. Who can dare humble the continually sought–after month of *Paüṣa*? None can.

(Folio 19 Verso)

In the month of *Māgha* (January–February), my friend and I used to sit by fire and enjoy each other's company.
I will never ever forsake such a dearer friend; May the Goddess offer me his company (for ever)!
I will for sure get the company of my friend;
After you left I have become (like) a lamp without oil.

Sanskrit Verse

After much effort, the month of *Māgha* (January–February), has successfully proven itself to be pleasure–giving, but, situated as it were in the midst of a cluster of bright lights, it has rendered itself into a feebly–flickering candle. In a similar way, even my body – once so admirable – is presently rendered lusterless due to the acute pain of separation from you i.e. Candraśeṣara.

In the month of *Phāguna*, (Sanskrit *Phālguṇa*; February–March), my sorrow increased ten–fold; this will for sure ruin my body.

Realizing the merits of my friend, I did not have the patience to imagine that I would ever take leave of his company.

If I ever take leave of you, O friend!

(Folio 20 Recto)

Then why would it be at all nice to let my ear–rings (continue to) dangle?

Sanskrit Verse

Just as with the advent of the month of *Phālguṇa* (February–March), the (mighty) Himalaya turns thinner due to the melting of the snow, similarly, my body has turned slimmer. Just as lord Viṣṇu turns lusterless without the *Kaüstubha*[3] gem dangling on his chest, so also my life is meaningless due to separation from my friend.

The month of *Caïta* (Sanskrit *Caïtra*; March–April) has extreme coolness of sandal wood powder and fragrance of tender *kesari* flowers; my friend and I experienced such happiness as one would expect to have in a spring season.

I would definitely rejoice in the company of my friend;

If by the grace of Mother–Goddess I get to be re–united with my friend again.

Sanskrit Verse

With the advent of the crooked month of *Caïtra* (March–April), the very–same objects, i.e. the fragrant and soothing sandal powder, the cold water, and the cool breeze – that once offered me cool comfort and great happiness in the company of my dear friend – have now tended to burn my heart with fiery pangs of separation from my friend.

(Folio 20 Verso)

In the (hot) month of *Mādhava* i.e. *Baïsākha* (Sanskrit *Vaiśākha*, also *Rādhā*); April–May), I can no longer bear to hear the plaintive love wails of a *koela*[4] bird.
Tears shed from my eyes and fell on the ground; my friend will (probably) hear the wail of my anguish from afar.
Who to would I speak about my feelings in a situation in which no one seems to trust each other?

Sanskrit Verse

In the (hot) month of *Rādhā* (April–May), even the sweetest song of a *koela* bird turns agonizingly unpleasant and inimical; my heart is shrouded with darkness as my glowing gem–like Candraśeṣara is hidden from me. In other words, my entire world is full of darkness.
In the month of *Jeṭha* (Sanskrit *Jyeṣṭha*; May–June), my friend left his body (for heavenly abode) and became invisible (in the sky).
All who are wise know it to be so, but that's where they are at fault.
The starry universe looked as sad as my face.

(Folio 21 Recto)

The Goddess gave me much sorrow indeed.

Sanskrit Verse

In the month of *Jyeṣṭha* (May–June), just as the sun rises from all directions with all its glory and bright light to ease the *cakavā*-bird's acute pain of separation from the beloved during night, similarly, the ever pleasure–giving jewel among the gems – Candraśeṣara – constantly resides in my heart with all his pure and pleasurable acts; he just cannot come out of my heart.
The month of *Āsāḍha* (Sanskrit *Āṣāḍha*, June–July) went by as I kept wishing for the company of my friend.
Being well–fated, I will re–meet my best friend and together we will have fun and amusement.
What use is the fun after all?
I will for sure strive hard to find a way to re–gain my friend.

Sanskrit Verse

With the advent of the month of *Āsāḍha* (June–July), new streaks of clusters of clouds appear and roam around in the sky. May these clusters of clouds put up a nice show of sixty–four arts of the play of love! May Candraśeṣara – the epitome of love of all wise men – create steadiness in my bewildered heart!

(Folio 21 Verso)

(At the end of the song of) the twelfth month says Prakāśa: I was very unhappy inside my heart;
After having received the company of Cā̃daśeṣara, I was extremely happy.
I will receive happiness in his company;
May the body of the dear friend rest in peace!

Sanskrit Verse

In this manner, I, the great king Jagatprakāśamalla, shining like Moon amidst the jewels of kings of the solar dynasty, make a fervent plea to you all that I am here to extol the fine attributes and good virtues of the ambrosia–showering Candraśeṣara with deep love and affection, and hereby declare that even after he is gone to the heavenly abode there is no difference between the two of us, and that we are both still together.

Knowing the merits of Candraśeṣarasiṃha and in a bid to extol and highlight them, I have composed the Gītapañcaka containing songs in Maithili and śloka in Sanskrit.

(Folio 22 Recto)

Thus ends the description of the fifth *yāma* 'canto' of śrīgītapañcaka composed by śrīśrījaya Jagatprakāśa in sad and loving memory of Candraśeṣara.

Now the description of the sixth yāma 'canto' begins.

(...) (...)
The first 'watch' (from dawn to morn) of the day was gone while playing with the friend; both of us came to realize that it was now the second 'watch' i.e. midday; (Then) both of us came over to my house from the house of my friend. *Refrain*

At night the stars shone amazingly wonderful; seeing it our love and joviality grew more and more.
The far–off moon offered us a little coolness; the moon–face of my friend shone hundred–fold more.
O Goddess! You must re–unite me with such a friend of mine; kindly give back our love again and show me his (beautiful) countenance.
Jagatprakāśa says: our bodies are but inseparable; may I have Cā̃daśeṣara as my brother in all subsequent rebirths.

(Folio 22 Verso)

Sanskrit Verse

I used to spend the first 'watch' i.e. the early part of the day playing all kinds of mirthful games with Candraśeṣara in a secluded grove–like house of mine; the same house now feels like a dense and dark forest to me and Candraśeṣara has turned invisible in darkness.

(...) (...)
My friend, who was equal to my life, left me for the heavenly abode.
Realizing his merit, I can no longer bear it; O lord! I am (suddenly) so sad.
He, whom I always thought of as a place of my headrest, without him night by night I am sleep–less.
All my happiness and love disappeared in absence of a glimpse of your arrow–like eyebrows.
O lord! I had to suddenly separate from such a friend – dear to my life.

(Folio 23 Recto)

I began to nourish doubts as to what for would I need my body any more in absence of my friend.
Jagatprakāśa sings (this song) with a very heavy heart: Cā̃daśeṣara is very handsome; since you left, my happiness is gone for good.

Sanskrit Verse

O friend! You were equal to my life (my second self as it were). Why did you forsake me so soon? I cannot bear to live in absence of you. I feel remorse in not being able to accompany you to your heavenly abode; pardon me for it.

(...) (...)
I knew that my friend was like a moon; without him my nights are shrouded in darkness.
I cannot bear to live a love–less (life); now all of a sudden very bad days are here for me.
When shall I (get to) hear his ambrosia–like sweet voice and have a full view of my dear friend?

(Folio 23 Verso)

Prakāśa says: my necklace is gone far away; Cā̃daśeṣara is the axis of my life.

Sanskrit Verse

O friend! Your face gleams like the beaming moon. I derive light from that moon as I am deeply shrouded in darkness from all directions. I am rendered lovelier owing to your loving face.

(...) (...)
My friend's complexion was very golden and he never quit performing his daily rite of passage.
What use is for me now to (continue to) live without such a friend? After all, day and night my mind is (constantly) in the company of my friend.
The more I look at my eyes, mistaking them to be of my dear friend's, the more I (tend to) lose my wealth and my men without you.

(Folio 24 Recto)

Jagatprakāśa says: My body is but for you; soon I will get Cā̃daśeṣara as my brother.

Sanskrit Verse

You were a person of a very fair (gold–like) complexion; I am extremely saddened to remind me of your fair complexion. O God! Now that gem–like Candraśeṣara is definitely no more, kindly turn me into a highly compassionate person in order for me to feel extreme sorrow in his death.

(...) (...)
Trees bearing yellow fragrant flowers such as *Campaka* (*Michelia Campaka)*, *Ketakī* (*Pandanus odoratissimus)*, and fragrant white flowers

which open towards the evening such as *Mālatī* (*Jasminum Grandiflorum)* are in full bloom; I cannot bear to see the garden in full bloom; (after all) the master of seasons – Spring – is right here.
My body burned without my friend, I (may even) swoon on the ground.
The sun heat is scorching, my body is shivering in sheer heat, and I feel like a typical forlorn lover.
It is difficult to bear (the heat of) the summer season, as I could not get to see the beauty of (the face of) my dear friend.

(Folio 24 Verso)

Do not ever forget me; give me the soothing moon beams i.e. Candraśeṣara at any rate.
Suddenly the sky was covered with clouds, and I heard the woeful wail of the *cātaka*[5] bird;
Hearing the wail of the love–lorn *cātaka* in absence of my friend, my sorrow grew and the earth was filled with my tears.
Without the love of my dear friend I would have nothing (that would please me).
Seeing the autumn moon the lotus is happy and all the stars are shining;
How would I spend the season without my friend? For sure, I will be ruined.
O! The object of my respect and devotion went far away; he alone is my dear friend.
Suddenly the cold wind blew in all directions; the earth was covered with frost/ice;
(I recall how) on arrival of the winter season my friend used to rejoice with happiness.

(Folio 25 Recto)

Without him I will no longer live; I will (instead) always serve and worship lord Śiva.
If during the winter season one is with one's friend, much happiness ensues.
In absence of his company I forsook all; all my happiness is turned into sorrow.
Prakāśa sings: he hopes to get Cā̃daśeṣara.

Sanskrit Verse

If I happen to return home in sad and loving memory of Candraśeṣara, then I would be proven untrue to my words. If I happen to wander into woods, then what would come of it? What would others think of me? Or, instead, if I choose to build a hut to live in a nearby forest, then too nothing would come of it. Therefore, O Mother Goddess! Cause me to re–meet my moon–like Candraśeṣara in the middle of the pathway.

Knowing the merits of Candraśeṣara and in a bid to extol and highlight them, I have composed the Gītapañcaka containing songs in Maithili and śloka in Sanskrit.

(Folio 25 Verso)

Thus ends the sixth *yāma* 'canto' of śrīgītapañcaka composed by śrīśrījaya Jagataprakāśa in sad and loving memory of Candraśeṣara.

Now the description of the seventh yāma 'canto' begins.

(...) (...)

While playing with my friend half of the night was gone; just then my friend began to fall asleep.

My friend took my hand as a headrest; I (on the other hand) took the friend's hand.

Such a dear friend is now away from me; in Three Worlds he alone was the pivot for me.

Jagatprakāśa says: You are my brother; (O Lord!) Cause me to re–meet with Cā̃daśeṣara soon.

(Folio 26 Recto)

Sanskrit Verse

Such a dear friend – my second self – who used to play with me mirthfully until midnight and sleep with me happily for fifty years and embrace me fondly with both of his tender hands was alas put to death by cruel God.

(...) (...)

O my friend! I won't do a thing; you alone ought to do something in order for me to live. *Refrain*

Or, I ought to go on a pilgrimage to earn merit and righteousness in the company of saints.

O friend! Why did you separate from me? The day you left me, my life–breath left my body.
Jagatprakāśa nourishes the hope; the brave Candraśeṣara is my brother.

Sanskrit Verse

Since the day my wonderful gem–like friend, Candraśeṣara, was abducted by the cruel God, there is no hope left in my life and there is no object that is dear to me any more.

(Folio 26 Verso)

(...) (...)
My eyes are hungrily pining for a glimpse of your face. *Refrain*
He with whom I didn't separate even for a moment I can no longer live without him;
You alone are dear to my body and mind; (all my life) I will keep singing in praise of you.
My friend! You loved me as the *cakora*–bird loves the moon;
Now that my friend is gone far away, who should I speak to (about my feelings)?
Jagatprakāśa (says): God knows that I always kept you in my heart;
Candraśeṣara, my brother! There is no sorrow when (and if) you are (around).

(Folio 27 Recto)

Sanskrit Verse

Earlier, I used to catch a glimpse of the face of the handsome and pleasure–giving lotus – born of the eye–mud – with utter delight; now, remembering the face of my life–like friend, my eyes are filled with tears.

(...) (...)
My friend, who was equal to my life, without him I filled the earth with my tears (of sorrow).
Your complexion was as golden as the *campaka* and *ketakī* flowers; your gem–studded ear–rings dangled (beautifully).
Your eyes were like lotus petals; who abducted those two (lovely) eyes (of yours)?

King Jagatprakāśa says in sorrow: C̃ādaśeṣara is my only (axis of) attraction.

Sanskrit Verse

O Candraśeṣara! My eyes are perennially pining to catch a glimpse of your beautiful face, but I am unable to do so as I am blind–like due to constant overflow of tears in my eyes. Kindly realize it to be so.

(Folio 27 Verso)

(...) (...)

Upon losing my friend my sorrow grew more and more just as the days of (the month of) *Caïta* (grew longer day by day);

For sure everything looks meaningless (to me) without my friend; I have become the poorer.

I had many happy times together with my friend; reminiscing about those happy times makes me unhappy;

May my friend never ever leave me just as a fish can never live without water!

Jagatprakāśa says (this) in sorrow, and God knows about it (too);

(O lord)! Give back Candraśeṣara to me again so that my sad days may be over.

Sanskrit Verse

O Candraśeṣara! The more deeply I realize and ponder over your good virtues and merits, the pain in my heart grows more and more, because, earlier, you offered me happiness of all kinds but, now, the fiery pangs of separation from you offer me excessive pain.

(Folio 28 Recto)

Knowing the merits of Candraśeṣara and in a bid to extol and highlight them, I have composed the Gītapañcaka containing songs in Maithili and śloka in Sanskrit.

Thus ends the description of the seventh *yāma* 'canto' of śrīgītapañcaka composed by śrīśrījaya Jagatprakāśa in sad and loving memory of Candraśeṣara.

Now the description of the eighth yāma 'canto' begins.

(...) (...)

My friend stayed with me twenty–four hours (day and night), and did many wonders as my mind wanted.

Where did such a dear benefactor disappear all of a sudden? Without him, my own body has become an enemy to my existence.

I have no patience/forbearance any longer;

(Folio 28 Verso)

I am likened to a beloved without a lover.

Jagatprakāśa says: you alone are my axis of hope; Cāṃdaśeṣara is the necklace of my heart.

Sanskrit Verse

My friend used to perform many kinds of playful and mirthful acts throughout the day and night; now, having to view the same friend in the image of a sequestered and wanton–eyed doe, I am unable to hold my life–breath i.e. I can no longer live (in absence of my dear friend).

(...) (...)

My whole life is devoted to the love of my dear friend; without him, of what use is my life anyway?

O friend! Don't you ever forget me; soon I will be reborn as you (and will be re–united with you).

Day and night (my) friend used to be with me; nonetheless now I must bear in mind that the very–same tender hands (of Candraśeṣarasiṃha) are gone far away.

(Folio 29 Recto)

Jagatprakāśa sings this sad song; Candraśeṣarasiṃha took away my happiness.

Sanskrit Verse

I was brought up with good care and deep love and affection by you (i.e. Candraśeṣara – the repository of high merits); the separation from you is the sole cause of my present sorrow and agony.

(...) (...)

My friend forsook me and went away I know not where; for sure my life is gone; who will offer me deliverance? *Refrain*

I cannot live without you even for the fraction of a moment; just as the *cakevā-cakora*[6] couple (never ever separate);

I witnessed new tender shoots (on trees); I heard the (sweet) voice of a *koela* (cuckoo), but the (sweet) voice of my dear friend is gone far away.

(Folio 29 Verso)

At night he (had) slept (well) turning on both sides without even covering his body, I could no longer sleep;

I realized that even his clothes in the middle part (of his body) were strewn apart; such was the state you were in, dear friend!

The friend left me with poignant pangs of separation; who will think of me (now)?

Realizing that I had lost my friend, I was naturally sad; (I also realized) that I had lost the necklace (of my heart).

(At night) the friend's locks of hair looked very dark; (but) his face beamed like pure and spotless moon;

Your lovely neck was as shapely as a conch–cell of gold; your heart was never cheerless.

Your forehead shone like a mirror, your hands were like lotuses and your two eyes were like those of a wagtail;

Ear–rings were suitably fixed on (your) shapely ears; gazing at the feet of my friend I spent the whole night until the morning dawned.

(Folio 30 Recto)

King Jagatprakāśa says about the sorrow of his self; do not rob me of my love;

Candraśeṣarasiṃha, my benefactor! You are my brother; I will do my duty and observe the rite of passage as much as I can.

Snnskrit Verse

The heat of the flaming fire of the pain of separation from you is burning me in all directions, and the pain is unbearingly acute. O Candraśeṣara! In a bid to alleviate my pain, kindly do something to offer me happiness.

(...) (...)
My friend may never forsake me, just as Lord Maheśa and Pārvatī (who never ever forsake each other);
My work will be done; I must do as much as I can; without that I will be full of sorrow.
He went away leaving his body, speech, and mind to me;

(Folio 30 Verso)

In my thoughts I am constantly with him;
O Goddess! Allow both of us to be under your two lotus–feet;
I will find my home there (i.e. under your feet).
Jagatprakāśa says: May no one's fate be as dull as mine!
Cā̃daśeṣarasiṃha, my brother! You are very brave and have a face beaming like a moon.

Sanskrit Verse

O friend! You discarded all your important duties for my sake and resolutely worked for me to give me delight. Remembering my only good friend of my liking, I am left with no desire any longer.

(...) (...)
Be it known that (our) life (lit. body) is as unsteady as a drop of water on a lotus leaf. *Refrain*

(Folio 31 Recto)

Gold palace, people, silver i.e. wealth, and everything else including every one will not remain steady;
I have come to know in my mind that one's son, friend, wealth, happiness, sorrow and body are all unsteady.
God is the master, and our body, our mind and our limbs are all subservient to God i.e. mind is the king and limbs slave;
It is through the mind that one finds around oneself merit, demerit, defamation, etc;
Jagatprakāśa pinned high hopes on you, Candraśeṣara, my brother;
May Mother–World put her feet here on both of our bodies!

Sanskrit Verse

O friend Candraśeṣara! All the worldly pleasures of wealth, home, brother, servant, etc. are as unsteady as a drop of water on a lotus–leaf. In absence of you, my body too is transitory; my fate has now made me realize it to be so.

(Folio 31 Verso)

Knowing the good virtues of Candraśeṣarasiṃha and in a bid to extol and highlight them, I have composed the Gītapañcaka containing songs in Maithili and śloka in Sanskrit.

Thus ends the description of the eighth *yāma* 'canto' of śrīgītapañcaka composed by śrīśrījaya Jagatprakāśa in sad and loving memory of Candraśeṣara.

May all be well!

Appendix 1a

Patrāṅka: Facsimile (MS. B 285/21)

Folio 1R

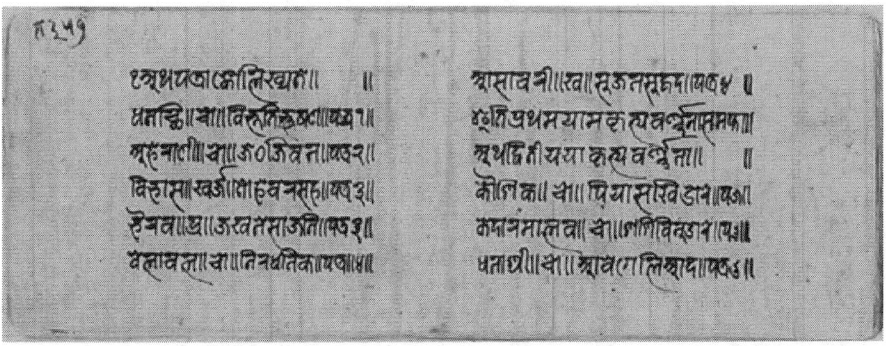

Folio 1V

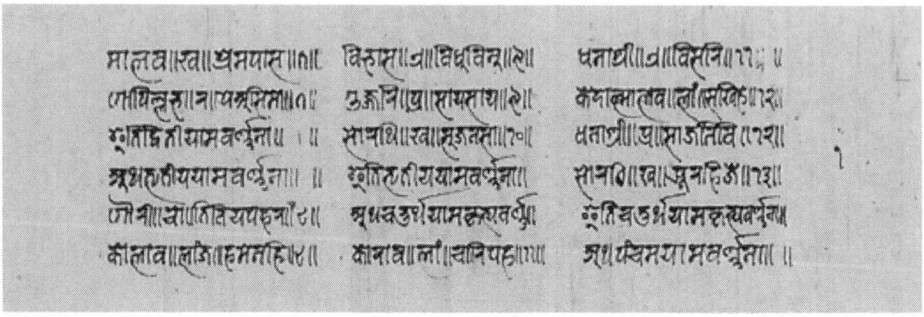

Folio 2R

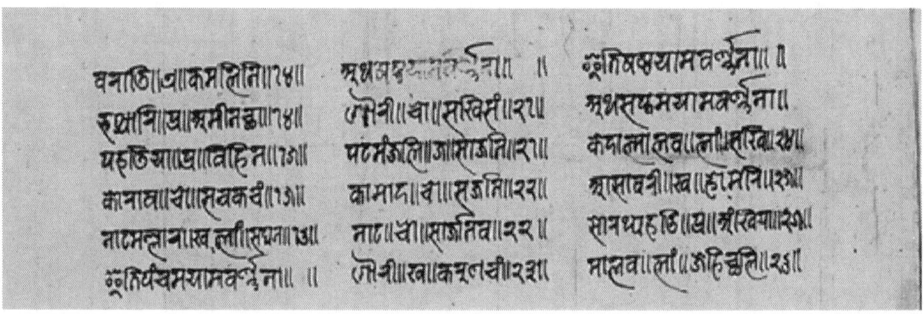

Folio 2V

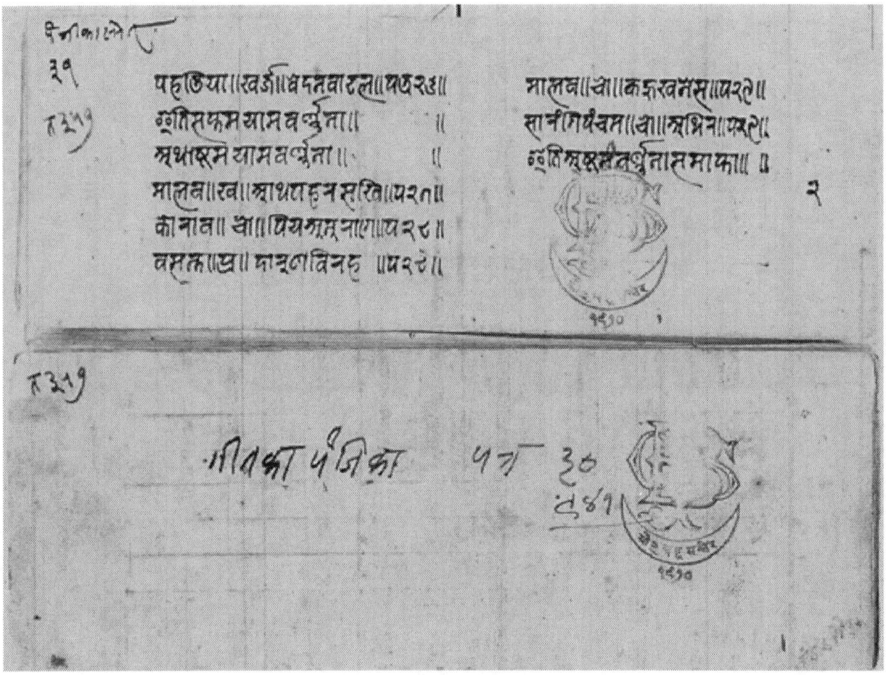

Appendix 1b

Transliteration of the *Patrāṅka*: into Devanāgarī Script

(पत्र १ अ, स्तम्भ १) अथ पत्राङ्को लिख्यते ॥ ॥
धनछि ॥ चो ॥ विभूति भूषण ॥ पत्र १ ॥
अहेराणी ॥ चो ॥ जेठ जिवन ॥ पत्र २ ॥
विभास ॥ खर्ज ॥ तोहे वर सह ॥ पत्र ३ ॥
भैरब ॥ प्र ॥ जखने साजनि ॥ पत्र ३ ॥
वेलावल ॥ चो ॥ निरधनिक ॥ पत्र ४ ॥
(स्तम्भ २) आसावरी ॥ ख ॥ सुजन सुहृद ॥ पत्र ४ ॥

इति प्रथमयामकृत्यवर्ण्णना सम(मा)प्ता ॥
अथ द्वितीयया(म)कृत्यवर्ण्णना ॥

कौशिक ॥ चो ॥ पिया सखि ओ रे ॥ प(त्र) ५ ॥
केदार मालव ॥ चो ॥ शशि विनु ओ रे ॥ प(त्र) ६ ॥
धनाश्री ॥ चो ॥ आवे गेलि आद ॥ पत्र ६ ॥
(१ प, स्तम्भ १) मालव ॥ ख ॥ प्रेम पास ॥ ७ ॥
गोपिल्लभ ॥ र ॥ पेअसि मो ॥ ७ ॥

इति द्विती(य)यामवर्ण्णना ॥ ॥
अथ तृतीययामवर्ण्णना ॥

गौरी ॥ चो ॥ तितिय पहर ॥ ८ ॥
कोलाव ॥ लांज ॥ हमे नहि ॥ ८ ॥
(स्तम्भ २) विभास ॥ ए ॥ विधु बिनु ॥ ९ ॥
गुज्जरि ॥ प्र ॥ साय साय ॥ ९ ॥
सोरथि ॥ ख ॥ सुजन स ॥ १० ॥

इति तृतीययामवर्ण्णना ॥
अथ चतुर्थयामकृत्यवर्ण्ण(ना) ॥

कोराव ॥ लां ॥ चारि पह ॥ ११ ॥
(स्तम्भ ३) धनाश्री ॥ ए ॥ विसरि ॥ ११ ॥
केदाल्मालव ॥ लां ॥ सखि हे ॥ १२ ॥
धनाश्री ॥ प्र ॥ साजनि वि ॥ १२ ॥
सोरठि ॥ ख ॥ झूरहि जे ॥ १३ ॥

इति चतुर्थयामकृत्यवर्ण्णना ॥
अथ पंचमयामवर्ण्णना ॥ ॥

(२ अ, स्तम्भ १) वराडि ॥ ए ॥ कमलिनि ॥ १४ ॥
भठ्यारि ॥ प्रं ॥ अमीन छा ॥ १४ ॥
पहडिया ॥ प्र ॥ विहिन ॥ १५ ॥

कोराव ॥ चो ॥ सेवक चं ॥ १५ ॥
नाटमल्लार ॥ ख, लां ॥ सघन ॥ १६ ॥

इति पंचमयामवर्ण्णना ॥
(स्तम्भ २) अथ षष्ठयामवर्ण्णना ॥

गौरी ॥ चो ॥ सखि सं ॥ २१ ॥
पटमंजलि ॥ ज ॥ साजनि ॥ २१ ॥
कामोद ॥ चो ॥ सजनि ॥ २२ ॥
नाट ॥ चो ॥ सार्जान व ॥ २२ ॥
गौरी ॥ ख ॥ करुण चं ॥ २३ ॥

(स्तम्भ ३) इति षष्ठयामवर्ण्णना ॥
अथ सप्तमयामवर्ण्णना ॥

केदाल्मालव ॥ लां ॥ सखिं ॥ २४ ॥
आसावरी ॥ ख ॥ हो मेरि ॥ २५ ॥
सोरथ्पहडि ॥ प्रं ॥ अंखिया ॥ २५ ॥
मालव ॥ लां ॥ जेहि छलि ॥ २६ ॥
(२ प, स्तम्भ १) पहडिया ॥ खर्जं ॥ वेदन बाढलं ॥ प २६ ॥

इति सप्तमयामवर्ण्णना ॥
अथ अथाष्टमयामवर्ण्णना ॥

मालव ॥ ख ॥ आथ पहर सखि ॥ प २७ ॥
कोराव ॥ चो ॥ पिय अनुरागे ॥ प २८ ॥
वसन्त ॥ प्र ॥ दारुण विरह ॥ प २८ ॥
(स्तम्भ २) मालव ॥ चो ॥ कहुखने स ॥ प २९ ॥
सारंगि पंचम ॥ चो ॥ अथिर ॥ प २९ ॥

इति अष्टमं(याम)वर्ण्णना समाप्ता ॥

Notes to Chapter 1

1. Ramdeo Jha (1971: 11) observes:

   nepālī vidvānaka dhyāna ehi disa viśeṣa jayabāka cāhaïta chala, kintu se bhela nahi achi.

   "The attention of scholars of Nepal ought to have been specifically drawn to it, but that does not seem to have been the case."

2. Mary Shepherd Slusser (1982: vii) describes a *maṇḍala* as given below:

   > A mandala [*maṇḍala*] is a circle, a mystic diagram of varied form, and in ancient Indian usage signified an administrative unit or country. From at least the sixth century AD., in conjunction with the word 'Nepal' it signified to the Nepalese the Kathmandu Valley and surrounding territory. (As quoted in Bell 2014: 405)

3. Mention, however, must be made of the publication of a Two–Act Sanskrit farce–play titled *Dhūrtta–Samāgamaḥ* (c.1320 CE) composed by a Maithili scholar of great repute, Kaviśekharācārya Jyotirīśvara Ṭhākura (c.1290–1350 CE), by a German scholar named Christian Lassen (Bonn: 1838) in *Anthologia Sanscritica* under the title of *Dhūrtta–Samāgamaḥ, Comoedia e Cod.Parisiensi Sanskrite cum Annotationibus Edidit*. Forty–five years later, another German scholar named Carl Cappeller also published a text–edition of this play under the title of *Dhūrtta–Samāgamaḥ*, *Herausgeben von Carl Cappeller* in Jena in 1883.

   We have also come to learn of two translations of this famous play – one in French by Ch. Schoebel and the other in Italian by Antonio

Marazzi – e.g. (i) *Dhūrtta–Samāgamaḥ, Piece d Theatre Hindou, Traduite du Sanscrit par Ch. Schoebel* (place and date of publication unknown) and (ii) *Dhortasaftiagama, Ossla il Congresso de Bricconi, Farsa di Giotirisvaro*, In: *Teatro Scelto Indiano Tradotto dal Sanscrito* da Antonio Marazzi, Vol. 2, Milan, 1874, pp. 189–321. (*Wikipedia – The Free Encyclopedia*)

4. Amazingly, as early as 1940, Suniti Kumar Chatterji – doyen of Indian linguistics – too had made a similar observation with regard to Grierson's indifference and lack of attention to Haraprasād Śāstri's search for Sanskrit and other manuscripts in Nepal and India. In his own words:

> The philologist who in a sense 'discovered' the Maithili and other Bihārī dialects, by first studying them properly and indicating their true position within the family of the Modern Indo–Aryan languages, namely, Sir George Abraham Grierson, curiously enough does not mention the MS. or the work either in his note on Maithili literature in the Linguistic Survey of India volume on the Bihārī dialects (L.S.I., V. II, 1903, pp. 17–18) or in his valuable grammar of Maithili (second edition, Asiatic Society of Bengal, 1909, pp. xiii, ff., where the L.S.I. account is repeated). It is likely that the notice of the work in Paṇḍit Haraprasāda Śāstri's Report escaped the attention of Sir George, who is truly the father of Maithili studies, and he missed examining the MS. when he was in India.
>
> Chatterji & Mishra eds. 1940: 'Introduction', xi–xii)

5. Jayakanta Mishra (1960: 'Introduction', p. 1) observes as follows:

   "This [second] trip [to Nepal in 1957] had been very successful as I found as many as 300 old Mss. in Maithili, including *a long elegy on Chanda–Shekhara the brother of Maharaja Jagatprakashamalla's wife and his chief minister and favourite man of letters* written by himself…" (Italics added)

6. D. R. Regmi (1966/2007: 221) mistakenly states as follows:

> On *Śrāvaṇa* 9 he completed *Nānāraṃgagītasaṃgraha*, otherwise known as *Gītapañcaka*.

Self–evidently, *Gītapañcaka* (c. 1662 CE) is an independent and complete collection of verse compositions of Jagatprakāśamalla. Nonetheless it is quite likely that a few of the songs contained in *Nānāraṃgagītasaṃgraha* (N.S. *Śrāvaṇa* 780/1660 CE) may also have been reincluded in the *Gītapañcaka*.

7. J. Mishra's (1977: 32, 'Footnote') observation is worth noting here:

> *rājā jagat prakāśamallaka candraśekharasiṃha abhinna mitra chalathina. bādame jagatprakāśaka vivāha candraśekharaka bahīna annapūrṇāsā̃ bhela chalani janikāsā̃ rāja mahalaka śobhā baḍhi gela chalani.*

> "Candraśekharasiṃha happened to be an intimate friend of king Jagatprakāśamalla. Later, Jagatprakāśamalla was wedded to Candraśekhara's sister Annapūrṇā by whose grace the prestige of the royal palace was enhanced."

8. Bh. Paudel (V.S. 2065/2008 CE, p. 37) speculates that the controversial and much–too–often referred to Candraśeṣarasiṃha (also *Cā̃daśeṣara* alias *Jagatacandra* or *Jagaccandra*) might be either the father–in–law or the elder brother–in–law, or that Candraśekhara might possibly have searched for a young girl (not necessarily related to him) and offered her to Jagatprakāśamalla in wedding solemnized in a *kanyādāna* ceremony performed by Candraśeṣarasiṃha:

> *yasabāṭa candraśekhara jagatprakāśa mallakā sasurā vā jeṭhāna pani huna sakchan athavā candraśekharale kunaï keṭī khoji lyāī jagatprakāśa mallalāi kanyādāna dieko pani huna sakcha.*

However, in an 'editorial' to his edition of Jagatprakāśamalla's *Nānārtha Deva Devī Gīta Saṃgraha*, Shastri (ed. V.S. 2029/1972 CE: p. '*kha*') vociferously refutes a few of the claims of Bholanath Paudel and cogently argues to assert instead that Candraśeṣarasiṃha might indeed have been *jeṭha sāra* 'the elder brother–in–law' to king Jagatprakāśamalla (as also suggested by Bholanath Paudel) implying thereby that Candraśeṣarasiṃha was indeed the elder brother to Jagatprakāśamalla's third and dearest queen Annapūrṇālakṣmī:

> *ī maïthilī kṛti sabha jaüṃ hunaka sva racita honi tathāpi preraka śaktike rūpame hunaka saṃbhavataḥ maïthili* [sic] *patnī śrīmatī annapūrṇā lakṣmī tathā hunaka jeṭhasāra śrī candra śekhara siṃhakeṃ ekara śreya chani.*
>
> *... ī suspaṣṭa achi je candra śekhara siṃha jagatprakāśamallaka prāṇābhinna maṃtrī chalāha tathā annapūrṇā lakṣmīkem jagatprakāśa mallaka hāthemṃ kanyādāna kaïnihāra seho vaïha chalāha.*
>
> *... kāraṇa je takhana jāhi tarahaka sneha dūnū goṭeka madhya parilakṣita hoicha evaṃ candraśekhara siṃha jāhi advitīya prakāraka prabhāvaśīlatā dekhaüne chathi se asvābhāvika bujhanā jāyata. ataḥ hunaka* [i.e. of Bholanath Paudel's] *dvitīya anumāna je o jeṭhasāra chalakhina tāhime hamarā pūrṇa viśvāsa achi.*
>
> "Even if these Maithili works are truly composed by the author himself, in all likelihood, all credit goes to his Maithil wife, Mrs. Annapūrṇā Lakṣmī, and to his elder brother–in–law, Candraśekharasiṃha, as potent sources of inspiration."
>
> "... It is all too clear that Candraśekharasiṃha was the most intimate Minister [of his royal court] and that Candrasekharasiṃha was indeed the very–same person who had offered Annapūrṇālakṣmī's hand to Jagatprakāśamalla in marriage solemnized through the act of a *kanyādāna*."
>
> "... The reason is: Considering the type of intimacy observed between the two of them and the rare influence that Candraśekharasiṃha is known to have exerted on Jagatprakāśamalla, it would be outrageous

> to conclude [that Candrasekharasiṃha might have been his father–in–law]. As a result, I tend to fully subscribe to his [i.e. Bholanath Paudel's] second view that Candraśekharasiṃha was indeed the elder brother–in–law of Jagatprakāśamalla."

About two decades later, refuting the above claim of Sundar Jha Shastri's, Ramdeo Jha (1990: 24; 1995: 22–23) hazarded an altogether different conjecture suggesting that Candraśeṣarasiṃha, allegedly a son to Jagajjyotirmalla's second son Śaśiśeṣarasiṃha, might have been instead the elder cousin brother (and naturally therefore neither the father–in–law nor the elder brother–in–law) to Jagatprakāśamalla. Ramdeo Jha's claim may hold water in view of the fact that at the very outset of *Gītapañcaka* in a Sanskrit *śloka* Jagatprakāśamalla addresses Candraśeṣarasiṃha as *mamāgrayo* and *mamāgrajo* 'my elder brother' (Folio 2 R: 5) and in a number of Maithili songs as *bhāi*, *bhāyi*, *bhaiyā* 'brother'.

The controversy wages on unabated and continues to remain unresolved as of now in absence of unequivocal and indisputable historical evidence with regard to Candraśeṣarasiṃha's ancestral lineage.

9. D. R. Regmi (1966/2007: 222) states as follows:

> … All these references to Chandraśekharasiṃha couched in terms expressing high regard and love for the man show him to be quite powerful in the kingdom. But we have yet to know more of him to be able to say definitely what he really did for his king and country. There is a suggestion from a passage in the above noted inscription of 787 [1667 CE] that Jagatprakāśa obtained his wife Annapūrṇālakṣmī through the efforts of Chandraśekharasiṃha.

As quoted in J. Mishra (ed. 1977: 32), a song of Jagatprakāśamalla's carved in N.S. 787/1667 C.E. on a stone tablet attached onto the southern side of the temple of Bhavānīśaṃkara situated in the Khaümāṭola near the Bhaktapur Royal Palace contains the following lines which clearly attest to Candraśeṣarasiṃha's pivotal role in arranging Jagatprakāśamalla's wedding with Annapūrṇālakṣmī:

jehi mori jivatula, candraśeṣarasiṃha,
sehi deli yahi dhanivāri.
jagata prakāśa bhūpa pāvola gharinivara,
annapuranā nāma nāri.

"Candraśeṣarasiṃha, who was equal to my life,
He offered me the great lady;
King Jagatprakāśa received the best wife,
A woman named Annapūrṇā."

Yogesh Raj (*Personal communication*, *Email* dated the March 3, 2015) has very kindly provided me with some extremely valuable information on Candraśeṣarasiṃha (and Jagatprakāśamalla), which is quoted verbatim within inverted commas below:

"1. NGMPP [Nepal German Manuscripts Preservation Project] Microfilm Number B 275. *नलीय नाटक* (Copy dated NS 780 Śrāvana vadi 2) has the following verse:

जगतप्रकाश भन चाँदशेखर धन भुगुति मुगुति देवि सारे
जगतजननि करु साधक अभिमत अपार करुणा सिंधु पारे (Folio 1b)

2. NGMPP Microfilm Number K 388/27. A list of ornaments donated to Taleju in Bhaktapur has a gold necklace with an inscription, which the guthi official in charge of listing made the following:

श्रीजगतप्रकासमल्ल श्रीचंद्रसेषरसीं राजाले सुनका सीकीमा उनेको सुनका मोहोर सुका ५१
छाप लागेको पातलो लाता (?) २ लाचकी (?) ७ नाउ लेखेको श्रीको ती (?) १ को माला १

3. A folded book, which describes an annual cycle of various Thaapujaa in Taleju, has the following entry:

भाद शुदि १५ चन्द्रसेखर उपाध्याय:

The text of the folded book has been published by Purushottam Lochana Shrestha as an essay in the journal *Rolamba, Millenium Issue*, published by Joshi Research Institute, Patan, with the title श्री ३ तलेजुस्के थापुजाया वाक्य: एक अप्रकाशित ठ्यासफू.

4. Janaklal Vaidya in his book नेपालभाषाया प्राचीन काव्य सिर्जना published by Nepal Academy in NS 1122 gives the following two songs on the relationships between the two:

(a) तवछ्रोत रास जेत दुख जार, तालेतर किंजाया शरीर ।
नेपालया संवाछ्रल न्हशर चये नश, मिथुन संक्रान्तिकुन्हु वीर ॥

(b) अपमान जगतस किंजान वाङान ॥धु॥
विपतिस याङा गुण नुगरस दाङ, जे मनस ओस तवधाङ
जे कारणस ओन जीन बिसे वङ, मुख सोसे जे दुख ताङ
सुथा बरन्हि न्हिस ओस नमवाक, रणस वीर जुसे ल्वाक
तलेजुस सेवा ओम्ह किंजा लाय, ताकार मते रे जे व फाय
परकास मल्लया देवि जुको ध्यान, चन्द्रशेखर बियान ॥

5. In a courtyard, called Bekvacuka: courtyard inside Bhaktapur Taleju complex, stand two life–size statues of Jagatprakash and Candrasekhar. These statues now adorn the south–opening door of the Bhairav courtyard, where Malla royalties breathed their last. The statues do not have inscriptions. But a stone inscription in another courtyard called Ganesh Cuka mentions the erection of these statues. It is possible that either the pair of statues or the inscriptions have been removed from the original location. The inscription consists of Maithili and Newari songs."

I have also come across a *bhaṇitā* 'author tag' attached at the end of a song in Jagatprakāśamalla's play entitled *Madana Caritra* that states as follows:

annapurana pati jagataprakāśa nṛpa
bhala kaya udhāraha mohi.

"May king Jagatprakāśa – husband to Annapūrṇā – do
me favors and offer redemption!"

10. The following utterance in Jagatprakāśamalla's play entitled *Prabhāvatīharaṇa* (L. Mishra ed. 1972: 3) confirms that Jagatprakāśamalla was indeed Nareśamalla's son, (and not of Jagajjyotirmalla as was erroneously claimed by S. B. Gyawali V.S. 2019/1962 CE: 105):

śrī śrī nareśamalla devaka hṛdayānandana

A *bhaṇitā* 'author tag' of Song # 34 in *Nānārtha Deva Devī Gīta Saṃgraha* (Shastri ed. V.S. 2029/1972 CE: 9) also attests to the fact that Jagatprakāśamalla was indeed the son of king Nareśamalla:

> *nareśa nṛpati suta prakāśa malla bhūpa i rasa kaütuka bhāna*
> *devi sevā binu kichu nahi pābia mora mana ehi paya jāna*

11. To quote Bholanatha Paudel (V. S. 2065/2008 CE: 28):

> *vi. saṃ.* १७२९ *mārga* २९ *gate rājā jagatprakāśa malla* ३४ *varṣako caḍhdo umeramā āphnā kalilā dui chorā choḍī, vipharako rogale svarge bhae.*

> "On 29 Mārga V.S. 1729, king Jagatprakāśamalla died [lit: left for the heavenly abode] from the effects of the disease of smallpox leaving behind his two young sons of tender age [namely, Jitāmitramalla and Ugramalla]."

12. A line in Jagatprakāśamalla's drama *Prabhāvatīharaṇa* (L. Mishra ed.1972: 3) provides the names of Jagatprakāśamalla's two previous queens as given below:

> *caṃdrāvati pahu padumāvatidayi kanta*

13. The actual number of plays written by Jagatprakāśamalla may exceed to 12, or even more, upon further exploration and research (R. Jha 1990: 48).
14. According to the *Viṣṇu Purāṇa*, the *aṣta vasu* 'eight saints/excellent ones' are: 1 *Āpa* 'Water' 2 *Dhruva* 'the Pole star' 3 *Soma* 'the Moon' 4 *Dhava/Dhara* 5 *Anila* 'Wind' 6 *Anala/Pāvaka* 'Fire' 7 *Pratyūśa* 'the Dawn' 8 *Prabhāsa* 'Light' (cf. Monier–Williams 1899/1999: 930).
15. For more information on an experimental phonetic study of Maithili phonetics in general and on [*a*] → [ə] sound change in Maithili in particular, the reader is referred to Yadav (1984a, b, c. 1996, 2013).
16. Mishra (1949: 77) translates the expression *chandaparaka* as "metrical verses fit to be recited rather than to be sung."

Notes to Chapter 5

1. George Abraham Grierson (1882: 165) defines *cakora* as "the mountain partridge, *Perdix rufa. Said to be enamoured of the moon: also to have a graceful gait and beautiful eyes, to each of which, either of these of a woman is often compared: hence used to signify* a beloved woman."

   An earlier account of William J. Kirkpatrick's (2007: 131) [1811] presents a rather hilarious description of a *cakora* (*chuckoar*) as such;

   > The Chuckoar is well known to the Europeans in India by the name of the Fire–eater; it is a species of partridge, and it derives its latter name from its reputed power of swallowing fire: the fact, according to the people of Nepaul, is, that in the season of love this bird is remarkably fond of red or chean–pepper; after eating two or three capsules of which, it will bite at a red–hot coal if offered to it.

2. Sir M. Monier–Williams' (1889/1999) *A Sanskrit–English Dictionary (Etymologically and Philologically Arranged with Special Reference to Cognate Indo–European Languages)* defines *kurara* as 'an osprey' and *kurari* as 'a flight of ospreys.' (p. 203)

   Govind Jha (*Personal communication, email*, 19 April 2015, 8: 33 pm) too describes *kurarī* as a bird of the category of a *papīhā* ("*kurarī eka pakṣī thika papīhā jātika*").

3. Sir M. Monier–Williams' (1889/1999) dictionary describes *Kaüstubha* as "a celebrated jewel (obtained with thirteen other

precious things at the churning of the ocean and suspended on the breast of Krishṇa or Vishṇu.") p. 318

4. Grierson (1882: 152) defines *koela/koili* as "the Indian cuckoo. *The song of the bird is supposed to be an incitement to love.*"

5. Sir Monier–Williams's (1889/1999) *A Sanskrit–English Dictionary* defines *cātaka* as "the bird *Cucculus melanolencus* (said to subsist on rain–drops)". p. 392

   Similarly, Vaudeville (1986: 126) defines *chātaka* <*cātaka*>, a water–bird, as follows:

   > ... According to popular belief, the Chātak bird is endlessly pining for the rain drop of Svāti, the tenth *nakshatra*, and will not drink any other water. His call is interpreted as "*piu kahāṃ*" "Where is my beloved?"...

6. Vaudeville (1986: 125) defines *cakavā* (*cakravāka*) as follows:

   > The Chakvā is a water–bird (the ruddy goose). According to popular belief, the Chakvā and its female, the Chakavī, are unable to meet as long as the night lasts and they suffer from the pain of separation (*viraha*). Therefore, the Chakvī, as a *virahini*, piteously moans throughout the night.

Bibliography

Allen, W. Sidney 1953 *Phonetics in Ancient India (A Guide to the Appreciation of the Earliest Phoneticians)*, London: Oxford University Press. London Oriental Series: Volume 1.

Bagchi, Prabodh Chandra 1938 "Materials for a critical edition of the Old Bengali *Caryāpadas*," *Journal of the Department of Letters* (Calcutta University Press): XXX, 1–156.

________1940 *Kuñjavihāra–nāṭaka* (of Jagajjyotirmalla), *Paricaya* (Calcutta University Bengali Monthly Journal).

________ & Śānti Bhikṣu Śāstrī (eds. 1956) *Caryāgītikoṣa of Buddhist Siddhas*, Santiniketan: Visva–Bharati.

Bandopadhyaya, Nanigopala (ed. Baṅgābda 1324/1917 CE) *Nepāler Bāṅgālā Nāṭaka*, Calcutta: Baṅgīya Sāhitya Pariṣada Mandira.

Basu, Dwijendra Nath 1976 *Functional Analysis of Old Bengali Structures*, Calcutta: Basudha.

Bell, Thomas 2014 *Kathmandu*, Gurgaon–Haryana: Random House India.

Bhattarai, Govinda Prasada (ed. & trns. V.S. 2032/1975 CE) *Rāmāṅka–Nāṭikā*, Kathmandu: Royal Nepal Academy. In Nepali

Brinkhaus, Horst. 1987a *Pradyumnavijayanāṭaka* (of Jagatprakāśamalla), In: *The Pradyumna–Prabhāvatī Legend in Nepal*, Stuttgart: Franz Steiner, Wiesbaden, "Appendix 1", 161–345.

________ (ed. 1987b) *Jagatprakāśamalla's Mūladevaśaśidevavyākhyāna–nāṭaka: Das Aelteste Bekannte Vollstaendig Ueberlieferte Newari–Drama*, Stuttgart: Franz Steiner, Wiesbaden.

Cappeller, Carl 1883 *Dhūrtta–Samāgamaḥ: Herausgeben von Carl Cappeller*, Jena.

Chatterji, Suniti Kunar. 1926 *The Origin and Development of the Bengali Language*, Calcutta.

________ & Babua Misra (eds. 1940) *Varṇa–Ratnākara of Jyotirīśvara–Kaviśekharācārya Edited with English and Maithili Introductions and Index Verborum*, Calcutta: Royal Asiatic Society of Bengal.

Chaudhary, Radhakrishna 1976 *Mithilā in the Age of Vidyāpati*, Varanasi: Chaukhamba.

Conrady, August (ed. 1891) *Das Hariçcandranṛityaṃ: Ein Altnepalesische Tanzspiel,* Leipzig: Druk von G. Kreysing.

Dalal, O. D. 1956 *Nemināthа–Phāgu*, In: *Gurjārarāsāvali*, G. O. S. CXIII, Baroda. [Second Edition]

Datta, Bijitakumara (ed. 1980) *Prācīna Bāṅgālā–Maïthilī Nāṭaka*, Burdhman: Viśvavidyālaya.

Devī, Kāmeśvarī (ed. 1999) *Saṃskāra–Gīta*, Navānī–Madhuvanī: Mohanabhavanam.

Grierson, George Abraham 1881 *An Introduction to the Maithilī Language of North Bihār, Part I, Grammar,* Calcutta: Asiatic Society of Bengal. [Second Edition 1909]

________ 1882a An *Introduction to the Maithilī Language of North Bihār: Part II, Chrestomathy and Vocabulary,* Calcutta: Asiatic Society of Bengal.

________ 1882b "Man'bodh's Haribans," *Journal of the Asiatic Society of Bengal*: 51, Part 1, Number 1, 129–150.

________ 1884a "Translation to Man'bodh's Haribans," *Journal of the Asiatic Society of Bengal* 53, Part 1 (Special Number as Substitute for Numbers III and IV), 1884, 1–36.

________ 1884 b "Some Bihārī Folk–Songs," *Journal of the Royal Asiatic Society of Great Britain and Ireland*, New Series, Vol. 16. No. 2, 196–246.

________ 1885 "Selected specimens of the Bihārī language, Part 1, The Maithili dialect, *The Gīta Dinā Bhadrik and the Gīta Nebārak,*" *Zeitschrift der Deustchen Morgenlaendischen Gesellschaft* (Leipzig, Germany) 39: 1, 617–673.

________ 1886 "Some Bhoj'pūrī Folk–Songs," *Journal of the Royal Asiatic Society of Great Britain and Ireland*, New Series, Vol. 18, No. 2 (Apr., 1886), 207–267.

________ 1917 "The *Pārijāta–Haraṇa* of Umāpati Upādhyāya," *The Journal of the Bihar and Orissa Research Society* 3: 1, 20–98.

________ 1935 *The Test of a Man: Being the Purusha–Parīkshā of Vidyāpati Ṭhakkura*, London: The Royal Asiatic Society.

Gupta, M.P. and A. Nahta (eds. 1953) *Bisaldev Rās*, Allahabad.

Gupta, Nagendranath (ed. 1909) *Vidyāpati Ṭhākurer Padāvalī*, Calcutta. In Bangla

Gyawali, S. B. V.S. 2019/1962 CE *Nepāla Upatyakāko Madhyakālīna Itihāsa*, Kathmandu: Royal Nepal Academy. In Nepali

Henry, Edward O. 1988 *Chant the Names of God*: *Musical Culture in Bhojpuri-Speaking India*, San Diego: San Diego State University Press.

________ 1998 "Maithil women's song: Distinctive and endangered species," *Ethnomusicology*, Vol. 42, No. 3, 115–140.

Ingemann, Frances & Ramawatar Yadav 1977 "Voiced aspirated consonants," In: Lance, D. M. & D. E. Gulstad (eds. 1978) *Papers from the 1977 Mid–America Linguistics Conference*, Columbia: University of Missouri (USA), pp. 337–344.

Jalil, Rakhshanda 2012 "Pity the pretty poem," *The Friday Times* (Pakistan): Vol. XXIV, No. 29, pp. 1–5.

Jha, Amar Nath (ed. 2008) *Vidyāpati Gīta–Ratnākara*, Kolkata: Viśva Maïthilīyam.

Jha, Dinabandhu Sāla 1353/1946 CE *Mithilā–Bhāṣā–Vidyotana*, Daḍibhaṅgā: Maïthilī Sāhitya Pariṣada.

________ Śāke 1872/1950 CE *Mithilā Bhāṣā Koṣa*, Isahapur: Dinabandhu Jha.

Jha, Govind 1968 *Maïthilīka Udgama O Vikāsa*, Calcutta: Maïthilī Prakāśana Samiti.

________ 1974 *Maïthilī Bhāṣā Kā Vikāsa*, Patna: Bihāra Hindī Graṃtha Akādamī.

________ 1979 *Uccatara Maïthilī Vyākaraṇa*, Patna: Maithili Academy.

________ 1981 *Vidyāpati Gītāvalī*, Patna: Maithili Academy.

________ (ed. 1999) *A Maithili–English Dictionary*, Darbhanga: Maharajadhiraja Kameshwar Singh Kalyani Foundation.

________ 2005 "Hariścandranṛtyaka bhāṣā," In: Govind Jha (2005) *Atītāloka*, Patna: Akhiyāsala Prakāśana, 91–102.

________ 2007 *Maïthilī–Pariśīlana*, Patna: Maithili Academy.

________ 2010 *Anucintana*, Patna: Navārambha.

________ 2011 *Bhāṣāśāstra–Praveśikā*, Patna: Dīnabandhu Prakāśana.

________ (ed. 2012) *Vidyāpati–Gīta–Samagra*, Mysore: Central Institute of Indian Languages.

Jha, Hetukar (ed. 2007) *India: Some Crucial Questions*, Maharajadhiraja Kameshwar Singh Memorial Lecture Series – 2, pp. 179–200.

Jha, Hetukar & Vedanatha Jha (eds. 2009) *Maithili Chrestomathy and Vocabulary by George A. Grierson*, Darbhanga: Maharajadhiraj Kameshwar Singh Kalyani Foundation, Kameshwar Singh Bihar Heritage Series – 13.

Jha, Ramdeo (ed. 1970) *Jagajjyotirmalla Kṛta Haragaürīvivāha Nāṭaka*, Laheriasarai, Darbhanga: Mithilā Research Society.

________ V.S. 2028/1971 CE "Nepālīya śilālekhame utkīrṇa maïthilī gīta," *Maïthilī* (Journal of Maïthili Sāhitya Pariṣada, Biratnagar): 4, 9–37.

________ 1976 *Kuñjavihāra–nāṭaka*, In: *Manīṣā* (Kāmeśvarasiṃha Darbhanga Sanskrit University Journal).

________ 1988 *Jagajjyotirmallakṛta Daśāvatāranṛtyam O Ṣoḍaśagītam*, Laheriasarai–Darbhanga: Mithilā Research Society

________ 1990 *Jagatprakāśamalla*, New Delhi: Sahitya Akademi.

________ 1995 *Jagajjyotirmalla*, New Delhi: Sahitya Akademi.

________ (ed. 2013) *Jagajjyotirmalla Kṛta Muditakuvalayāśva Nāṭaka*, New Delhi: Sahitya Akademi.

Jha, Ratneshwar V.S. 2037/1980 CE *Nepāla Rāṣṭrīya Abhilekhālayamā Bhayekā Maïthilī Pustaka tathā Lekhaharūko Vivaraṇātmaka Sūci ra Viśleṣaṇa*, A Mini–Research Report Submitted to the Tribhuvan University Institute of Humanities and Social Sciences, Kirtipur, Kathmandu, Nepal, pp. 106. MS. In Nepali

Jha, Shailendra Mohan 1969 *Siddhi Narasiṃha Malla*, Lālabāga–Darbhanga: Pustaka Kendra.

Jha, Subhadra (ed. 1954) *Vidyāpati Gīta Saṃgraha or The Songs of Vidyāpati*, Banaras: Motilal Banarsidass.

________ 1958 *The Formation of the Maithilī Language*, London: Luzac.

Jośī, Satyamohana & Hemarāja Śākya (eds. N.S. 1090/1970 CE) *Juju Bhūpatīndramallajuyā Vikrama Carita*, Kathmandu: Cvasā Publication # 45.

Kasā, Premabahādura (ed. N.S. 1084/1964 CE) *Juju Jayaprakāśayā Ratneśvara Prādurbhāva*, Ombahāla, Yaṃ (Kathmandu): Cvasāpāsā # 27.

Kāyastha, Chatrabahādura (ed. N.S. 1103/1983 CE) *Kṛṣṇacaritra* (of Raṇajitmalla), Patan: Sāhityayā Mūlukhā.

Kirkpatrick, William J. 2007 [1811] *An Account of the Kingdom of Nepaul*, New Delhi: Rupa Publications India Pvt. Ltd.

Kitada, Makoto 2012 "*Cacā* songs: The oral tradition in Kathmandu," In: Nagasaki (ed. 2012), pp. 103–228.

________ 2012 'Middle Bengali Metres," In: Nagasaki (ed. 2012), pp. 329–342.

________ 2014 "Manuscript of a Maithili play preserved in the Kathmandu Valley: *Madālasāharaṇa–nāṭaka,* Part 1," *Indomizokukenkyu* (*Indian Folk Culture Research*): 13, 65–84, Osaka University Knowledge Archive: Osaka university. In Japanese

________ 2015 "Jagajjyotirmalla's play *Madālasāharaṇa–nāṭaka,* Part 2 (Latter half)," *Indomizokukenkyu* (*Indian Folk Culture Research*): 14, 45–84, Osaka University Knowledge Archive: Osaka University. In Japanese

Kværne, Per 2010 [1977] *An Anthology of Buddhist Tantric Songs: A Study of the Caryāgīti*, Bangkok–Thailand: Orchid Press. [Earlier published by Der Norske Videnskaps–Akademi in Oslo–Bergen–Tromsø in 1977]

Lassen, Christian (ed. 1838) *Dhūrtta–Samāgamaḥ, Comoedia e Cod.Parisiensi Sanskrite cun Annotationibus Edidit*, In: *Anthologia Sanscritica*, Bonn.

Lienhard, Siegfried (ed.1992) [1974] *Songs of Nepal: An Anthology of Nevar Folksongs and Hymns*, Delhi: Motilal Banarsidass.

Malangiya, Mahendra 2004 "Pratināyaka Cūhaḍa Mallaka mūlyāṃkana," *Ghara–Bāhara* (Journal of the Cetanā Samiti, Patna, India) 1: 3–4, 54–58.

_______ 2015 *Śabdaka Jaṃgalame Arthaka Khoja*, New Delhi: Malaṃgiya Arts.

Malla, Kamal P. 1981 *Classical Newari Literature*, Kathmandu: Nepal Research Centre. Mimeograph

Marazzi, Antonio 1874 *Dhortasaftiagama, Ossla il Congresso de Bricconi, Farsa di Giotirisvaro*, In: *Teatro Scelto Indiano Tradotto dal Sanscrito* da Antonio Marazzi, Milan, Vol. 2, 189–321.

Masica, Colin P. 1976 *Defining a Linguistic Area: South Asia*, Chicago and London: The University of Chicago Press.

Maüna, Praphulla Kumar V.S. 2028/1971a CE "Nepālaka maïthilī sāhityaka itihāsa," *Maïthilī* (Journal of Maïthilī Sāhitya Pariṣada, Biratnagar): 6, 1– 99.

_______ V.S. 2028/1971b CE "Sampādakīya: Śilotkīrṇa maïthilī gītāñjalī," *Maïthilī* (Journal of Maïthilī Sāhitya Pariṣada, Biratnagar) Sāhitya Saṃkalana: 4, 1–8.

Mishra, Jaimant (ed. 1977) *Maïthilī Abhilekha Gītamālā*, Patna: Maithili Academy.

_______ 1978 *Maïthilī Nāṭakapara Saṃskṛtaka Prabhāva*, Patna: Maithili Academy.

Mishra, Jayakanta 1949 *A History of Maithili Literature–1*, Allahabad: Tirabhukti Publications.

_______ (ed. 1368 Sāla/1960 CE) *Maïthilī–Dhūrttasamāgama* (of Jyotirīśvara), Allahabad: Akhila Bhāratīya Maïthilī Sāhitya Samiti.

_______ (ed. 1965) *Vidyāvilāpa: Nepālīya Maïthilī Nāṭaka*, Allahabad: Akhila Bhāratīya Maïthilī Sāhitya Samiti.

Mishra, Lekhnath. (ed. 1972) *Prabhāvatīharaṇa Nāṭaka*, Paunā–Arerāhāṭa–Darbhanga: Lekhnath Mishra.

_______ & Bhaktishwar Jha (eds. 2010) *Jagajjyotirmalla Padāvalī*, Patna University, Patna: Maithili Development Fund.

Mishra, Mithilesh Kumari and Govind Jha 2012 *Vidyāpati–Śabdakośa (Avahaṭṭa–Khaṇḍa)*, Patna: Bihar–Raṣṭrabhāṣā–Pariṣada.

Mishra, Tarakant 2008 *Maïthilī Loka Sāhitya Kā Adhyayana*, New Delhi: National Publishing House. In Hindi

Mishra, Taranand V.S. 2062/2005 CE "Nepāla upatyakāka maïthilī hastalikhita granthaka viśeṣatā," *Āṃgana* (A Maithili journal of the Royal Nepal Academy): 1, 53–59.

_______ V.S. 2072/2015 CE "Cikitsāśāstra, Simaraünagaḍhakā vaïdya Śrīcakradatta ra devapāṭanakā malla rājavaïdyamājha aṃtaḥsambandha," *Abhilekha* (Journal of the National Archives, Kathmandu) 33: 33, 44–55. In Nepali

Mishra, Umesh and Jayakanta Mishra (eds. 1961) *Gorakṣavijaya–nāṭaka* (Containing a facsimile of the 24–page Manuscript in Tirhutā), Allahabad: Akhila Bhāratīya Maïthilī Sāhitya Samiti.

Mishra, Vishweshwar (ed. 2014) *Vidyāpati–Gītāvalī*, Sarisaba–Pāhī–Madhubanī: Sāhityikī.

Monier–Williams, M. 1999 [1899] *A Sanskrit–English Dictionary (Etymologically and Philologically Arranged with Special Reference to Cognate Indo–European Languages)*, Delhi: Motilal Banarsidass.

Mukherji, Amulyadhan 1976 *Sanskrit Prosody: Its Evolution*, Calcutta: Saraswat Library.

Mukherji, Tarapada 1963. *The Old Bengali Language and Text*, Calcutta: University of Calcutta.

________ (ed. 1970) *Gopīcandra Nāṭaka,* The Cambridge Manuscript of a 17th Century Bengali Play from Nepal, Calcutta.

Nagasaki, Hiroko (ed. 2012) *Indian and Persian Prosody and Recitation*, Delhi: Saujanya Publications.

Nepāla, Jñānamaṇi (ed. V.S. 2040/1983 CE) *Jayataracita Mahīrāvaṇavadha Nāṭaka: Vivecanātmaka Adhyayana*, Kathmandu: Tribhuvan University Research Centre for Nepal and Asian Studies (CNAS). In Nepali

________ (ed. V.S. 2057/2000 CE) *Kavimaṇikaracitam Bhaïravānandanāṭakam*, Belḍāṃgī, Dāṃga: Mahendra Sanskrit University. In Nepali

________ V.S. 2062/2005 CE *Nepālako Mādhyamika Kālako Itihāsa*, Kathmandu: Makālu Prakāśana Gṛha. In Nepali

Niwa, Kyoko 2012 "Samples of Bengali Metre," In: Nagasaki, (ed. 2012), 343–369.

Orsini, Francesca 2010 "Barahmasa in Hindi and Urdu," In: Orsini, Francesca (ed. 2010), *Before the Divide: Hindi and Urdu Literary Culture*, New Delhi: Orient BlackSwan. pp. 142–177.

Paudel, Bholanath V.S. 2065/2008 CE "Jagatprakāśa Malla," In: *Bhaktapurako Rājakulo,* Kathmandu: Āgama Prakāśana, 20–28. [Originally published in *Pūrṇimā*: 6 (Vol. 2, No. 2), V.S. 2022/1965 CE, 29–37.] In Nepali

________ V.S. 2065/2008 CE "Jagaccandra," In: *Bhaktapurako Rājakulo,* Kathmandu: Āgama Prakāśana, pp. 37–43. [Originally published in *Pūrṇimā*: 8 (Vol. 2, No. 4), V.S. 2023/1966 CE, 20–25.] In Nepali

'Rākeśa', Rāmaiqbālasiṃha (ed. V.S. 1999/1942 CE) *Maïthilī Lokagīta*, Prayāga: Hindī Sāhitya Sammelana. [Second Edition, V.S. 2012/1955 CE] In Hindi

Rakesh, Ram Dayal V.S. 2056/1999 CE *Maïthilī* [sic] *Saṃskṛti*, Kathmandu: Royal Nepal Academy. In Nepali

'Ramaṇa', Ramanand Jha (ed. 2014) *Maïthilī Lokasāhitya evaṃ Lokasaṃskṛti*, Patna: Cetanā Samiti.

Regmi, D. R. 2007 [1966] *Medieval Nepal–2*, New Delhi: Rupa & Co.

Schoebel, Ch. *Dhūrtta–Samāgamaḥ, Piece de Theatre Hindou, Traduite du Sanscrit* par Ch. Schebel. Place and year of publication unknown

Sen, Nilratan 1973 *Early Eastern New Indo–Aryan Versification: A Prosodic Study of Caryāgītikoṣa*, Simla: Indian Institute of Advanced Study.

________ (ed. 1977) *Caryāgītikoṣa: Facsimile Edition*, Simla: Indian Institute of Advanced Study.

Shāstrī, Mahāmahopādhyāya Haraprasād 1911 *Report on the Search for Sanskrit Manuscripts (1906–1907 to 1910–1911)*, Calcutta: Asiatic Society of Bengal.

________ 1916 *Hājār Bacharer Purāṇa Bāṅgālā Bhāṣāy Bauddha Gāna O Dohā*, Calcutta: Baṅgīya Sāhitya Pariṣat. In Bangla

Shastri, Sundar Jha (ed. V.S. 2029/1972 CE) "Śrī Jaya Jagatprakāśa Malla Kṛta *Nānārtha Deva Devī Gīta Saṃgraha*," *Phūla-Pāta* (A Maithili Journal, Kathmandu: Vijayā Daśamī Viśeṣāṃka) 4: 8, viii + 38.

Singh, Shrutidhari 2013 *History and Order in Mithila: Reflections on Continuity and Change over the Last Millennium*, Darbhanga: The Mithila Institute of Post–Graduate Studies and Research in Sanskrit Learning.

Situ – a Newari Journal in Kathmandu – N.S. 1091/1971 CE, Jayaprakāśamalla's *Vīradhvajopākhyāna* (only a fragment published).

Slusser, Mary Shepherd 1982 *Nepala Mandala: A Cultural Study of the Kathmandu Valley*, 2 Vols. Princeton. [Mandala Book Point Edition, Kathmandu, 1998]

Smith, W. L. (ed. 2003) *Maithili Studies: Papers Presented at the Stockholm Conference on Maithili Lamguage and Literature*, Stockholm: Department of Indology, University of Stockholm.

Snell, Rupert 1983 "Metrical forms in Braj Bhāṣā verse: The *Chaurāsī Pada* in performance," In: Thiel–Horstmann (ed. 1983), pp. 353–383.

________ 1991/2006 *The Hindi Classical Tradition: A Braj Bhāṣā Reader,* London and New York: Routledge.

Śreṣṭha, Rājitabahādura (ed. N.S. 1124/2004 CE) *Kāśīvijaya*, Nhū Hisu Pucaḥ: Tāpāhiti, Yala (Patan), Nepal.

'Śrīśa', Durganatha Jha 1983 [1968] *Maïthilī Sāhityaka Itihāsa*, Darbhanga: Bhāratī Pustaka Kendra.

________ (ed. Śāke 1896/1974 CE) *Nṛpatijagajjyotirmalla–Kṛta Gīta–Pañcāśikā,* Kaṭaharabāḍī–Darbhanga: Cetanātha Jhā.

Stump, Gregory T. & Ramawatar Yadav 1988 "Maithili verb agreement and the Control Agreement Principle," In: *Chicago Linguistic Society Parasession on Agreement in Grammatical Theory* 24: 2, 304–321.

'Sumana', Surendra Jha & Ramdeo Jha (eds. 1977) *Maïthilī Prācīna Gītāvalī*, Patna: Maithili Academy.

Thakur, Shivanandana (ed. 1941) *Mahākavi Vidyāpati*, Laherasarai: Pustaka Bhandāra. In Hindi [A Maithili version published in Vidyapati Thakur 1979]

Thakur, Upendra 1956 *History of Mithilā (From the earliest times to 1556 A.D.)*, Darbhanga: Mithila Institute. [Second Revised & Enlarged Edition, 1988]

Thakur, Vidyapati (ed. & trns. 1979) *Mahākavi Vidyāpati* (*Revised Maithili Edition*), Patna: Maithili Academy.

Thiel–Horstmann, Monika (ed. 1983) *Bhakti in Current Research, 1972–1982*, Berlin: Dietrichner.

Vajrācārya, Śāntaharṣa (ed. N.S. 1103/1983 CE) *Kṛṣṇacaritra* (of Raṇajitmalla) Kathmandu: Bimalā Vajrācārya.

________ (ed. N.S. 1103/1983CE) *Madanacaritra* (of Raṇajitmalla), Kathmandu: Bimalā Vajrācārya.

Varma, Satyajivan (ed. V.S. 1982/1925 CE) *Bisaldev–rās*, Banaras: Nāgarī Pracāriṇī Samiti.

Varma, Siddheshwar 1961 *Critical Studies in the Phonetic Observations of Indian Grammarians*, Delhi: Munshi Ram Manohar Lal. [Originally published in 1929 by Royal Asiatic Society, London]

Vaudeville, Charlotte 1986 *Bārahmāsā in Indian Literatures: Songs of the Twelve Months in Indo–Aryan Literatures*, Delhi: Motilal Banarsidass.

WWW.exoticindiaart.com 2009 "Barahmasa: Songs of Twelve Months," *Exotic India Newsletter,* Article of the Month – September, 2009.

Yadav, Ramawatar 1979a "The influence of aspiration on vowel duration in Maithili," *South Asian Languages Analysis* (Urbana–Champaign, USA): 1, 157–165.

________ 1979b **Maithili Phonetics and Phonology**, Doctoral Dissertation Submitted to the University of Kansas, Lawrence, USA.

________ 1981 "Maithili language and linguistics: Some background notes." *Kailash – A Journal of Himalayan Studies* 8:1, 71-87.

________ 1982 "Acoustic characteristics of vowel nasalization in Maithili," *Indian Linguistics:* 43: 1–2, 1–8.

________ 1984a "Voicing and Aspiration in Maithili: A fiberoptic and acoustic study," *Indian Linguistics* 45: 1–4, 1–30.

________ 1984b "Maithili phonology reconsidered," *Studien zur Indologie und Iranistik* (Germany): 10, 155–168.

________ 1984c *Maithili Phonetics and Phonology*, Mainz (Germany): Selden und Tamm.

________ 1985 "Causativization in Maithili: A preliminary enquiry," *SAIS Arbeitsberichte (aus dem Seminar für Allgemeine und Indogermanische Sprachwissenschaft)*: 8, Kiel (Germany): Christian–Albrechts–Universitaet, 201–221.

________ 1986 "Acoustic correlates of word stress in Maithili," In: Bh. Krishnamurti *et al* (eds.) *South Asian Languages: Structure, Convergence and Diglossia*, Delhi: Motilal Banarsidass, 1986, pp. 101–107.

________ 1991 "Clitic versus affix: Maithili *e* and *o*," *Contributions to Nepalese Studies* 18: 2, 123–132.

________ 1996 *A Reference Grammar of Maithili* (Trends in Linguistics: Documentation 11), Berlin & New York: Mouton de Gruyter. [An Indian edition was also published in Delhi by Munshi Ram Manohar Lal in 1997]

________ 1998 "Markers of (in)definiteness in Maithili." *Contributions to Nepalese Studies* 25: 1, 1–14.

________ 2000 "Maithili linguistic research: State–of–the–art." *Contributions to Nepalese Studies* 27: 1, 71–87. Also published in Jha (ed. 2007).

________ 2001 "The morphology of the Maithili conjunctive participle," *Contributions to Nepalese Studies* 28. 2, 2001, 269–275.

________ 2003 "Maithili," In: Cardona, George & Dhanesh Jain (eds. 2003) *The Indo–Aryan Languages,* London & New York: Routledge, pp. 470–490.

________ 2004 "On diachronic origins of converbs in Maithili," *Contributions to Nepalese Studies* 31: 2, 215–241.

________ 2011 "Medieval Maithili stagecraft in the Nepālamaṇḍala: The Bhaktapur school," *Contributions to Nepalese Studies* 38: 2, 171–190.

________ (ed. 2011) *A Facsimile Edition of a Maithili Play: Bhūpatīndramalla's Parśurāmopākhyāna–nāṭaka*, Kathmandu: B. P. Koirala India–Nepal Foundation.

________ 2013 "Grierson reevaluated: Is there a rule of 'Short Antepenultimate Vowel' in Modern Maithili?" *Contributions to Nepalese Studies* 40: 1, 1–10.

________ 2014a "Maithili phonology revisited: Vowel hiatus, glide insertion, and diphthongization," *Nepalese Linguistics*: 29, 42–51.

________ 2014b "A hitherto undiscovered and unstudied hand–copied Newari manuscript of a Maithili *bārahamāsā* song by king Jagatprakāśamalla (1643–1673 CE) of Nepal: Preliminary analysis," *Contributions to Nepalese Studies* 41: 2, 153–172. [A revised version is forthcoming in *Proceedings of the 4th Annual Kathmandu Conference on Nepal and the Himalaya*, Kathmandu]

________ 2015 "Metathesis in Maithili," *Contributions to Nepalese Studies*, 42: 2.

________ 2016 *Maïthilī Ālekha Sañcayana (1989–2015)*, Janakpurdham: Maïthilī Vikāsa Koṣa.

________ *Aspects of Maithili: Selected Papers of Ramawatar Yadav, 1976 –2016.* In preparation

________ *Francis Buchanan's* ***Comparative Vocabularies***: *Facsimile Edition.* In preparation

Zbavitel, Duśan. 1961 "The development of the Baromasi in the Bengali literature," *Archiv Orientalni*: 29, 582–619.

About the Book

A thoroughly researched facsimile–cum–critical edition of the Newari MS. of a collection of intensely elegiac and panegyric Maithili lyrical songs, *Gītapañcaka*, of king Jagatprakāśamalla, the book presents an exhaustive literary and linguistic description of the text – the chief highlight being an in–depth analysis of probably the oldest extant hand–written MS. of a *bārahamāsā* folk–song of the Maithili language composed as early as c. 1662 CE.

Two–time Academy Award winner: the ***Royal Nepal Academy Pāsāṅg Lhāmu Award–1996*** and the ***Nepal Academy Nepāla Prājñā Bhāṣā Puraskāra–2017***, and the winner of the ***Baïdyanātha–Siyādevī Foundation Maithili Award–1999***, the first ***Nepal Vidyāpati Maithili Research Award–2011***, and the ***Nepal Academy of Music and Drama Saṃgīta tathā Nāṭya Rāṣṭriya Prajñā Puraskāra–2018,*** Professor Yadav has authored four books: *Maithili Phonetics and Phonology* (Mainz: Selden und Tamm, 1984), *A Reference Grammar of Maithili* (Berlin & New York: Mouton de Gruyter, 1996), *A Facsimile Edition of a Maithili Play: Bhūpatīndramalla's Parśurāmopākhyāna–nāṭaka* (Kathmandu: B. P. Koirala India–Nepal Foundation, 2011) and *Maïthilī Ālekha Sañcayana (1989–2015)* (Janakpurdham: Maïthilī Vikāsa Koṣa, 2016). Two more of his books are in preparation: *Aspects of Maithili: Selected Writings of Ramawatar Yadav, 1976–2016*, and *Francis Buchanan's* ***Comparative Vocabularies***: *Facsimile Edition.* Professor Yadav has published a total of more than 75 research papers in journals of language and linguistics in Nepal, India, USA, and Germany; he has also contributed a chapter titled "Maithili" in George Cardona and Dhanesh Jain (eds. 2003) *The Indo–Aryan Languages* (London & New York: Routledge).

Recipient of the British Council Scholarship (1970–71), the Fulbright–Hays Scholarship (1974–79), the British Council Visitor Award, London (1989), Senior Fulbright Visiting Scholar, Council for International Exchange of Scholars, USA (1989), and the Alexander–von–Humboldt Postdoctoral Senior Research Fellowship, Germany (1983–84, 1989, 2000–2001, 2013, 2018), Professor Yadav has also been honored with ***Mithilā Ratna*** (International Maithili Conference, Chennai, India, 2008), ***Mithilā Vibhūti*** (Vidyāpati Sevā Saṃsthāna, Darbhanga, India, 2011), and the ***Pahila Śabdakoṣakāra Paṇḍita Bhavanātha Miśra Sāhitya Śikhara Sammāna–2017***. (Sāhityāṅgana, Jhanjharpur, Bihar, India, 22 November 2017).